REPORTS FROM A WILD COUNTRY

DEBORAH BIRD ROSE is a senior research scholar and prize-winning author. An anthropologist by training, she has worked with Aboriginal people in their claims to land, in protecting sacred sites and in collaboratively documenting their relationships with totemic landscapes. Her work in both academic and practical arenas is focused on social and ecological justice. Her previous books include *Country of the Heart: An Indigenous Australian Homeland*, *Dingo Makes Us Human: Life and Land in an Australian Aboriginal Culture* and *Hidden Histories: Black Stories from Victoria River Downs, Humbert River and Wave Hill Stations*.

REPORTS FROM A WILD COUNTRY

ETHICS FOR DECOLONISATION

Deborah Bird Rose

A UNSW PRESS BOOK

Published by
University of New South Wales Press Ltd
University of New South Wales
Sydney NSW 2052
AUSTRALIA
www.unswpress.com.au

© Deborah Bird Rose 2004
First published 2004

This book is copyright. Apart from any fair
dealing for the purpose of private study,
research, criticism or review, as permitted under
the Copyright Act, no part may be reproduced
by any process without written permission.
Inquiries should be addressed to the publisher.

National Library of Australia
Cataloguing-in-Publication entry

Rose, Deborah Bird.
 Reports from a wild country : ethics for
 decolonisation.

 Includes index.
 ISBN 0 86840 798 4.

 1. Decolonisation – Australia. 2. Aborigines,
 Australian – Attitudes. 3. Aborigines,
 Australian – Social life and customs.
 4. Australia – Race relations. I. Title.

325.30994

Cover design Di Quick

CONTENTS

Acknowledgments   vii
Introduction: Into the Wild   1

PART 1   HERE AND NOW   9
1. Recuperation   11
2. Wounded Space   34
3. The Long Transitive Moment   53
4. Cattle Kings and Sacred Cows   73

PART 2   BATTLEFIELDS   95
5. Gender of the Gun   97
6. The Fellowship of Mates   115
7. Battles, Betrayals, and Resilience   131
8. The Transformation of Culture into History   149

PART 3   TRACKS   163
9. Footprints   165
10. Journeys   179
11. Love and Reconciliation in the Forest   193

Afterword   213
Notes   215
References   217
Index   232

ACKNOWLEDGMENTS

Aboriginal people in many parts of Australia have taught me more than I could ever have dreamed. The generosity I have encountered has been warm, and rich with opportunities to expand my thinking and my sense of self. They have shaped many research questions, changed my writing, and taken me in unexpected and delightfully challenging directions. In this book I acknowledge particular teachers by name, but people live within families, communities, and country, and my debt is to all those domains. Special thanks are owing to the people in the communities and countries surrounding Yarralin, Lingara, Pigeon Hole and Daguragu in the Northern Territory, and Wallaga Lake and Narooma in New South Wales.

My interest in the Daly River region was sparked by my work on land claims and land disputes in the region. I owe a debt of thanks to the Aboriginal people with whom I worked, especially Raelene Singh and her family (Kenbi Land Claim), Nancy Daiyi and her family (Wagait dispute), and Marjorie Foster and Maxine Hill and their family (Kamu dispute). Thanks as well to the talented lawyers who achieved so much: Ross Howie, Dominic Toomey, and Paul Walsh. I am also grateful to the Jesuits in the Hawthorn headquarters; they were kind and helpful during the time it took me to read the Daly River diaries.

Scholars in a number of disciplines have offered collegiality and intellectual stimulation over the years that this work has been taking shape. I am particularly grateful to my anthropology colleagues and mentors, including Aletta Biersack, John Bradley, Paul Faulstich, Jane Goodall, Michael Lieber, Fiona Magowan, Francesca Merlan, Elizabeth Povinelli, Alan Rumsey, Nonie Sharp, and Franca Tamisari. Among historians I owe particular debts of comradeship and inspiration to Jay Arthur, Bain Attwood, Dipesh Chakrabarty, Ann Curthoys, Geoff Gray, Tom Griffiths, Klaus Neumann, Peter Read, Libby Robin, Tim Rowse and Christine Winter. In philosophy my outstanding debts are to the Australian eco-philosophers Freya Mathews and Val Plumwood. Among cultural studies scholars my particular debts are to Roland Boer, John Docker, Chris Healy and Steve Muecke. Thanks to all of you, and thanks to my colleagues at the Centre for Resource and Environmental Studies. My ability to deal with ecological issues in the ways that I do in this book are quite specifically indebted to our conversations and seminars.

Several key ideas in this book were first explored in the beautiful intellectual environment of the Centre for Cross-Cultural Studies and Humanities Research Centre at the ANU. I have presented some of my ideas in the context of Visiting Scholars programs at the Centres, and I thank in particular Bain Attwood and Dipesh Chakrabarty ('Trauma and Memory' Visiting Scholars Program), and Greg Dening and Donna Merwick ('Challenges to Perform' Visiting Scholars Program); in addition the visiting scholars themselves asked questions and made comments that were perceptive and inspiring. Most of the ideas in this book have been tried out in seminars on several continents. I am grateful to all the people who have listened to and engaged with my ideas as they were forming. Special thanks as well to Jessica Weir, who brought her many skills to bear in helping me finalise the manuscript.

Thanks go most profoundly to Darrell Lewis and Chantal Jackson. Not only did they live with this book for a long time, they also discussed many of the ideas with me, and helped me hold my focus and maintain my patience.

The research was funded in part by ARC Discovery Grant 'Nature and Nation', awarded to Libby Robin and myself, reference: DP0208361. The book was written during the time I have been Senior Fellow at CRES, ANU.

Portions of some of the work in this book have appeared elsewhere, and I acknowledge the earlier publication:

Chapter 6 appeared as 'Australia Felix Rules OK' in G. Cowlishaw and B. Morris (eds), *Race Matters; Indigenous Australians and 'Our' Society*, Aboriginal Studies Press, Canberra, 1997. Portions of chapter 2 were first published as 'Rupture and the

Ethics of Care in Colonised Space' in T. Bonyhady & T. Griffiths (eds), *Prehistory to Politics: John Mulvaney, the Humanities and the Public Intellectual*, Melbourne University Press, 1996. Portions of Chapter 3 were first published as 'Hard Times, An Australian Study' in K. Neumann, N. Thomas & H. Ericksen (eds), *Quicksands: Foundational Histories in Australia and Aotearoa New Zealand*, University of New South Wales Press, Sydney, 1999. Portions of chapter 7 were first published as 'Signs of life on a barbarous frontier: intercultural encounters in North Australia', in R. Torrence and A. Clarke (eds), *The Archaeology of Difference: Negotiating Cross-Cultural Engagements in Oceania*, Routledge, London, 2000.

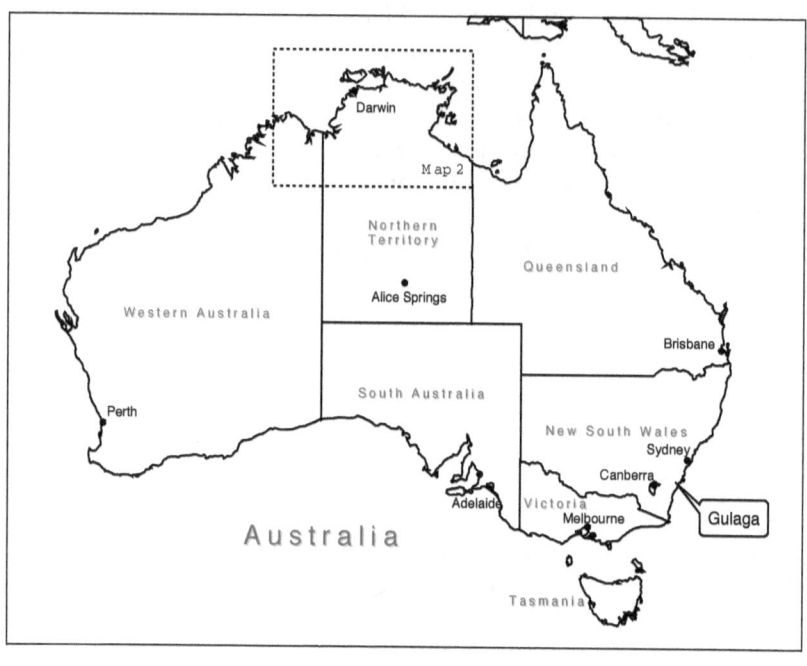

INTRODUCTION: INTO THE WILD

Dark times, Hannah Arendt tells us, surround us when the past cannot guide us into the future. Our work towards decolonisation is taking place in just such a dark time, both because it cannot be theorised in advance (there is very little received wisdom), and because we are now in an extremely unstable time of ever more rapid change. The beauty of Arendt's work for me is that she affirms the possibility of moral action in dark times. If we cannot see into the future, we can still look around us and into our past. If our world is uncertain, it is also richer than any single story would lead us to believe.

Accepting that there is no single clear path towards decolonisation, my purpose is to trace the contours of some of the tracks with which I am familiar. Conversations with Aboriginal people have led me to these tracks. I came to Australia in 1980 to study with Aboriginal people, and the people of Yarralin, Lingara and Pigeon Hole communities in the Northern Territory took particular responsibility for me. From their teachings, our conversations, my questions, and our shared work together on land claims, sacred site registrations, judicial matters, and written work, they have offered a set of questions concerning the major issues of our time and place. This book offers some responses to a number of those questions. Their insights have particular value because these people, situated at the margins of the nation and yet also bearing the brunt of a particular type of colonisation, speak from perspectives that are almost invisible from the centre. In that sense, theirs is a privileged perspective (Bar On 1993).

I use the pronoun 'we' to refer primarily to the conquerors and their descendants in settler societies. I also use the terms 'Whitefellas', 'White people' and 'Kartiya' (in its various spellings this is the North Australian Kriol term for non-Aboriginal people). Many of my teachers used the word 'Blackfella' to refer to themselves. Except in quotations, where a number of vernacular terms are used, I have opted to use the terms 'Aboriginal' or 'Indigenous'. In addition, I have slipped into the use of first names with some of my closest friends and teachers. I could press myself to be more formal, but my greater hope is that readers may also find ways to feel close to people who they may only ever meet on the written page.

Within a few months of arriving in Australia I was in an Aboriginal community, and I would stay in that region, the Victoria River District, for years, returning regularly. Aboriginal people took me into their homes, taught me about country, sites, Dreamings, history, and kinship with Nature and with human beings. As a new Australian, I was socialised into the country, the history, and the culture by Aboriginal people in the first instance. Their teachings have remained primary for me, not only as a matter of fidelity but equally as a matter of sequence. The Australia I came to know and love was always a place of invasion, death, betrayal, hardship and cruelty, and of resilience, survival, and storytelling, and of an unswerving belief that things could be different.

I understand and agree with the critique of White people's efforts to find their own redemption in Aboriginal people's culture, Law, and teaching, as if those we had conquered should now save us. And yet it is also true that there is much to be learned. At the very least, consider gratitude. Starting with an initial premise that conquest was always meant to be complete, we know that the conquest of Indigenous peoples, like the conquest of Nature, was undertaken in a mode of replacement. From the first it was imagined as a project that would be finished when the replacement was fully accomplished. There would always be space in museums and zoos for surviving remnants, but the remnants would have no autonomous life of their own.

Today we are in a different cultural time-space; there may be people who continue to envision Australia in a homogeneous mode of conquest and replacement, but they can hardly be thought to constitute a majority. Rather, in this time of ecological crisis, globalising hegemony, and threats of terrorism and escalating warfare, our work towards alternatives to crisis and chaos depends on decolonisation. Our ability to make peace depends on there being people and places with whom we can make peace. I experience an immense gratitude towards the people and places whose resilience has withstood conquest, and an enduring sense of awe at the fact that these people and these places continue to hold open a moral place for settlers, both old and new.

Wild People: Wild Ecologies

The concept of the wild pervades the book. The idea of wild people was brought to my attention by Hobbles Danaiyarri; he was a historian and political philosopher by inclination, and a Lawman and community leader by education, birth, and community demand. He told the history of the colonisation of his region of North Australia through the saga of Captain Cook, as is by now well known. Chris Healy (1997) works with Indigenous people's stories of Captain Cook and contrasts them with settler forms of memory and memorialisation. His view is integral to the work I am doing here (chapter 1, in particular):

> These histories [of Captain Cook] are concerned with the place of history-making, with the ethical dilemmas bequeathed by the past. These histories seem closer to the spirit of social memory in caring about the importance of being able to live with, rather than simply accumulate knowledge about, the past in the present. (Healey 1997: 7)

Like many of the people with whom I have spoken, Hobbles enjoyed taking the words of the settlers and turning them back on themselves to make a political and moral point. Some of his turns are so subtle that they run the risk of being missed, but others are quite explicit. He describes Captain Cook, the emblematic figure of invasion, running amok in country that is not his, and thinking that the original inhabitants are wild while failing to recognise his own wildness:

> Because Captain Cook order: You got to clean that people up, right up. And put all my whitefellows on top. This my country. Good people this I bring in one day. They all ready for the Aboriginal people. He's the wild one. No good keep this land. (in Rose 2001b: 66)

As Hobbles liked to say, Captain Cook was the real wild one. He failed to recognise Law, destroyed people and country, lived by damage, and promoted cruelty (see Rose 1984, 2001b).

The concept of wild country was brought home to me in a conversation with Daly Pulkara. We had stopped to look at some of the extreme erosion on Humbert River Station, and I asked Daly what he called this country. He looked at it long and heavily before he said: 'It's the wild. Just the wild.' Daly went on to speak of quiet country – the country in which all the care of generations of people is evident to those who know how to see it. Quiet country stands in contrast to the wild: we were looking at a wilderness, man-made and cattle-made. This 'wild' was a place where the life of the country was falling down into the gullies and washing away with the rains.

Daly was the son of warriors, both men and women (chapter 5). His ancestors lost the war, and sometimes he brooded on loss and death. Perhaps because of his occasional preoccupation with death, he often articulated an on-going truth: that social and ecological impacts of conquest can be analysed together as one process. Wild people (colonisers) make wild country (degrading, failing). Colonisation and the wild form a matrix: settler societies and their violence. We cannot avoid the knowledge that conquest requires death and dispossession. Indeed, in many ways we fetishise the violence, glamorising the frontier and erecting hegemonic silences around facts that are taken to be too demanding or too demeaning. Richard Slotkin's (1992: 11) analysis of American violence speaks to the specifically American love affair with guns and fighting, but his main point can be generalised across settler societies: violence is central both to conquest and to progress.

The idea that civilisation is founded in violence has been central to 20th-century thought, from Sigmund Freud to Walter Benjamin to the post-World War II philosophers writing in the afterwash of 'man-made mass death' (Wyschogrod: 1985). It is not new, and nor is it newly linked to colonisation. Tacitus wrote of the Roman conquest of Britain. He put some of his most damning critique into the voice of one of the natives, Calgacus:

> 'Pillagers of the world, they have exhausted the land by their indiscriminate plunder, and now they ransack the sea. A rich enemy excites their cupidity; a poor one their lust for power ... To robbery, butchery, and rapine, they give the lying name of "government"; they create a desolation and call it peace.' (Tacitus in the *Agricola*, 1970: 80–81)

What is new is the technological power and the calculus of progress that together promote loss of ecological sustainability, and ongoing social violence in rapidly amplifying dynamics. In chapter 1, I discuss in much greater detail the concept of violence that I am working with here, as well as the ethics that would replace violence with responsive attentiveness.

Catastrophe

As a member of two powerful settler societies, the United States and Australia, I find myself with a heightened awareness of the patterns that cross these two nations, nations that in many other respects are quite dissimilar. The core problematic for Australia and America, and other settler societies, is that we colonisers and settlers, the conquerors of new worlds, are paradoxically situated. Most of us are here because of hope. Our ancestors hoped to make better lives for themselves and their families. They hoped to build societies that would be more equitable and more generous than those they left behind. Their optimism was channelled into migration, settlement, hard work, and a faith in progress, science, technology and, for some, the guiding hand of God or the destiny of Empire. Their callous indifference to the dispossession, death, and despair they generated for the Indigenous peoples and the ecosystems of their 'new worlds', and for the many others who were caught up in their projects, rendered their whole enterprise hope-destroying right from the start. The result for us is that we are here not only by violence, but also by a misguided and misleading hope for the future.

A further consequence is catastrophe. New World settler societies loosen moral accountability from the powerful constraints of place and time. In detaching people from place these societies enable action to escape feedback from the place. Settlers imagine themselves free to depart, indeed many of us make a virtue of departing, and both geographical and economic mobility are fuelled by people's efforts to escape the results of their actions, to search yet again for that better future. In detaching people from continuity in place they also loosen people from the feedback of time. Founded in disjunction ('new' worlds), settler cultures posit an endless overcoming in which the present is always already about to be superseded. Detached from organised moral accountability in two of the most fundamental domains of human life, New World settler societies generate catastrophe.

We see this process within a larger set of settler societies that includes Australia, America, Canada, and New Zealand. There have been catastrophes of major consequence, and we settlers barely know what to make of that. Equally, however, awareness of the ruptured alienation of settler societies is becoming ever more apparent. Our generations alive today may be the first wave of settlers to try to grasp the enormity of conquest, and to understand it as a continuous process. In consequence, many of us really search to understand how we may inscribe back into the world a moral presence for ourselves.

The process of decolonisation, as I pursue it, concerns exactly this problematic. We cannot help knowing that we are here through dispossession and death. What does this mean, for us and for country? What alternatives exist for us, and what is asked of us? I am working with a statement made by Hobbles Danaiyarri that to me says what decolonisation is all about:

> I'm speaking about now. We can come together, join in, make it more better out of that big trouble. You know, before, Captain Cook bin making a lot of cruel, you know. Now these day, these day, we'll be friendly, we'll be love meself [one another], we'll be mates. That be better. Better for make that trouble. (in Rose 2001b: 77)

Time and Life

One of the main premises underlying this book is that time is neither homogeneous nor linear (in any social sense). Alternatives to the wild can be found in the past, and in the present. The alternatives are not sorted out into an 'us' (wild) and 'them' (non-violent). Rather, alternatives arise unexpectedly in relationships among peoples and between people and place. Alternatives are entangled in the midst of the wild, and may depend on the wild even as they resist it (chapters 4 and 11). In some instances alternatives are only a shadow of things left unsaid (chapter 6).

Four major themes run through this book: resilience, doubling up, countermodernity, and ethics. The term 'resilience' is used in a technical way by ecologists. It refers to relationships within ecosystems and is attuned to the instability of living systems. Each living thing has its own will to flourish, its own 'conatus' in philosophical language. The will to flourish brings every living thing into relationship with other living and non-living parts of its environment. When those relationships work to enable life to flourish, the system itself may be said to be resilient. As I discuss in chapter 2, it will be self-organising and self-repairing. In human terms, resilience has a similar meaning, referring to the capacity of groups of people to sustain themselves in flourishing relationships with their environment, to cope with catastrophe, and to find ways to continue.

The second theme concerns doubling up. I am particularly concerned with doubled violence. The doubling I refer to is a continuing act of wounding that not only kills parts of a living system but actually disables or kills the capacity of a living system to repair itself. Doubling up goes beyond the normal process of death which is inherent in life, pushing death further and further so that greater and greater damage and loss ensue. Doubling up is an amplification of death, such that death exceeds a balance with life and becomes a self-amplifying process itself. In more personal contexts, doubling up refers to the amplification of pain through repetition and denial.

The third theme, countermodernity, is not the same as anti-modernity. Whereas anti-modernity is reactive against modernity, countermodernity is generously responsive. It seeks to offer radical and challenging alternatives to the modernity that underlies so much of contemporary social and ecological violence.

Ethics is the fourth theme. The basic definition derives from the philosopher Emmanuel Levinas. He states it most explicitly in negative form: 'For an ethical sensibility ... the justification of the neighbor's pain is certainly the source of all immorality' (Levinas 1988: 163). Doubling up, the amplification of pain, depends on indifference to ethics since it depends on indifference to or justification of the suffering of others. The callousness that underlies damage, whether inter-human or ecological, requires an absence or suppression of ethics.

As I discuss in the first chapter, the 'provocation' of Levinas (to borrow from Bernasconi & Wood 1988) is to assert in philosophical terms that ethics precedes ontology. In practical terms this means that we humans (perhaps other living things as well) are brought into being already called into ethics by others. Furthermore, the primacy of ethics means that while ethics can be talked about with some degree of abstraction, ethics are properly always situated. In the words of John Roth (1999: xiv): 'Any ethical system that thinks it has the solution to every problem has the potential to be genocidal. Ethics must no longer be a closed system, but a way of living ... in openness to the vulnerability of others ...' Like the living beings who call and respond, ethics are situated in bodies and in time and in place. Situatedness poses significant challenges for our New World societies. Our immersion in concepts of disconnection, our future-orientation, our seeming indifference to the losses that colonisation entail – these and other specificities of our way of conceptualising and actualising time and place ensure that ethics place particular, perhaps unique, demands upon us.

Throughout this book I aim to offer wide-ranging and nuanced accounts and contexts of ethics. The book is divided into three sections, each of which is focused on a different aspect of time and place. Part I, 'Here and Now', examines issues of time and place in the mode of the past. Part II, 'Battlefields', examines claims to the future, as evidenced in struggles over the bodies, souls, and country-relationships of Aboriginal people. Part III, 'Tracks', works within the present moment, and explores the idea that the ground itself – the earth and its living things – holds traces not only of our damage but also of our alternatives. Throughout the book the stories and analysis diverge in some places and converge in others; in Part III I bring the various strands together in the interest of more densely woven accounts. Chapters 10 and 11 speak quite specifically to reconciliation and to countermodern alternatives. My purpose is to show that ethics for decolonisation work with harm, twisting violence back into flourishing and life-affirming relationships.

PART ONE

HERE AND NOW

Many of my Aboriginal teachers in the Northern Territory expressed views that I understood to indicate that they believed that Whitefellas were in a state of epistemological crisis. In particular, they pointed to actions and ideas which to them indicated that Whitefellas were trapped in a state of confusion about their own past and their own place. Not knowing what to remember and what to forget, Whitefellas, according to Victoria River people, follow dead laws, fail to recognise living ones and, in our power and denial, continue to promote death. Similarly with regard to place, people spoke of Whitefellas 'coming up blind' and bumping into everything. The living presence of the living country in its own flourishing particularity was not noticed by Whitefellas, whose mission was conquest. Their purpose was to 'put the flag' (to quote Anzac Munnganyi of Pigeon Hole, in Rose 1996a: 18).

Aboriginal people's questions and analysis arise from contexts in which the here-ness of the place is vividly present, and in which the now-ness of the living moment is the time of life and encounter. These chapters look to some of the ways in which Whitefellas have deflected the living 'here and now'. The analysis focuses on structures and processes of distance – on ways of pushing away the people and places and times that truly are close to us.

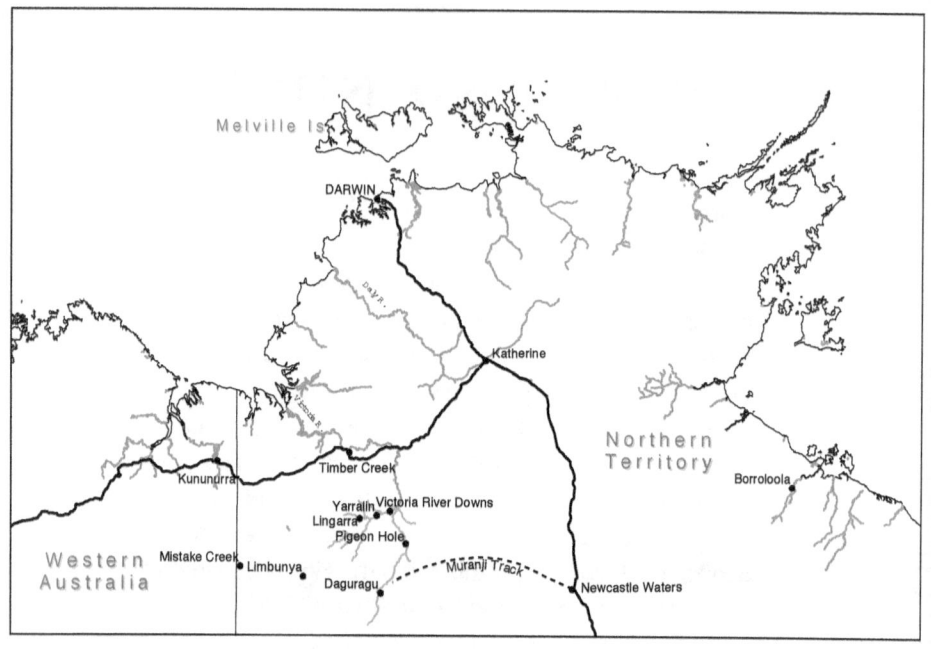

1

RECUPERATION

> Historians must also consider how the past has become the present and how the present relates to the past. Nations rest on such historical consciousness – on a chain of connection between 'them' and 'us' – and so we need histories that create a sense of moral engagement with the past in the present.
> (Attwood & Foster 2003: 26)

Hobbles Danaiyarri spoke of efforts to conceal and contain the histories of colonisation as they affected Indigenous people: 'Captain Cook bin coverem up me gotta big swag.' He spoke out of the knowledge that much has been silenced, that history is contested, and that knowledge has been and will continue to be manipulated. His intention was to promote the kind of moral engagement Attwood & Foster call for in the succinct statement of purpose just quoted.

The past is contested territory, and so memory, ethics, and narratives are also contested. Some politicians, for example, exhort us to accept an account of history that enables us to feel 'comfortable and relaxed' (John Howard, quoted in Attwood & Foster 2003: 13). Remembrance, it would seem, should focus on that which causes no discomfort. By default, amnesia should surround that which causes discomfort. My Aboriginal teachers in the Victoria River District would have understood this exhortation as further evidence of both epistemological chaos and the colonising practice of concealment – of covering people with a big swag.

In this chapter I take up Attwood & Foster's challenge to explore the basis of a moral engagement with the past in the present. Three main themes draw my attention: ethics and history, practices that entice us to abandon our moral presence, and the project of recuperation.

The Weight of History

Ann Curthoys (2003: 186) links Australia's contestation over history to similar debates in countries such as Japan, Germany and the United States. She reminds us that our debate is about more than the suppression or partial representation of certain strands of history: 'It is a debate about the moral basis of Australian society.' Among the issues at stake is a perception of White Australian innocence (p. 187). The argument seems to be that if settler Australians' conquest of the continent meant death, dispossession, perhaps genocide for Indigenous people, then an aura of guilt must hang over White Australian people, and the nation must rethink its moral basis.

Along with many other scholars, I have encountered and published various forms of evidence concerning death, dispossession, and actions that could reasonably be termed genocide (see Curthoys & Docker 2001 and other essays in the same volume). I have not, however, aimed to produce a tour guide for guilt trips. My purpose is more challenging. In linking knowledge of the violence of the past with an ethics that demarcates a path towards decolonisation, I work with the distinction proposed by the great 20th-century philosopher of ethics, Emmanuel Levinas. James Hatley, in his excellent analysis of 'testimony and history', discusses Levinas's distinction that guilt 'is the burden I or the other may carry for our specific actions or comportment', while responsibility 'is the burden upon me of the other's vulnerability to suffering' (Hatley 2000: 104). The distinction to be made is that between one's own actions (concerning which one may have cause for guilt), and the human condition of living with and for others.

To lift even a corner of the 'big swag' is to move into a realm of ethics and moral challenge. I reject concepts of collective guilt and descendants' guilt, but there are quandaries nevertheless. The immediacy of quandary was articulated beautifully by Miloš Vasič, one of the founders of the Yugoslavian independent weekly *Vreme*.

His situation was acutely uncomfortable: having been a member of the minority opposition to Milosovich's policies and practices, he could absolve himself from personal guilt. And yet he said that he felt ashamed 'as a human being' – not as a Serb but as a human being. He went on to say that 'history sometimes hangs over us in terrible ways' (reported in Paris 2000: 454, 462).

A moral engagement between past and present must acknowledge violence, and having done so, must acknowledge the moral burden of that knowledge. Levinas defines violence as acting as if one were alone; it denies relationship, denies responsibility, and thus effectively denies others. The physical manifestations of violence create pain, destruction, and catastrophe. Discursive practices equally can cause pain and may be a first condition for catastrophic destruction. 'Totality cannot stand alterity', Hatley (2000: 81) writes, concisely summing up Levinas's thought on violence.

Bernhard Casper (1988: 104) connects the ethical thought of Levinas with that of Rosenzweig and Buber. He writes that these scholars, Levinas pre-eminently, have articulated a new sense of ethics that brings two millennia of dedication to the absolute into the here and now of the contemporary western world, connecting our ethics to our lives as they unfold within relationships of responsibility.

The radical turn that Levinas articulates for us is an intersubjectivity in which each of us is always, already, responsible for others. 'Self is not a substance but a relation', Levinas writes (1996: 20). There is no self without other. Life with others is inherently entangled in responsibility. Levinas thus claims the primacy of ethics as an inherent and inalienable aspect of the human condition. He teaches an ethic of human connectivity: 'consciousness and even subjectivity follow from, are legitimated by, the ethical summons which proceeds from the intersubjective encounter. Subjectivity arrives, so to speak, in the form of a responsibility towards an other ...' (Newton 1995: 12).

This ethic of connection, of mutually implicated humans whose primary duty is to respond to the calls of others, particularly those who are vulnerable, does not demand a suppression or denial of one's own self. Rather to the contrary, the argument is that one finds one's own self in responding to others, and so both self and other become entangled in ethical relationships, or, if responsibility is abjured in favour of violence, in abuse of ethics. The self includes one's capacity for moral knowledge and action: 'I become a moral agent and not a power instrument, when I understand that my existence is entangled with other lives and is, therefore, responsible' (Kaplan 2000: 71).

In one sense one is always situated as a moral agent: 'self is a relation not a substance.' What this means for how one goes about acting in relation is not, however, straightforward or easy. Bauman states the condition plainly: '[the] self finds itself alone in the face of moral dilemmas without good (let alone obvious) choices, [with] unresolved moral conflicts and the excruciating difficulty of being moral' (1993: 249). In spite of the severity of the challenge, Bauman, along with others, contends that moral responsibility is one of the most important forms of action we can take in a world in which our humanity is under assault.

It may be easier to define what is immoral than to prescribe what is moral. Levinas takes it as given that murder and the infliction of pain are immoral. In the domains of our everyday lives, he states that relational closure marks immorality. As discussed in the introduction: 'For an ethical sensibility – confirming itself in the inhumanity of our time, against this inhumanity – the justification of the neighbor's pain is certainly the source of all immorality' (Levinas 1988: 163; see also Hatley 2000: 97).

Our Australian context presses us to consider not only the justification of others' pain, but the denial of it as well. It follows that part of our moral burden is an injunction to hold the memory of violence within our texts. To write as if the suffering of those who were harmed never mattered would be to perpetuate violence in the present. A moral engagement of the past in the present thus resists closure, whether that closure aims to decree that the violence in the past (or even in the present) is finished, or whether it claims more specifically to outlaw or ridicule historians and others who seek to remember violence. Each of these two powerful forms of closure – time and monologue – is embedded in mainstream contemporary practice surrounding the relationships between past and present. I will briefly examine each of them, analysing ways in which they deflect responsibility for others. My argument is that these forms of closure alienate us from our own moral capacities and thus work to produce immorality as Levinas defines it. They diminish us as human beings even as they may promise the illusion of a 'comfortable' life.

Past and Present

An examination of practices of discontinuity and continuity in Whitefella cultural constructions of time indicates the links between closure and the deflection of responsibility. The hypothesis that there is a link between time concepts and violence is, on the one hand, self-evident. If there were no links, there would be no controversy over the meaning and punctuation of history. On the other hand, the links go deeper than a struggle for who gets the last word concerning the European conquest of Australia. A seemingly commonsensical orientation towards the future, in a society built upon destruction, enables regimes of violence to continue their work while claiming the moral ground of making a better future.

Punctuation and intertemporality are two lenses for examining western time-constructs. How are moments of time differentiated from each other, and what are the relationships between different moments? As there is far more to be said about time than can be conveniently packed into one chapter, I restrict myself here to the western conventional moments labelled past, present, and future, and take up a more nuanced analysis in chapter 3.

Two core features of early medieval Christian Europe's cultural construction of time – disjunction and irreversible sequence – are the core properties of modern punctuation and intertemporality (Gurevich 1985: 111). In that period the life of Christ was held to be the major ontological disjunction for Christians, as the western calendar still indicates. With the concept of disjunction it was possible to break up the history of the world into epochs, each of which was differentiated not just by duration by also by inner value – from the promise made, to the promise fulfilled, to the final re-creation of Heaven on Earth (Gurevich 1985; Baudrillard 1994; Cohn 1993).

The second core feature is the concept of irreversible sequence within a teleological frame. Zoroaster ($c.3500$ BP) is credited with introducing to the world the idea that through conflict the world is moving towards a conflict-free state (Cohn 1993: 220). These concepts were incorporated into Christianity, and gave to western history a teleological and apocalyptic structure and content (Gurevich 1985: 143). The final goal for both individuals and the world was the achievement of eternal life in a post-historical new heaven and new earth (Cohn 1993: 218).

The stretching of time between two key moments of ontological significance (life of Christ, return of Christ) had the effect of 'shrinking' the present to a moment of transition in which the future became the past. According to Gurevich (1985: 112), 'past and future were of greater significance and value than the present, which was fleeting'; he quotes Augustine's view that history unfolded itself 'in the shadow of the future'.

With the secularisation of western culture under the Enlightenment, many Christian concepts, values, and root metaphors were taken across from religious thought to socio-cultural thought, or abstracted into vague notions such as 'spirit'. Indeed, Boer & Conrad (2003) pursue an analysis initiated by Certeau to argue that Christian discourse not only 'dissipated into society at large' but also that Christian theology transformed itself into the secular academic disciplines that took shape after the Enlightenment. Thus even the more modest claim that Christian discourse transformed itself into secular discourse gives us good ground for examining the continuities across religious and secular time concepts.

The core features of disjunction and irreversible sequence continue to be constitutive of both modernist philosophies of history and everyday time-constructs. Rather than postulating major disjunctions brought about through eruptions of the divine into human history, modernity has privileged a paradigm of progress within which human agency is the driving force. Walter Benjamin gives us the most succinctly perceptive assessment of the links between progress and violence. His ninth thesis on the philosophy of history deploys the now famous image of the Angel of History who 'sees one single catastrophe which keeps piling wreckage upon wreckage'. The Angel is caught in the storm of violence, and that 'storm is what we call progress' (1969: 257–58). Where the Angel of History sees one ongoing catastrophe, and where scholars such as Benjamin see an ongoing sequence of catastrophes, apologists for progress would focus on a bright and beautiful future.

Within the paradigm of progress, history is a process of conflict and change such that the present emerges from, and is differentiated from, the past, and such that the future will emerge from, and will be differentiated from, the present. It puts a positive value on change, and posits that history, or society, is moving towards the resolution of conflict and contradiction. There is thus held to be an 'end' in the sense of a goal: a future point towards which our lives are directed.

This secular paradigm of violence and redemption expresses the kind of thought and behaviour that Hobbles and others characterised as 'the wild'. Much of that assessment derives from the apparent disregard that progress-oriented people have for the damage they do in the present. This paradigm has been subject to analysis by key thinkers throughout the 20th century and recently has been linked with Al Qaeda (Gray 2003). It is perhaps best known in social practice through the analysis of the revolutionary applications of Marx's philosophy of history. Whether it was Hegel developing the dialectic of 'spirit' fulfilling itself in history, or Marx developing a dialectical materialism, we see a disrespect for human or other suffering. Present distress can be claimed to be leading towards, and thus to be justified by, a more perfect future. In a brilliantly argued essay, Glowacka (2000: 39) reminds us of 'Hegel's slaughter-bench model of history'. Hatley (2000: 33) expands this pungent point, saying that Hegel felt justified in arguing 'that the suffering of those who are "immolated upon [history's] altar" is secondary to the larger work of spirit in history'.

In our post-Hegelian, post-Marxist period, the progressive paradigm of history continues to excuse any number of troubling actions and thoughts. Bauman (1993: 225) contends (drawing on Lyotard) that emancipation, the grand idea of the Enlightenment, draws its power 'from the shackles it wants to fracture, the wounds it wants to heal'. He connects the ideal of emancipation with future-oriented thought that discounts present suffering, and concludes that 'future bliss [is] served as the cover-up for the repulsiveness of the present'. That 'repulsiveness' includes the loss of one's moral presence in a world of ethical encounter.

The vision of a future which will transcend the past, a future in which current contradictions and current suffering will be left behind enables us to understand ourselves in an imaginary state of future achievement. It thus enables us to turn our backs on current social facts of pain, damage, destruction and despair which exist in the present, but which we will only acknowledge as our past. It is not necessary to our time-constructs that we shall be indifferent to others, but for Marxist revolutionaries as much as for the people engaged in 'New World' conquest, suffering was justified by reference to the future. Following Levinas's assessment that immorality is constituted in the justification of others' suffering, it is clear that future orientation has been a major tool in deflecting us from moral responsibility.

These time concepts support a peculiarly dizzy detachment of agency in human affairs. The past is always already discontinuous with the present. The discontinuity that marks what we choose to call the past is reflexive: the past is not necessarily that which has already happened, but equally a label to be applied to that which we wish to finish and forget, or from which we wish to differentiate ourselves and thus to absolve ourselves from responsibility.

In future orientation we hasten on our way to fulfilment. Resolution in any large or permanent sense, however, is framed as a forever imminent tomorrow. It always lies just ahead of us, and thus there is a sense in which we will never achieve the resolution we may believe to be our future state precisely because it is always already posited as a future state. It is becoming increasingly clear pragmatically that resolution is unachievable because the damage we do on our way to the future is already destroying the future we hope to inhabit. And yet we keep doing more of the same, not least because of the sense of hope we attach to the future.

Our lives are thus suspended in a web of time concepts that hold us always about to be that which we would believe we truly are. The qualitative differentiation of past and future means that the present is discontinuous with both. In this disjunctive moment, it can appear that our responsibilities can be understood to be most properly directed towards the future rather than towards the people and places of this moment because the present is always already becoming the past which is in the process of being transcended.

The present becomes a place in which we are estranged from the actual conditions of our lives, where agency is alienated, responsibility cast elsewhere, and morality subjected to a double deflection as it aims towards a future which will, in due course, become the past. The 'now' becomes a site of such alienation that it hardly bears thinking about, and that is my point. We are suspended in a bereft and hapless moment. The headlong rush towards the future may be an attempt to escape accountability, but even for those who seek responsibility, the most plausible action often appears to be to look to the future and thus to act towards a moment that our time-constructs enable us to think may yet be remediable.

The very justification made possible by orientation towards the future enables another attitude, that of complacency. Arendt (1969: 47) notes the amoral quality of complacency in her summarising statement that 'we need only march into the future, which we can't help doing anyhow, in order to find a better world'. Whether idealistic or complacent, the idea of disjunction can be deployed to evade responsibility. The logic is to declare the present disjunctive with the past, and then to declare that the present is about to be transcended and that we will soon live in a period that is disjunctive with our 'now'.

This benighted 'now' in which we actually live our lives is circumscribed and rendered largely irrelevant through progress ideology. What is most demeaning for us is that it displaces ethics, as if, in a secular mimicry of Messianism, the mere passage of time will somehow alleviate us of present responsibilities and will restore our true moral capacity to us in that illusory unblemished future.

The project that Attwood & Foster call for – creating a sense of moral engagement with the past in the present – is thus a much larger task than it might initially appear. It involves rejecting a paradigm of future social perfection or some form of redemption, and revaluing the present as the real site of action in the world.

'Us' and 'Them'

A further challenge to closure builds on the violence of totalising monologue. Whose past and whose present are implicated in the moral work of engaging the past in the present? Monologue is another primary form of closure. Critical theory of recent decades has shown western thought and action to be dominated by a matrix of hierarchical oppositions which provided powerful conceptual tools for the reproduction of violence. In this matrix the world is formed around dualities: man/woman, culture/nature, mind/body, active/passive, civilisation/savagery, and so on in the most familiar and oppressive fashion. In fact, however, these dualities are more properly described as a series of singularities because the pole labelled 'other' (woman, Nature, savage, etc.) is effectively an absence. This point is articulated extensively by feminist theoreticians. Luce Irigaray (1985), for example, shows that the defining feature of woman under dualistic thought is that she is not man.

Ecofeminists extend the analysis to include 'Nature', and show that the same structure of domination controls women, Nature, and all other living beings and systems that are held to be 'other' (Warren 1990; Salleh 1992). Val Plumwood (1994: 74) speaks directly to the centrality of this structure: 'the story of the control of the chaotic and deficient realm of "Nature" by mastering and ordering "reason" has been the master story of Western culture.' Within that 'chaotic and deficient realm' were all those others who were classed outside the 'Us' that is the hero of the story.

Stripped of much cultural elaboration, this structure of self/other articulates power such that 'self' is constituted as the pole of activity and presence, while 'other' is the pole of passivity and absence. Presence is a manifestation both of being and of power, while absence may be a gap awaiting transfiguration by the active/present pole, or an enabling background; in either case, without power and presence of its own (Plumwood 1997).

A crucial feature of the system is that others never get to talk back on their own terms. Communication is all one way as the pole of power refuses to receive the feedback that would cause it to change itself, or to open itself to dialogue. Power lies in the ability not to hear what is being said, not to experience the consequences of one's actions, but rather to go one's own self-centric and insulated way. Plumwood (2002: 27) notes two key moves in sustaining hierarchical dualism and the illusion of autonomy – dependency and denial. The pole of power depends on the subordinated other, and simultaneously denies this dependence.

The image of bi-polarity thus masks what is, in effect, a singular pole of self. The self sets itself within a hall of mirrors; it mistakes its reflection for the world, sees its own reflections endlessly, talks endlessly to itself, and, not surprisingly, finds continual verification of itself and its worldview. This is monologue masquerading as conversation, masturbation posing as productive interaction; it is a narcissism so profound that it purports to provide a universal knowledge when in fact its violent erasures are universalising its own singular and powerful isolation. It promotes a nihilism that stifles the knowledge of connection, disables dialogue, and maims the possibilities whereby 'self' might be captured by 'other'. Levinas equates these totalising monological narratives with war.

This is not to say that monologue itself lacks debate and conflict, but more deeply that it is self-totalising in only including what it can accommodate within its own narrative, and by insisting that others, if they appear at all, appear as they are construed by that monological narrative. Indeed some monological narratives are so broad as to be able to encompass everything, but only within the terms of the narrative. Elizabeth Povinelli's (2002) brilliant new study of Australian multiculturalism gives a much more complex face to public monocultural discourse than I am able to present here. She focuses on the 'cunning of recognition', examining the impossible necessity for Aboriginal people in certain contexts to be able to produce for the nation an identity that the nation defines as authentic (see also Merlan 1998). This is one of many ways in which monological narrative scoops up others on its own terms and within its own self-understanding (see chapter 3).

The dismantling of the warlike theory of 'self' is a necessary step in moving towards decolonisation. The consequence of unmaking narcissistic singularity is that we embrace noisy and unruly processes capable of finding dialogue with other people and with the world itself. In doing so we shake our capacity for connection loose from the bondage of monologue. As Povinelli (2002) analyses in depth, plurality poses seriously disjunctive moments for individuals, and for states. Plurality is an ethical direction but by no means is it a paradox-free or conflict-free zone.

The ethical alternative to monologue is dialogue. And this dialogue is not the Platonic or Socratic dialogue, which Arendt (1970: 10) describes as a 'silent dialogue between me and myself'. It is specifically a form of dialogue that requires difference. It seeks relationships across otherness without seeking to erase difference. Emil Fackenheim (1994: 129) draws on the work of Franz Rosenzweig to articulate two main precepts for structuring the ground for ethical dialogue. The first is that dialogue begins where one is, and thus is always situated; the second is that dialogue is open, and thus that the outcome is not known in advance. Fackenheim developed this paradigm of dialogue in this era after the *Shoah*, asking, as have other philosophers, whether any dialogue can again take place between those who have been radically harmed and those who harmed them. Because he develops a form of dialogue that can work across chasms of radical harm, his paradigm is especially appropriate for our settler societies.

Our situatedness as settlers is clear. In Australia, settler-descendants are situated in damaged places; we bear the burden of the violent history of conquest, and oscillate between hope and despair. Aboriginal people are also situated in damaged places, have borne the brunt of social violence, and are similarly urged to link their hopes to practices that are linked to destruction. These are harsh situations, and as I have argued elsewhere, ethical dialogue requires that we acknowledge and understand our particular and harshly situated presence (Rose & Ford 1995; Rose 1999).

From a situated perspective, what lies between us are these terrible histories: the invasions, the dominations, the deaths and exclusions. Violence, both legal and extra-legal, wars, dispossessions, extinctions and invisibilities lie between us. Silence, the big swag, also lies between us. Before we lose heart, however, we must also consider that violence is not the whole story. What lies between us, or between some of us some of the time, is love, respect, sympathy, and the determination to act together. The possibility of dialogue, and its accomplishment in many contexts, rests in the fact that our situatedness is neither wholly violent nor wholly non-violent. Entanglements give us grounds for action.

The concept of openness may sound obvious, but it is equally challenging. Openness is risky because one does not know the outcome. To be open is to hold one's self available to others: one takes risks and becomes vulnerable. But this is also a fertile stance: one's own ground can become destabilised. In open dialogue one holds one's self available to be surprised, to be challenged, and to be changed.

Openness also challenges us because it contains a contradictory set of injunctions. On the one hand openness is unlimited, since one always wants to try to understand others, and to listen with an open mind. On the other hand, openness has limits: an ethical position does not remain open to assisting violence or to sustaining the silences that oppress. Openness, in brief, is both unlimited in its even-handedness and at the same time is counterbalanced by commitment to the decolonising process.

The connection between temporality, monologue, and ethics can be demonstrated vividly through consideration of past violence and continuing pain. We live our lives in the present, as our bodies tell us even when our minds are cast into the future. Along with other scholars, I see a doubled violence: the practices that hurt others, and the sustained indifference to the hurt of others that is a key index of power. Elaine Scarry (1985) works with an analysis of torture to develop the point that pain is amplified through denial. My point is that monologue constitutes an equally pain-amplifying denial. In Australia, the injuries of colonisation stand as concrete evidence of a violence which monological settler ideology denies or trivialises. Moreover, the articulation of injury comes to be represented in some public discourse as itself an act of aggression: as if Aboriginal people sought explicitly to destroy White Australians' comfortable attitude towards history. Aboriginal people's injuries testify to an ongoing war. Their existence calls forth rejection and denial, both of which are injurious in their own right. Inescapably, denial reinflicts past harm and sustains present injuries.

Monological history derives from a singularity and must seek to protect that singularity. The results are themselves catastrophic; Hatley is eloquent:

> Only humans can conspire to repress, to destroy the future of human [groups]. In doing so, humans show the reprehensible capacity to turn their history, their remembrance of time across the aeons, the generations, into a sort of narcissistic mirror. One eliminates all the strangers, all the disruptions of one's own vision, so that one's history only articulates one's own concerns, one's own needs. One writes the past and the future as a mode of colonisation. All the other times are resources for one's own. (Hatley 2000: 63)

A consequence for the human person who finds herself or himself situated near the pole of power is that in assenting to a monological history and abandoning one's own moral agency, one explicitly or implicitly becomes an instrument of the violence that excludes, denies, suppresses, abandons or destroys. Monological history, ideologically driven to protect power, is written as if the victims of power never mattered (Hatley 2000: 204). Prime Minister John Howard's idea that monological history could leave us feeling comfortable is as violent as it is appalling. It attacks our moral presence in the world.

Recuperative Work

Hannah Arendt used the term 'dark times' to refer to periods when the construction of law-like generalities and theoretical models is cut loose from human knowledge (Luban 1983). Her work is pertinent to our time now for three reasons. First, our postmodern condition is one of failed master narratives; we no longer desire the great stories that once may have made sense of the world for us because we have been required to understand the violence they conceal. Second, we are entering a period of deep uncertainty, in which many unthinkable things have happened, are undoubtedly happening right now, and will continue to happen. Arguably, current levels of risk and terror exceed our capacity to plan rationally in order to avoid or manage them. The third reason concerns my specific focus on decolonisation. The process of decolonising modern settler societies is a new phenomenon; we have no models from the past to guide us. It is equally a dialogical project; we cannot theorise in advance just how it will happen and still be committed to openness. We have to work it out step by step dialogically with and among each other. If it happens at all, it will unfold in real time, and will be shaped by the Indigenous, 'old' settler, and recent migrant peoples who share the here and the now of our homelands.

As stated, the beauty of Arendt's work for me is that she insists on affirming the possibility of moral action by proposing that what sustains our understandings in dark times is the web of stories we are able to weave out of our historically grounded experience. My recuperative project is based on the premise, articulated so elegantly by Arendt (1970: ix), that even in dark times there will be some illumination. Recuperative histories and ethnographies are not aimed towards dialectical opposition or overcoming; rather they trawl the past and the present, searching out the hidden histories and the local possibilities that illuminate alternatives to our embeddedness in violence.

I use the term 'recuperation' in preference to more familiar terms such as 'recovery' or 'restoration' because in contemporary usage it seems to communicate the humility of the project. Central to my argument is the proposition that there is no former time/space of wholeness to which we might return or which we might resurrect for ourselves (chapter 10). Nor is there a posited future wholeness which may yet save us. Rather, the work of recuperation seeks glimpses of illumination, and aims towards engagement and disclosure. The method works as an alternative both to methods of closure or suspicion and to methods of proposed salvation.

Recuperative work is oppositional in several major senses of opposition and encounter. I will examine time and monologue in a recuperative mode, and will then contextualise the analysis through analysis of time and the dead, the position of witness, and the existential question of hope and intent.

Time

Recuperative work takes an ethical stance in opposition to the temporal and monological practices that cause suffering and damage and that exclude or deny the reality of that suffering and damage. Breaking up the linearity of past → present → future, recuperative work imagines all accessible time as rich with possibility. Time work impels one immediately into moral responsibility. As Benjamin tells us in his sixth thesis, the past makes urgent moral claims on us (1969: 255). So too does the present, and so, we increasingly understand, does the future (in particular, see chapters 10 and 11).

There are alternatives to linear time. Like many scholars today, I want to consider the time of the generations of living things, including ecological time, synchronicities, intervals, patterns, and rhythms, all of which are quite legitimately understood as forms of time (Adam 1994). Similarly, ecofeminists such as Ariel Salleh (1997: 137) argue that complex time concepts are necessary to understanding ecological processes. In attending to the world of 'Nature' she makes a case for a concept of enduring time – a time of continuity between past and future. In my work I have sought to understand more deeply Aboriginal concepts of time (Rose 1999, and chapters 3, 8 and 9).

As Salleh's analysis suggests, analysis of relationships across moments of time and across kinds of time is significant. Concepts of heterogeneous time demand the understanding that different kinds of time are coeval, that is, coexisting (Fabian 1983). Dipesh Chakrabarty uses the beautiful metaphor of time-knots. In his analysis of subaltern histories he proposes that 'the writing of history must implicitly assume a plurality of times existing together, a discontinuity of the present with itself' (Chakrabarty 1997: 28–29). In contrast to modernity's privileging of linear sequence in which the past is overcome and consigned to the past, time knots are the entanglements of real life in time: we do not move through 'homogeneous empty time' (Benjamin's phrase, 1969: 261), filling the fleeting 'now' with our homogeneous presence. Rather, the entanglements to which Chakrabarty directs our attention draw us into complex and co-mingled times. Our understanding is enhanced, Chakrabarty contends, through engagements with plurality, and we learn more about 'the disjointed nature of our own times' (1997: 27).

Along with time's heterogeneity, there is also the question of the quality of relationship between life and death as they are situated in time. I take up this issue in chapter 10 from the perspective of my understanding of Aboriginal time concepts; here I want to lay the groundwork for thinking about time across generations from a western perspective.

In another article (Rose 2003) I have discussed some of the issues that arise for me in thinking about how Aboriginal people's narratives of the past configure life and death. Western culture pervasively imagines the relationship between life and death as a battle. In this battle the grave will always claim at least a temporary victory, as death is inevitable, but numerous cultural practices seek to redeem life. The conceptualisation of death as sacrifice is foundational not only to theology, but also to society and nation (for example, see Inglis 1998; Muecke 1999). Paul's triumphal assertion to the Corinthians that through the resurrection 'Death is swallowed up in victory' (I Corinthians 15:54) sets out the matrix of the war with death. In the contemporary world, historians are deeply implicated here, as Curthoys and Docker (1999: 6–7) note in their analysis of 19th-century history's desire 'to defeat time and death'. History, they contend, is a continuing act of defiance.

My Aboriginal teachers know the pain and grief that death entails for both the living and the dying. They do not give the grave victory, and in part this is because life is not at war with death. Stephen Muecke (1999: 34) ventures a generalisation with which I would agree: Aboriginal philosophies 'are all about keeping things alive *in their place*'. Aboriginal stories are living traditions. As long as they are told, life has the last word. As often as they are erased – in texts, in the courts, in public discourse – the sting of death walks the land.

The dead

The sting of death has been massively amplified, and perhaps given qualitatively different valence, under conditions of modern 'manmade mass death' (Wyschogrod 1985). Hatley (and others) contend that mass death is an attack on death itself. Hatley's specific focus is on genocide and the corresponding process of aenocide. Aenocide refers to cross-generational deaths, and directs attention to the fact that genocide curtails all the future generations. The claim is that in killing the future, mass death also kills death as we experience it in a non-mass death manner. The argument is that one's death belongs not only to one's self but to others as well: to those who mourn, to those who remember, to those who incorporate the death into a community of memory. Aenocide obliterates those who mourn; it obliterates the community of memory. In this way it can be thought to obliterate death (Hatley 2000: 24).

These propositions take on a further urgency in thinking about relationships across numerous generations. Hatley argues that generations are connected through transmission of wisdom, memory, and traditions. Younger generations receive what is offered and take on the work of the previous generations in its complexity: 'Because each generation dies, the next generation takes up with the lives of the preceding generation in a spirit of commemoration and reverence, as well as criticism and shame' (Hatley 2000: 60). The relationship across life into death, and death into life (through memory, transmitted wisdom and other cross-overs) is a gift, in Hatley's analysis:

> Precisely because one is not one's forebearers, [*sic*] one experiences one's time as a gift, the proffering of one's own existence from out of the bodies and lives of the beings who preceded one. One in turn offers this gift to those who come after one. Time is in this offering the articulation of a generosity beyond primordiality. (Hatley 2000: 61)

Aenocide can thus be said to kill death because it kills the possibility of connectivities across generations. It can also, in this way, be thought to kill time.

The moral burden of the past in the present includes the work of sustaining the heterogeneous gifts of time. No one foresaw or expressed the implications of the ramifying effects of mass death more eloquently than Walter Benjamin (1969: 255) in his sixth thesis: '*even the dead* will not be safe from the enemy if he wins.' Recuperative work thus seeks to tug on whatever may remain of life's gifts, pulling them from the annihilation of the multiple deaths and enabling them to be rethreaded into the fabric of decolonisation.

Monologue

Recuperative work breaks up monologue; the purpose is not to replace one monologue with another, but rather to reveal a rich diversity of events and people. One result is utilitarian. This work allows us to expand our repertoire of possibilities by enlarging our thinking. Just as heterogeneous time can be understood as rich with possibility, so heteroglossic narratives are richly complex and diverse. Here we enter domains of moral responsibility in relation to truth, public memory and the dead.

If the totalising structure of monologue is resisted there is discursive space for conflicting arguments. Does this mean that everything is relative? Povinelli (2002) provides a complex analysis of limits. In contrast, I take an approach that, while logically problematic, is ethically required. The parameters of my approach – problematic and necessary – are well known to philosophers. Povinelli (2002: 8) explains the issue as the gap or contradiction between 'the seemingly unconditional nature of ethical and moral obligations and its relation to the enlightenment obligation to public reason (critical rational discourse)'.

Pursuing my ethical necessity, I note that FC DeCoste (2000) identifies the problem with extreme relativism in relation to radical harm: that historical 'truth' would always simply be a matter of opinion. Clearly this extreme position is not adequate. Wyschogrod (1998: xi, 1) articulates the proposition that truthfulness is about matching an account of an event with the event or pattern; the proposition is commonsensical, and as she says, is at the same time mundane. While homology may be mundane from an historical view, it is not mundane from an ethical view. In developing moral engagements with the past in the present, truth is absolutely necessary. There must be some degree of certainty about events in the past – certainty about what happened, although there may be different interpretations of why things happened. As Hatley (2000: 110) tells us: 'If nothing can ever be unproblematically characterized as having actually occurred, then no moral judgement about what occurs could ever matter.' Facts matter because they enable us to exercise our moral capacity. The creation of confusion incapacitates us.

Another moral domain concerns public remembrance and the dead. As numerous scholars have suggested, the dead are a powerful part of community (for example, Taussig 2001; Margalit 2002).

Michael Ignatieff (1997) reminds us that there is nothing inherently ethical in this relationship. The dead are mobilised in community interests, and the politics of terror mobilise the dead just as surely as ethics for decolonisation. Muecke (1997: 227) contends that death 'is at the heart of the formation of the nation ... States can be set up as political entities, but they only become nations through the magical or spiritual agency of death ... A people recognises itself as a people, that is as a culture, through the symbolic treatment of its dead.'

Monological definitions of the dead are thus central to monological narratives of nationhood. National histories that commemorate some deaths, but not others, rework monologue, as Tom Griffiths explains with elegance in a recent essay. Griffiths (2003: 138) takes up the issue of white silence, contending that 'the great Australian silence was often "white noise": it sometimes consisted of an obscuring and overlapping din of history making.' The white noise of history-making concerns the dead in extremely immediate ways. Griffiths notes the paucity of public memorials to Aboriginal people who died defending family and country, and he links debates over war memorials to the 'Us' and 'Them' exclusions of past and contemporary cultural life. Here is his discussion of responses to Ken Inglis's proposal that Indigenous–settler conflict should be included in the Australian War Memorial:

> Inglis's proposal came out of his lifelong study of the settlers' culture of commemoration and in a book steeped in intelligent sympathy for the rituals of war. It wasn't a war, wrote his critics. And even if it was a war, then it wasn't an officially declared war and both sides didn't wear uniforms. And even if it still rated somehow as a real war, then Aborigines were the other side, and they were the losers, and victors don't put up monuments to the losers. Aborigines are not Us. Here speaks the real politics of separatism in Australia today. (Griffiths 2003: 147)

There is, I believe, another distinction to be made: there are the dead who are members of community (and thus those whose deaths matter), and then there are the dead who are outside the community and thus whose deaths matter to the extent that they can be excluded. The first is social and commemorative, the second harks back to the relationship between violence and progress. If progress emerges from violence, and if conquest is not complete, then deaths that are treated as if they do not matter actually still do matter. They mark progress. Nicholas Thomas (1997: 28) contends that settler societies seek simultaneously to exterminate and exhibit Indigenous people. Arguably, Aboriginal deaths are necessary to Australian nation-making even as the dead are dishonoured through denial and through chilling debates about how much blood has been shed and whose bloodshed counts.

Dialogue works counter to monological separatism; it requires a 'we' who share a time and space of attentiveness, and who bring our moral capabilities into the encounter. It seems we must also bring the dead into the dialogue. It is not yet possible to know, dialogically, what they may say to us.

Witness

To listen with attentiveness is to take a first step in witnessing. Thus to break out of monologue and into a ground of encounter across difference and harm is suddenly to encounter one's self as witness. In his study *Suffering Witness,* Hatley (2000: 3) defines witness as 'a mode of responding to the other's plight that exceeds an epistemological determination and becomes an ethical involvement. One must not only utter a truth about the ... [person] but also remain true *to* her or him.'

The demands of witnessing are demands of memory. Fackenheim, among many scholars, asserts that memory work is a refusal to participate in violence. If the purpose of violence was to extinguish certain people, knowledges, and perspectives, then memory continues to resist that violence. Thus the moral burden of the past in the present includes this refusal to succumb to the world of violence and amnesia; witnessing promotes remembrance and works against death and against the comfort of monologue.

The past has a moral claim on us, and so do the people in the present whose memories and actions we witness. The claim is often phrased in terms of the dead, but it is often put to us by the living. I do not here deny the direct claims of the dead. Who, for example, can look at a recent photo of mass graves being exhumed and not find one's self morally claimed by the eye sockets that still seem to search out some connection with the living? In our everyday lives in Australia and other settler societies, however, we are more likely to encounter such claims as they are mediated by the living.

Moral claims are thrust upon one, and then a response is due.

Throughout his study Hatley discusses the problematics of the witness's moral response, and while I do not want to play down the ambiguities of the situation, I also want to draw attention to the dialogical potential at work here. To be claimed is to be called into connection; to respond is to start to actualise that connection. Muecke (1997: 184–85) contends that connections lead to commitment. Connection, in his view, is a new way of reasoning, a way that leads into engagement and purpose. I am saying that decolonisation depends on this process: the moral claim, the response, the recognition of connection, the commitment.

Intention and Hope

Recuperative work takes its intention from the demonstrated fact that violence and damage are not the only things we are capable of. Many of us really do seek to find ways to generate a moral presence for ourselves. Such a presence is founded in the 'now' of our lives, engages with our moral relationships with the past, acknowledges our violence, and works dialogically towards alternatives. Accordingly, this work demands that we consider an ethics of intention.

The ethics I am developing around decolonisation acknowledge the claims of others (thus far I have only dealt with human others), and to acknowledge the existence of such claims is itself a provocation. Response to a claim is itself a call – of refusal of violence, of further claims of responsibility. And so the question must be asked: does it matter if anyone is listening?

Avishai Margalit (2002: 155), for example, argues that people witness as an act of hope, or perhaps of faith, 'that in another place or another time there exists, or will exist, a moral community that will listen to their testimony'. I am absolutely certain that this form of faith informed the decision of Hobbles Danaiyarri and other North Australian historians to share their stories with westerners (discussed in Rose 2003). Indeed, they were quite explicit in asserting their belief that there were others, including White people, who would hear the stories in their moral context and would find ways to make a moral response. For myself, I understood my position as scribe to be a moral claim on my own life, and this book continues my exploration of that claim.

But what if one had no faith that there were others who would listen? Would it still be important to witness? Margalit leaves this question open, seeming to conclude that there must be some level of faith in order to warrant witnessing. Other scholars of memory and witnessing contend that one must proceed as if there were hope, whether one can be sure of that or not. Glowacka, for example, works with Fackenheim's (1978) study of hope and suggests that one must continue *as if* there were hope because to do so is still to refuse violence, and to work towards some sort of mending of the assault on humanity brought about by man-made mass death (Glowacka 2000: 39).

Still others are even more stern, claiming that there is always a moral duty to remember and witness. From this perspective, even if one were certain that there was no reason to hope, there would still be reason existentially to define one's self as one who refuses violence. It seems to me as well that as long as there is one person who refuses violence, then there could be some grounds for hope, but that is not really the point. Levinas is the best representative of this most extreme position. He contends that memory and witnessing attest not only to the past and to harm but to the good in the present moment. One is commanded to goodness even if it is futile. In his wisdom, Levinas contends that there is no nuanced philosophical argument for this position. It is given in the nature of ethics: the claim is always there (discussed in Hatley 2000: 99).

The stronger statements of moral response and possible futility take us away from hope and towards an existential ethics of claim. I think this is a good thing. A few years ago I was working with the idea of an ethics of hope, and I offered a short paper on the subject at a symposium at Pitzer College in Claremont California. One of the Native American participants, Robert John, took me up on my use of the concept of hope, and we spent quite a few hours discussing it. In his view 'hope is wishy washy'. He contended that if you really care that something may happen, then you offer your intention. You put your will into it. You do what you can to make it happen. From his intention- and action-oriented perspective, I had to agree that hope does seem banal, and I started thinking about an ethics of connection rather than hope (Rose 1999).

A complementary perspective on hope is put forward by Paul Ricoeur (1995), although he argues for hope whereas I would now argue against it. In Ricoeur's view, hope is connected to concepts of time that look towards future redemption. History directed towards a vision of a better future is a history of hope (1995: 204–205). I would contend, in contrast, that the evidence for alternatives exists in the present, and that intention towards alternatives does not have to rely on hope. From this perspective, hope could be seen to be implicated in time-concepts that deflect us from our moral presence in the here and now, and thus engage us in violence. This violence consists in ignoring the diversity of life in the present moment in favour of an imagined life in a future moment.

The recuperative project seeks to demarcate a path towards decolonisation, and we can be grateful that here in Australia one does not have to consider in a practical way what one would do if there were no one with whom to share the path and put their footprints alongside ours. Our decolonising work leads us directly into claim, connection, and commitment.

2
WOUNDED SPACE

> How many of us can really imagine that the war against nature will be over and we will come out alive in a world where continuing ecological destruction is not the order of the day? (Nicholson 2001: 147–48)

Two issues capture my concern: these are wounded space, and seduction. By wounded space I mean geographical space that has been torn and fractured by violence and exile, and that is pitted with sites where life has been irretrievably killed. Seduction arises from the quality of the terrains of one's life, and lies in one's longing for immunity. There is a uniquely Australian temptation that sits on one's shoulder and whispers the maddening little mantra 'she'll be right, mate'.[1]

In analysing geography as a cultural system I aim to uncover some of the ruptures that impede our attentiveness to the here-ness of the here. I examine the dissonance and double binds that Imperial geography creates for this settler society in which the colonisers are also colonised. This analysis leads me to a brief look at the savagely satirical aspect of Australian identity, the continuing desire for immunity, and the work of witnessing for Nature. My argument is that the moral engagement with the past in the present must include the natural world, and I work with the ethics discussed in chapter 1 to include the natural world within the moral community of encounter, responsibility, and witness.

Ecocide[2]

Settler societies are built on a dual war: a war against Nature and a war against the natives. Each has been devastating. In both the

United States and Australia, the evidence for dual warfare is found in written material and in the vernacular. In 1801 Pierre Du Pont de Nemours wrote to Thomas Jefferson: 'The inhabitants of your country districts regard Indians and forests as natural enemies which must be exterminated by fire and sword and brandy, in order that they may seize their territory' (quoted in Churchill 1992: 139). White Australians say much the same thing in their succinct vernacular: 'If it moves shoot it, if it doesn't move chop it down.'

Our legacy includes both genocide and ecocide. It is well known that settlers cleared the land of both native people and native ecologies in order to establish what they took to be civilisation. The idea that our history is marked by genocide is widely debated, and if not widely accepted, at least is recognised as a possible interpretation of our history (see, for example, Curthoys & Docker 2001 and other contributors to the journal *Aboriginal History*, vol. 25). The idea that our history is marked by ecocide may be far less familiar although it has been well documented over decades (for example, Bolton 1981; Lines 1991; Marshall 1966; see also Wilson 2002). We also have an excellent literature on the links between colonisation, modernity, development, and devastation (Mies & Shiva 1993, for example). As well, there is now a new and excellent study of 'the ecological crisis of reason' (Plumwood 2002).

In summary form, the evidence for ecocide goes like this: conquest has brought about a devastation so sudden and massive that we will never fully grasp its extent or its consequences. Many of my Aboriginal teachers indicated that White people just didn't seem to get the sense of it at all. Devastation includes the loss of around 90 per cent of the original Aboriginal population, the loss of all but a small number of Aboriginal languages, and the loss of earlier cultural coherence of the continent through Aboriginal networks of cultural exchange. It includes the loss of large numbers of plant and animal species, including the highest rate of mammalian extinctions in the contemporary world. Globally, a recent study predicts that by 2050 one quarter to one third of all land animals, plants will become extinct (Brown 2004). Indeed, EO Wilson (2002: 99) contends that the rate of extinctions today is between 1000 and 10 000 times the rate prior to recent human patterns of production and consumption. In his view we are now at decisive point; the legacy of the 21st century could well be an 'Age of Loneliness' (p. 77).

There is the regular loss of topsoil as it washes out to sea or is blown across to New Zealand. Water tables are rising in some areas, falling in others, and large amounts of agricultural land are lost to salinity, while large amounts of pastoral land are lost to erosion and scalding. There is widespread loss of surface water, barely documented as yet, and extensive desertification, also as yet barely documented; in many areas water is just running out (Fullerton 2001). Then, too, there are the invasions: feral animals, weeds and transported exotics invade and displace indigenous plants and animals (Low 1999). As systems change, there is loss of habitat, loss of biodiversity, and, increasingly, the loss of life support systems that make life (including that of the settlers) possible. Losses amplify, generating more death, damage and disorder.

We experience these losses, if we experience them at all, in our own local areas, but we know about them at a range of scales including global systems within which life and damage are embedded. Vandana Shiva (1993) connects colonisation with development, asserting that development is a continuation of colonisation. In her analysis, development continues the colonising project of wealth creation at the cost of water, soils, plants and animals, and marginalised people.

Australia is very much part of the global scene, both in the numbers of extinctions and in the production of the waste and damage (including greenhouse gases) that promotes extinctions. The violence wrought on indigenous Australian ecosystems, the practice and making of the 'wild', is both long-standing and ongoing. Much of the past can be known in the present as absence – the mammals that are no longer here, the plants that are gone; or as danger – all those species that are on a trajectory towards extinction. Only some of the endangered ones can and will be swerved back onto a trajectory of life through changes to human practices. In the wake of settler ecocide, Australian settlers, by our own actions, can only inhabit what is for us 'wounded space' (Blanchot 1986: 30).[3] The further consequence, of course, is that these terrains are damaged for Indigenous people, too, as I discuss in chapter 9.

Geography as a Cultural System

The analysis of the culture of place, or of the geographical dimension of culture, has produced many excellent Australian studies that have taught us about exploration and encounter, master narratives, and perception of place (for example, Carter 1988, 1996; Gibson 1992, 2002; Ryan 1996; Arthur 2003; Thomas 2003). Here I consider the mythic and cosmological structures of orientation, horizon, narration, and culturally defined 'deixis' (see below) that constitute an architecture of geographical ways of knowing.

Mikhail Bakhtin (1981) developed the idea of the 'chronotope' to refer to a set of culturally constructed time-space co-ordinates. He analyses novels, but his ideas have a much broader scope. In the webs of our lives, as much as in novels, 'the chronotope is the place where the knots of narrative are tied and untied', and where time is bound into space (Bakhtin 1981: 250). Every culture develops its own manner of fashioning time and space into social and symbolic configurations, and these configurations become part of the 'common sense' social knowledge of a given group.

The assumptions, presuppositions and understandings of geography and society constitute taken-for-granted information about the world, and as such constitute some of the most powerful and largely unexamined strands in the webs of stories in which Arendt contends that human life is always already enmeshed (Arendt 1958: 181–88; see also Geertz 1973). The givenness of a system of cultural geography underlies early European imagining of the southern hemisphere. The antipodes had been thought about for two or three millennia (Gibson 1992: 87), and long before the people of the British Isles had a concept of a round world, they had a concept of an other world which was sometimes identified with the antipodes. Called Otherworld, and Underworld, this place was located beyond the sea in the west, or it was located beneath the surface of the earth; it was hidden in mists or located far to the south. It was like the ordinary world, but enhanced: it was the place and source of health, youth, wealth, wisdom, perpetual spring and summer, fruits and feasts, music and joy. Bright, fabulous, and sensuously delightful, it was the place where trees have silver branches and golden apples, and birds sing songs of such peace and beauty that sick people would find sleep (MacCulloch 1991: 380). In many accounts it was, of course, the place of King Arthur, from whence he would return to defeat the enemies of his people (Rees & Rees 1989: 71).

Accounts first recorded in the 1100s assert that Arthur was

lord over the antipodes during the course of his lifetime, and that the local antipodean king (the King of the Dwarfs, in one account) paid homage to Arthur. Welsh tradition peopled the antipodes (or lower hemisphere) with 'high-minded dwarfs', while others portrayed the place and people in forms grotesque and ridiculous, using the place as a site of satire directed towards contemporary figures and events. In 12th-century Europe both traditions were extant: the antipodes were the home of wise, honoured and noble dwarfs, and, alternatively, of grotesque and ridiculous beings (Loomis 1956: 65, 68).

Christianity demonised the Underworld, labelling it Hell, and recasting its symbolism in grotesque fashion, but visions of and longing for the Celtic Underworld persist and coexist. An example that makes the point perfectly is Bernard Smith's epitomisation of the artist Drysdale's landscape imagery as 'alien to man, harsh, weird, spacious and vacant, given over to the oddities and whimsies of nature, fit only for heroes and clowns, saints, exiles and primitive men' (quoted in Mulvaney 1991: 113).

Along with ways of conceptualising the southern land and its inhabitants, European settlers also brought with them their fixed points of reference. In *The Road from Coorain*, Jill Ker Conway describes the people of the region she calls 'The West', that is, the western plains of New South Wales:

> At night when they sat with their wives beside their crackling static-blurred radios, they waited for Big Ben to chime and then heard the impeccable British accents of the BBC announcer reading the news. With that voice they absorbed a map of the world which placed their near neighbour, Japan, in the Far East, and located distant Turkey in the Near East. (Conway 1989: 13–14)

I take this basic disjunction to be one of the foundations of the never-ending discussion of the question 'where are we?' Are we part of Asia or part of the Pacific? Part of the western world? Somewhere else entirely? Are we south of the west, as Gibson (1992) contends, or south of the east, as maps indicate? The only location that seems stable is that we are unambiguously Down Under, and this label only makes sense as a colonised position. We can say with certainty that Aboriginal people did not consider themselves to be Down Under.

The World, the Body, and the Social

Europeans were able to 'know' about this place they could only imagine because their imagining was created out of a system of understandings of orientation and polarity which already structured the world. Linguists use the term 'deixis' to refer to words which specify aspects of communication whose interpretation depends on knowledge of the context in which communication occurs (Lyle 1990: 88). Words such as 'here', 'there', 'now', and 'then' are deictic – one has to know the context in order to understand. Ego is the centre of standard deictic communication. 'Here' and 'now' are time-space co-ordinates that are contingent on the speaker's own siting.

In contrast, socio-centric deixis refers to temporal and/or spatial co-ordinates that are held as social/cultural constants. I am exploring two main aspects: socio-centric zero-point, and polarity. Socio-centric zero-point is a set of time and/or spatial co-ordinates that are held constant irrespective of individuals. A clear example of spatial zero-point is found in sacred cosmic geography. For example, Semitic and Indo-European traditions speak of an *axis mundi*, a sacred topos consisting of a mountain or tree from which flow the four rivers of the world (Clifford 1972: 95, 190–91). In both sacred and secular geography the zero-point is not an empty space, in spite of the term 'zero'; it is the pivot of the system (Lyle 1990: 91).

Polarity involves spatial parameters of right and left, front and back, up and down. Spatially it involves the direction of facing and the site from which a society is held to face. Thus, for example, the archaic old-world socio-centric orientation was towards the east. This orientation is evident in Hebrew and Arabic languages, as well as a number of Indo-European languages, such as Gaelic, in which the terms for 'south' and 'right' are the same (Lyle 1990: 153). Before the introduction of Christianity in Europe, this orientation situated the person and the society towards the rising sun. With Christianity, this orientation placed the person with their face towards their sacred origins, looking towards the sacred sites in and around Jerusalem, and beyond, perhaps to the 'garden in Eden, in the east' (Genesis 2:8). A few of these basic parameters of European-centred geographies of East and West are outlined by Fiedler in his study of American cultural identity:

> For a long time Europeans thought of themselves as inhabiting a world without a West; a three-fold *oecumene* made up of Europe itself, Asia, and Libya, which is to say a ruling and redeemed North plus a subsidiary and redeemable East and South. The fourth direction they considered closed off to colonisation and the hope of salvation by the impassable barrier of the River Ocean, which could be glimpsed through the terminal Straits of Gibraltar or from the shores of those peripheral European Isles, Ireland and Iceland ... What Homer and Hesiod described to themselves as the Isles of the Blest or Elysium becomes the Hesperides, the Fortunate Isles, eventually the Earthly Paradise ... And it is the Celts, the Irish in particular, who, from their home on the very verge of the West, have dreamed most variously and convincingly of that other Place, naming it ... [among others] Avalon: the Island of apple trees where Good King Arthur sleeps and awaits his second coming. (Fiedler 1968: 27–28)

Spatial orientation cannot be separated from its corresponding temporal orientation. To the extent that the east constituted the sacred source, it must also have constituted a founding moment in time, and while the sacred centre undoubtedly was thought to exist through all time, movement away from the centre constitutes movement through time. In Western European thinking the direction of time is towards the west. That which is closer to the origin is older than that which is further away. European culture placed a positive value on the quality of youth, and Western Europeans saw themselves as privileged with youth, promise and energy in comparison with the older cultures to the east. Westward position is thus linked to the agrarian myth; new beginnings enable release from the depravity of the old, and the escape from an earlier civilisation is the opportunity to transcend it (Worster 1991).

This geography was possible as long as the world was understood to consist of the north, east and south. With the discovery of the New World (originally, of course, thought to be the east, hence the labelling of the Indigenous people as 'Indians'), a new orientation was brought into being. In Fiedler's (1968: 30) words: 'All that is necessary to make Celtic and Christian fantasy one is to realize that the earth is mythologically as well as geographically round, that the paradise lost in the East can be regained by sailing West.'

With round-world geography the western world shifted orientation and now faces west, the zone of the future, rather than east, the zone of the past. Americans all face west, because that is the direction of the future, and in facing the future, and in being the vanguard of the move towards the future, Americans claim to transcend the past. The linearity I discussed in chapter 1 is given extremely literal geographical expression in American landscape poetics (see Rose, in press a). Western Europe now finds itself positioned between the ultimate west (America) and its own west. Once securely positioned to encompass the whole of the known world, Europe is now positioned ambiguously by round-world geography; it is of the west but no longer the unambiguously definitive site of the west. Again, age is brought into the discourse, and Europeans now seek to privilege their position on the grounds of their relative maturity in comparison with the United States.

World geography is reinforced by, and itself reinforces, the mapping of society and the body. Social mapping in ancient Indo-European cosmogony is based on a tripartite division of society – ruling elite, warriors, labourers – as Georges Dumézil and many others have shown (see Littleton 1982). The pervasive quality of this division cannot be underestimated; it survived and influenced Christianity, and it has survived and influenced secularisation (Lyle 1990: 231). Social strata are mapped onto the human body with metaphors that are entirely contemporary. 'Priests' (intellectuals) were associated with the head and with thought, perception, and speech. 'Warriors' were associated with the upper torso and with strength, energy, and courage. Labourers (commoners/producers) were associated with the lower torso, with physical labour, and with an exuberant appetite for food, drink, and sex (Lincoln 1986).

The waist is the zero-point of the body, and the two upper divisions belong together over and against the lower division. Thousands of years ago this imagery was brought to bear by priests and warriors to explain why the lowest stratum needed to work and to be ruled, and why it could not be trusted to think or act for itself. The lowest stratum was said to consist of the people who, all brawn and no brain, were appropriately to be engaged in manual labour, and who would be unable, so the theory goes, to put the products of their labour to sensible use. They were the people who could not control their powerful urges for food, drink, and sex, and who therefore needed to be controlled by their superiors. Their labour was taken for granted as being there to be used by upper classes (Lincoln 1986).

The geographical potential of microcosm and macrocosm was extended and, one might say, fulfilled during the period of colonisation. Like the body, the earth is also divided into above and below, with a socio-centric 'waist' that is notionally fixed at about the Tropic of Cancer. The region north of (or above) that notional line is valued along one set of criteria; the region south of (or below) that notional line is valued along another set of criteria.

Mapping these symbolic associations onto the globe, one finds the north (upper body, two upper classes) associated with mental labour, rulership and reason, while the south (lower body, lower class) is associated with manual labour, rule by others, and appetite and emotion without reason. Going towards the east and down, you found backward races and lower civilisations. East and south (down) could be conceptualised as the past; west and north (up) could be conceptualised as the future. These orientations were linked into a linear framework, in the sense that there was only one future for everybody. Any person, group or culture that was going to move 'forward' or 'progress' upward was going to follow the lead of the west. (See also chapter 8.)

In the era of colonisation the north created its wealth through conquest of the south, and the south was confirmed in its inferiority by the fact of being conquered. Exploitation of resources and labour was comfortably conceptualised as the productive use of a region which (in theory) was a source of limitless supplies of raw materials, including human labour, which could only be put to proper use by those advanced cultures of the north (for example, Baudrillard 1994: 66–71).

Savagery Down Under

The cultural constructions of East/West and Down/Up, linked to class, culture, labour, and resources pervade issues of Australian identity to this day, framed still by the ambivalent positioning of settlers as both coloniser and colonised, and by the heterogeneity of settlers' attitudes towards and relationships with overseas places. Ross Gibson (1992) constructs a compelling postcolonial narrative of Australia that seeks to revivify the fabulous conceptions of the Great South Land and position this continent south of the west. I think it is fair to say, however, that when the English mapped Australia into their Empire they located it very far east and very far down. It is not called Down Under by accident. In English Imperial imagery England was mapped as Home (zero-point), and Australia was mapped as colony. The oppressive logic of hierarchical opposition was integral to the geography of Empire: Australia was not-Home – that is, everything Home was not, and deficient in everything properly belonging to Home. It was associated with natural resources to be taken elsewhere, with manual labour, and with the kind of coarse earthiness (or uncouth boorishness, depending on perspective) deemed to be characteristic of the lower orders of society. The socio-centric Home remained fixed in the British Isles, and the whole weight of the category 'lower' was brought to bear in defining Australia. The category 'lower' is the non-self to the powerful pole of self (as discussed in chapter 1). Plumwood (1973: 117) explains that this and other binary separations are actually 'hyper-separated': they work on the idea that the two poles of separation really have nothing in common. In this social context, as in others, lower people, ecologies, and places are there to benefit the pole of power, and their contributions are either denied or taken for granted (Plumwood 2002: 27). The colonising project of wealth creation analysed so vividly by Shiva (1993) was, we can see retrospectively, wildly wasteful of the water, soils, plants, animals, and people, particularly, but not exclusively, Indigenous people. Much of today's development continues this wastage.

White Australians are ambiguously positioned in this structure. In their role as colonisers they represent Home; the discontinuity between home and colony positions them on the side of Home and thus alienates them from the place where they actually live and from the Indigenous people whose homes are here. In their role as settlers who come to stay, however, they are positioned as colonials. The discontinuity between Home and colony now positions them on the side of the colony, alienating them from their own origins and kin, and assigning them a lower-order identity. In the first position they share a Home-based subjectivity which distances them from the continent and the Indigenous people. In the second position, they find themselves excluded from the subjectivity of Home, and objectified as a disjunctive fragment transported to an unfavourable part of the globe. Australians' long insistence on their 'whiteness' may have been stimulated by their desire to find a clear and seemingly natural code by which to assert what was at heart completely ambiguous.

Several founding myths have competed in defining the relationship between Home and Australia. Australian nationalistic ideology sought to found the nation within a mythology that bore a loose, and never thoroughly pursued, relationship to the Exodus story which is America's foundation myth. Americans, early and recent, have conceptualised themselves as being freed from tyranny and delivered into a New Promised Land (Bercovitch 1978: 65–66). Australia, in contrast, was from the first conceived as hell on earth, and from an American perspective its foundation owes as much to the myth of Expulsion as to myths or dreams of liberation. In the first decades the majority of the people who settled here did so not to escape tyranny, but at the precise will and directive of the monarch. Henry Parkes (1890: 74) spoke of the original settlers as 'a despairing group of outcast persons of British origin'. The Expulsion myth situates Home as Eden, the monarch as God, and the convicts as fallen people doomed, like Adam and Eve, to a life of toil and sweat amid thorns and thistles (Genesis 3:17–19).

Ann Curthoys (1999) brings new insight to the Exodus myth in Australia, arguing that it enabled settlers to cast themselves in the role of victim, and thus to emphasise their own suffering and harden their hearts to the suffering of Indigenous people. She links Exodus and victimology to the pioneer legend; both focus on 'the hardships endured by white people ... [who] are at the heart of the narrative' (Curthoys 2003: 191). Her work thus offers a strong cultural foundation for the monologue that excludes Indigenous people.

According to Russel Ward (1970), the convicts were the people among whom were formed the values and attributes which would become the Australian national identity, and for whom Australia became home. They wore the imagery of the lower sphere and lower body as a badge of honour, subverting and rejecting the old-world hierarchies, the arrogance of the 'high born', and the subservience of the lowly. They were the levellers, the equalisers, the mates. Their humour deflates the pompous and glorifies nobody. In Ward's (1970: 40) view, 'the lower orders were singularly unimpressed by the self-proclaimed superiority of the colonial "gentry"'. Their language is rich in inventive terms which scoff at pretension, heaping insult upon insult: toffee-waffies, silver tails, Lord Haw Haws and jumped up Poms populate the Australian vocabulary.

Australians' behaviour as well as their language disrupted and burlesqued the taken-for-granted social order of Home. The ancient tripartite social division was inverted, mocked, fashioned as grotesque and rendered ineffectual in many pragmatic ways, although the sense that the source of value in the world does not emerge from Australia but rather from overseas still lives in parts of the public arena and presumably in the hearts of some Australians.

The field of Australian identity is wide and disparate. Complexity is related to the heterogeneity of experience and longing, and also to subversion. One of the most perceptive analyses of nationalism and the destabilisation of White Australian identity is Andrew Lattas's (1990) article 'Aborigines and Contemporary Australian Nationalism'. Lattas contends that the public discourse which focuses on Australians' purported alienation from the land is related directly to their purported lack of national identity. He further argues that the 'ascribed lack of national identity is used continuously to authorise discourses which are concerned with giving us a sense of national self'. Paradoxically, he says, 'this sense of being without meaning is itself a system of meaning' (Lattas 1990: 55, 67).

The cultural production of an alleged void busily fills the alleged void with a continuing discourse about the 'problem' of the void. There is another side of this alleged void, and that is that Australian identity and sense of belonging are actualised and affirmed, for some Australians at least, in the rejection of any single subjectivity. Among the main strategies Australians have developed in attempting to produce a unique subjectivity are mimicry and satire. I use the word 'satire' as a general gloss to include sarcasm, parody, and Gibson's (1992: 10) eloquent 'sardonic utopianism'. The term also covers vernacular expressions such as 'taking the mickey out of', or 'sending up'. Identity in this mode is always being debunked and reinvented.

Australian satirical identity depends on the ambiguity of Home. A reflection must bear some relation to the source, and in Imperial geography a settler colony must be a distorted reflection of Home. In fact Home will insist on both: that its colony mirror it, and that the colony fail accurately to mirror it. Superiority is produced and authenticated precisely through this double bind. Australians have grasped and subverted the logic, creating a hall of mirrors which reflects images only to destabilise them, and fundamentally and thoroughly to subvert the authenticity of Empire-inspired narratives of inferiority. Further, the destabilisation of meanings becomes its own reward; meaning is found in the inability of any set of meanings to encompass Australia.

This is the code: that all totalising narratives concerning White Australian identity will be destabilised and debunked. The result is a wild and contentious sense of place, a mimicking mockery of Hell, Home and Otherworld that enables an Australian, for example, to stand in a desert, sunburnt, parched with thirst and covered with flies, surrounded by thorns and thistles, and call the place Godzone. This disruptive sense of place, simultaneously self-mocking and self-affirming (who but a native-born Australian, Aboriginal or settler, could call such a place God's Own?), is continuously being created and contested. The continuity of invention and contestation depends on the failure of meanings, on gaps and discontinuities, on narratives satirised, disrupted, and rendered inadequate, and its power is sustained in part because it is still found to be loathsome by those who continue to hold that the zero-point of the globe, the apex of history and culture, is Home in Europe.

For a number of years I puzzled over an appropriate term for this Down Under position. It is very far east and so very far down; it is savage in its self-mockery and affirms itself provocatively through self-satire; it is disrespectful of the cringing towards Home, and yet never loses sight of itself as the object of Home scrutiny. In 1994 Prime Minister Paul Keating was reported to have described Australia as the arse-end of the world. There is absolutely no improving on this brash, provocative, bodily situated and mirroring term. It mingles defiance, resistance, recognition and complacency, associating itself intimately with the strangeness of the place (from a northern hemisphere perspective), and all the while mooning off at Britain. This complex and resilient identity resists totalisation and yet establishes its own possibilities for a totalising presence through its shifty and unstable dynamic.

Resilience and Countermodernity

The great Australian mantra 'she'll be right' speaks to a mode of quietism that can go in two major directions. One is the direction of amnesia and the illusion of progress. In this direction the seduction is to lull us into a sense that somehow it is all going to be okay. The other direction takes us into a philosophy of Nature and place that calls for quietism and demands activism.

Amnesia can be seen as a response to the view that this broken world is our destiny in the sense that it is the result of all the actions that brought us here. To be responsive to the vulnerability of living beings and living systems is to become exposed to responsibility, and to the possibility of intense suffering as well as to the possibilities of serenity, joy and belonging. Peter Read explores these issues with sensitivity to the fact that settlers are settling in where others have been dispossessed, in his perceptive trilogy *Returning to Nothing* (1996), *Belonging* (2000), and *Haunted Earth* (2003). The seduction of comfort, if such there be, lies squarely here in a desire to avoid suffering. As self and place are interwoven for most of us, self-protection would require insulation from other living beings and from place itself. Self-protection would thus promote the fragmentations of modernity and while insulating us, would also leave us stranded in a hapless no-where.

The problem for memory is this: if we are to forget all the things that may make us uneasy, then we have to forget even to think about the places where uncomfortable things happen. If we were able to do that, then we would find ourselves forgetting the losses for which we are ultimately accountable, and insulating ourselves against the absences that surround us. Worse, perhaps, we would have to forget what is vulnerable, endangered, under threat. We would have to forget the accountability which gives our lives moral gravity. We would have to forget who and where we really are.

And yet many, probably most, Australians have come to love not just their built or otherwise transformed environments but their natural world as well. Freya Mathews (1999b: 95) puts the case that here in Australia '"Nature" is still bigger than "culture"'. She describes us as 'a settler society ... set down arbitrarily in a country bigger than' our society. Mathews points out that Australia produced some of the earliest critiques of human supremacism (in relation to Nature) and that Australian philosopher Val Plumwood was a key figure in the first wave of radical ecophilosophy (1993: 96). To this one would now add that Plumwood has written a powerful new study of contemporary crisis (2002), and one would add that Mathews herself is making wide-ranging and important contributions to eco-philosophy (Mathews 1991, 2002, and other work in press). This side of Australian identity rejects amnesia and engages with a passionate critique of man-made mass destruction.

Resilience

In considering resilience we need to make a crucial set of distinctions between types of human action: anti-resilience, engineered resilience, and facilitated resilience. The first type is most evident in large-scale schemes of mass destruction of ecosystems: dams are a good example, but so are engineered forests and other plantation monocultures (Scott 1998 provides numerous excellent examples). The key feature is that humans actively oppose and seek to suppress Nature's own resilience. The second type, engineered resilience, comprises those efforts to force Nature to behave as humans would like Nature to behave. Suppression of fire in national parks is a good example: the parks are there to protect Nature, but fire suppression damages Nature in the long run. Other examples include efforts to reclaim damaged places in order to put them in the service of human efforts. This type of human engineering works selectively to promote aspects of resilience deemed valuable to humans. In contrast, the third type, resilience facilitation, involves observing Nature's own processes and then working to facilitate the conditions under which Nature's resilience can flourish. This could mean leaving the place alone, or it could mean some form of active engagement with the place. In either case, it is almost certainly going to involve struggles with other people to try to prevent interventions that diminish or incapacitate resilience. These types are not totally discrete; there is overlap and there are fluctuations in thought and action.

In considering the war against Nature, the existential condition is that what is extinct will not be brought back to life, and some ecosystems are so damaged that they are unlikely to be capable of self-repair in any human time-frame. Nevertheless, the beautiful resilience of the natural world can be astounding. It is experienced in the wake of many catastrophic events, such as the Mount St Helens volcano that exploded in 1980. Ecologists documenting the return of life to areas that were blasted clear of all life have been impressed at the rapidity and vigour with which life seeks to organise itself into patterns of growth and regeneration (Franklin et al. 2000). They note, however, that there are significant differences in the biological legacies left after natural 'disturbances' when compared with man-made disturbances. The latter tend to leave far less of a legacy for resilient recovery.

I would take the concept of resilience further, perhaps, than many ecologists might care to go; I would put forward the idea that resilience is extraordinarily countermodern in its implications. Resilience works with connectivity and commitment. It acknowledges the force, or desire, of living things to flourish, to be in connection, to find their mutually beneficial patterns, and to restore in the world the power of life which is always in delicate relationship with death. My words put a human slant on a biological concept, and I do this in part to work across the discursive divide that often prevents such lateral thinking. This divide is arbitrary, and usually unhelpful. It is also dangerous to the extent that it cuts us off from understanding our place in the world by thinking that knowledge concerning 'Nature' does not apply to us, and vice versa. In addition, I mingle languages because whatever the language, the facts referred to are the same: life does want to live, it does want to be in connection, it does want flourishing relationships, it does want pattern and community. If we are to facilitate resilience we need to understand not only the specifics of individuals, but also the larger patterns of life.

The concept of resilience brings us back into the here and the now. Life processes take place in time, and are emplaced. The same must also be said of loss. Most scientific analysis of environmental crisis deals in agglomerated figures that are largely abstracted from place. In contrast, loss is primarily experienced *in place*. We are unlikely to experience the predicted loss of twenty-one out of twenty-four species of butterflies in Australia (Brown 2004), but we are almost certain to encounter absences – places where butterflies used to be and are no more. These places may be forests or paddocks, but may just as well be one's own backyard.

Places marked by loss, by the absent ones whose presence is now only memory, are sites of wounding. Tumarkin (2002: 5) uses the brilliantly evocative term 'traumascapes' to refer to places that are repetitively bound by violence. She writes that 'any examination of place history and place making in this country is bound, sooner or later, to come face to face with traumatic legacies of colonialism [lying] silent in or addressing us through the continent's ground' (p. 41). She calls us to relieve some of the burden of traumascapes by 'taking on our responsibility for the histories and memories that they have come to embody' (p. 42). The further point is that while we cannot take up responsibility for a set of statistics, we can take up responsibility for place and action, and can assist others to take up their responsibility. We can act, and we can witness.

Australians and love

I am holding my focus on ecologies and working with a concept of place that is not confined to the natural. Sense of place attaches equally to natural and to built environments – to homes, neighbourhoods, and towns, for example (Read 1996). Mathews analyses the philosophical implications of resilience, quietism, and activism in an exquisite essay, 'Letting the World Grow Old' (1999c). She asks the question: 'What is nature, and how are we to live *with* it rather than *against* it?' (p. 119). Her answer is to consider Nature as a process rather than a thing, and thus to consider that the 'natural' is the undisturbed (by humans) unfolding of events, as distinct from the intentional redirection of the course of events (p. 121). Mathews is thus able to argue that it is 'never too late to return to nature' (p. 126). She sets her philosophy of reinhabitation within an action domain in which 'respect for the world' hinges on the capacity of the world to unfold in its own way (p. 133), and is demonstrated by permitting what exists to continue to endure. She specifically develops her analysis within an urban context to make the point that Nature is everywhere (see also Low 2002).

'Letting nature be' is a recuperative project that facilitates resilience; it does not offer a licence for negligence. The quietism of working with resilience is potentially countermodern, as Mathews describes it (1999c: 133). Modernity, she contends, seeks to remake the world in accordance with abstract ideas; it posits man against Nature in a drive towards continuous overcoming. 'Letting things be' thus challenges and works against modernity. The further consequence of 'letting things be' requires political and other forms of action in defence of the given (see also chapter 11). The clear moral duty is to seek to prevent actions that fight against Nature's resilience.

Report from Lake Pedder

People are called to defend the places they love, witnessing to their meaningfulness and, in the worst cases, witnessing to loss. The power and presence of lost and damaged places is eloquently attested to by the hundred or so people who spoke to Pete Read as part of his research into 'the meaning of lost places'. Read (1996: xii) advises us: 'Let us not underestimate the effect which the loss of dead and dying places has on our own self-identity, mental well-being and sense of belonging.'

Those who witness to the loss of place, especially when place is lost to the colossus of development, take up a moral burden. They break up monologue and sustain a moral engagement with the past in the present that gives voice, presence, and power to that which has been lost, abandoned, or destroyed. The burden of witnessing to ecological loss brings Nature into a moral community, implicitly asserting in the context of place the injunction described by Hatley (chapter 1): not only to speak truthfully, but to remain true *to* the place. In remaining true to place, one remains (or seeks to remain) true to non-human living things, ecosystems, and processes of resilience.

The terms 'non-human living things', 'ecosystems', and 'processes of resilience' are abstract; we encounter their reality in the world, in place. Acting in defence of, and witnessing to, place opens a gateway to conflict and to further moral dilemma. It also opens further one's own vulnerability to suffering through the vulnerability of others to suffer. Kevin Kiernan (1990) has written eloquently about his relationship of love and loss with Lake Pedder. This mountain lake in the island state of Tasmania was dammed in 1973. The purported reason was for hydro-electricity. Opposition to the plan was vigorous. As Read (1996: 126) puts it:

> Dodgers, posters, clothing, newsletters, books, poems, public meetings, political parties, committees, films, scientific reports, inquiries, stickers, vigils, depositions and petitions were among the measures employed to halt the inundation. All failed.

Arguments based on reason failed: it was clear that there were perfectly viable alternatives, and at one point the Commonwealth offered to pay for one of them in order to save the lake. Arguments based on science, on poetry, love, and passion also failed. Opposition continued well after the lake had been dammed in the hope that it could be restored (Kiernan 1990; Read 1996: 126–27).

Kiernan is articulate about his role in opposing the dam, and about the pain of loss:

> I cannot speak for others. But I saw my temple ransacked by my own community. Pedder was the cradle of my adult life. Many of us were matured by the experience. I have seen friends grow up, and some have aged terribly. My own soul seems haunted by an unwanted legacy of cynicism and distrust.

Kiernan's activism in defence of 'letting things be' was an existential stand with strong intent towards both past and future. He witnesses to the place and to his love, his action, and his intent even in the face of loss. Considering that perhaps one day he will see his daughter playing in a renewed and restored lake, he writes:

> Yet these things take time. Perhaps it will be she, not I, who sees a child regain its heritage. My solace is that even if she does not see that heritage regained, the Earth may finally restore Lake Pedder, when the dams have become dust and none of us remains here to destroy. (Kiernan 1990: 30)

3

THE LONG TRANSITIVE MOMENT

> 'But I think that was finished now for the Captain Cook ... That time been gone. It's finished now. But really, the land belongs to Aboriginal people.'
> (Danaiyarri, quoted in Rose 2001b: 67)

Paul Ricoeur (1985: 16) defines the now as being 'constituted by the very transition and transaction between expectation, memory, and attention'. His approach is important because it avoids the idea that 'now' is given in 'Nature', as well as the idea that it is only a mental construct. Rather, in Ricoeur's thought, 'now' is a practice. In this chapter I look at practices that support a strange process by which the insignificance of 'now', produced by disjunction, is stretched across chronological time and geographical space. My aim is to develop the connections between messianic time, the time of progress, and the frontier. This time work contrasts with Vic River Aboriginal time practices, and I conclude by showing both the ongoing war of totalising monologue and a twist into new forms of social life.

A Story about Time

A small mob of us went fishing once, and trigger-happy Morgan raced down the river bank, saw a snake in a tree, and shot it. He missed, and the snake disappeared into the river. We discussed this incident over and over while we fished and camped, because some of us thought that it might have been a Rainbow Snake. In Aboriginal Australian cosmology, Rainbow Snakes are powerful beings, and are said to inhabit all the permanent waterholes in the Victoria River region of the Northern Territory. Sometimes they wrestle people into the water to drown them. Only the most gifted people can pull back drowned individuals and restore them to life.

Rainbow Snakes are part of the monsoonal drama of dry and wet seasons. As the hot weather builds towards the point of desiccating life on earth, the Rainbow rises up from the permanent waterholes and starts travelling across the skies making clouds and rain. Conscious, powerful and in control of whirlpools, episodic rains, monsoons and floodwaters, the Rainbow Snake is a world-sustaining being. It is dangerous too: anything that can sustain life on earth can just as well destroy it.

About a week after the fishing trip we had heavy unseasonable rains. By then the story of Morgan's shot had been told all around our immediate communities. In the telling, the snake was becoming less ordinary and more Rainbow-like all the time. A few weeks later our same little mob made a trip to several more distant communities, and the story was told again and again. Regional opinion was tending towards the interpretation that the snake had been a Rainbow. A very old and knowledgeable woman in one of the more distant communities pronounced the verdict: the snake had been a Rainbow; the unseasonable rains had come as a result of its being 'humbugged'. She asserted that it had been a mistake to have shot at it, and everyone was profoundly relieved that the shot had missed.

My understanding of the time concepts of the Aboriginal people who shared their knowledge and life experience with me in the Victoria River District developed from incidents like this, and out of stories of events and creation. Aboriginal stories and negotiations of meanings suggest that time is not an entity in itself, existing outside life. Rather, time seems to be a quality of life. Victoria River people do not distinguish kinds of time, but kinds of life, and I have applied this distinction – Dreaming and ordinary – to time.

Ordinary time, the temporal dimension of ordinary life, is sequential and bounded. Evidence for sequence in human life is found, for example, in the terms for the periods of life that begin with infancy, move through childhood, articulate various levels of adulthood, and finish in old age. Further evidence is in the rituals of life that shift people through sequences. Sequences coexist with patterns that recur. Seasons are one such pattern: hot weather, followed by rains, followed by cold weather, followed by hot weather. These cyclical patterns are marked by regular events that erase the particular. The annual rains, for example, wash away the traces of life, the footprints, campfires, dead plants, animal and fish bone, and all the other marks and remains of ephemeral life. On a broader scale, human and other lives are 'washed away', as Vic River people put it, with death.

Orientation is towards origins. We here now, meaning we here in this shared present, are distinct from the people of the early days by the fact that they preceded us and made our lives possible. We are the 'behind mob' – those who come after. The future is the domain of those who come after us. They are referred to as the 'new mob', or as those 'behind us'. It seems that we face Dreaming, and live our lives moving closer to Dreaming; those behind us walk in our footsteps, as we walk in the steps of those who precede us. Vic River people's time-space matrix of country and their canonical orientation towards origins (rather than towards a future state), ensure that from time to time a western person experiences a dizzying sense of historical inversion – of the past jumping ahead, or of time running backward.

That which endures is not ordinary. Dreaming (or creator) beings brought life into being and continue to empower the presence of life in the world. One key point of difference between Dreaming and the ordinary is that the latter is ephemeral, while Dreaming endures. Enduring yet contingent, Dreaming songs, stories and life force are held in the present world in sacred sites, and are moved around in the present by the actions of ephemeral beings who, in their ordinary lives, carry Dreaming power through sequential and repetitive patterns. Dreaming and ordinary times are separated by something that could reasonably be called a temporal boundary. Dreamings walked the earth in human form, making, shaping, and bringing into being the world of form and difference, as well as the relationships that cross these boundaries. At some point, they changed over into the species they now are. The flying-fox Dreamings, for example, are the source for the flying foxes in the world today, and at the same time are the source for the flying fox people (a 'totemic' connection) who are also descended from the ancestral creators. The Dreamings changed over; this was a major disjunction, and it happened not so long ago. Most of the senior people who taught me took their genealogies back about three generations to their grandparents. There the genealogies stopped. Grandparents, for most people, came straight from the Dreaming. The point at which Dreaming became ordinary, then, may be only about a hundred years back. The changeover created a boundary of difference, and time work in present-day life involves cross-cutting, but not obliterating, this boundary. Difference is brought into relationship, and the moral engagements of past in present work this boundary to hold on to that which matters and to sustain relationships across it.

The old woman who made the public statement about Morgan's shot at the snake took responsibility to assert public regional consensus. Within the limits of memory, however, it remained possible that new events might occur that would require a re-examination of this event. The event might be forgotten (and perhaps by now it is, except by me and those who read about it), and thus would be 'washed away' with the debris of that which does not endure. Alternatively, it might be coded into a form of remembrance that would hold it as a story or song for those who come behind us. It would become part of the past that endures and is kept alive within social memory.

The period I call a one hundred-year present can be understood precisely as a kind of 'now' – a set of transitions and transactions. Memory, expectation, and attention are brought to bear in social life as tools for understanding the meaning of events, for determining their moral valence, if any, and for finally determining whether they are to endure or be left to wash away. Some events are lost to memory, others remain in connection with memory and place. Dreaming action continues in the present in the bodies of all living things whose origins are in Dreaming. And Dreaming action continues in the present through ceremony, creation, song and other forms of creative memory and connection. The boundary between Dreaming and ordinary is cross-cut by ceremony, site-based action, story and song, and the ecological experience of ongoing life.

Conquest has added another dimension to these practices of memory and forgetting. One of my teachers, Old Johnson Bididu, told me that he stayed at Lingara, a little outstation with marginal land and uncertain tenure, because there they camped on the blood and bones of their people who had been murdered. He often spoke in an oratorical manner, but he was not being allegorical. The evidence of violence that White people sought to eradicate through fires or drownings, or unmarked graves, or through silence, has for Old Johnson and others become part of the place. Memory, place, dead bodies and genealogies hold the stories that tell the histories that are not erased, and that refuse erasure. Painful as they are, they also constitute relationships of moral responsibility, binding people into the country and the generations of their lives.

The impact of conquest includes the problem of trying to find a place within Dreaming for actions that clearly are so destructive that they do not belong in the living world of thriving life (Rose 1984). In addition, it poses the problem that 'forgetting' could become a form of capitulation that gives the final word to the conquerors. If people decided to cease to tell the stories of what happened, the implication could be that deaths and the pain no longer matter. I have written elsewhere: 'When Hobbles said that Victoria River people remember Captain Cook, he was asserting that lies cannot be allowed to engulf the present ... As long as those who need to change cling to the dead past, those who are hurt must remember' (Rose 2000a: 229).

Year Zero

With the western concept of temporal disjunction it is possible to break up the history of the world into epochs, each of which is differentiated by disparate inner value (Gurevich 1985: 118). The time regime of progress reduces 'now' to insignificance because it is always about to be overcome or transcended, and thus will become disjunctive with the next moment. An awareness of disjunction would seem to be primarily retrospective; one looks back and realises that there was a time when a fundamental shift occurred – that is, that which followed differs significantly from that which preceded. The colonisation of the New World is an exception to retrospection; the projects were undertaken precisely with a future-oriented awareness of disjunction. Settlers specifically held the intention of leaving the old behind and creating new societies. Their presence, like their terminology ('new worlds'), signalled their sense of themselves as agents of disjunction. Equally, their many efforts to generate continuities (New England, New South Wales) speak eloquently, and mercilessly, of disjunctions.

Looking to practices of time that underlie the making of new worlds, I find a regime of violence, a neutralisation of moral action, and a bruising indifference towards pain. Settler societies are brought into being through invasion; death and silence pervade and gird the whole project. This fact is most evident in those regions of immediate conquest known as the frontier. In settler societies, nationhood is asserted in the wake of the frontier; thus the frontier is quite explicitly not the nation, but rather a site for the making of the nation. An examination of the practices of 'now' in the frontier zone throws into relief the shape and consequences of those practices more generally.

I have suggested that punctuation and intertemporality are two constitutive frames for analysing time. How are moments of time differentiated from each other, and what are the relationships between different moments? I use the term 'punctuation' to refer to closure, and I am most concerned with attempts to define a break which determines that the past is finished. Intertemporality refers to the relations between moments, and here I am especially concerned to consider how moral accountability is managed between punctuated moments.

In chapter 1, I suggested that modernity, with its emphasis on progress and the new, has harnessed the concept of disjunction in a socially and technologically powerful fashion. Unlike its Christian counterpart, which postulates major disjunctions brought about through divine action in human history, modernity has privileged a human agency. The frontier, however, is marked by a mingling of human and divine agency that would be astounding if it did not somehow seem so natural. The Australian writer Mary Durack, descendant of one of Western Australia's prominent pioneering families, depicts her grandfather as a patriarch blessed by the Almighty:

> And who could say that he had not been blessed when he rode into the lonely land with his hand in the hand of God? He had loved the country and its wild people and both had served him well. His family had grown up about him with strong bodies and good minds, his flocks and herds had increased and multiplied. He had brought people and life to the wilderness. There were homes now on the inland rivers and roads criss-crossed the vast, grass plains. (Durack 1986: 280)

In an equally self-conscious mode, an American cowboy song links biblical patriarchs with life on the open range. This verse follows from a series of verses in which city folk look down on pastoralists, and the songwriter defends cowboys by reference to the Bible:

> But why it is I can ne'er understand,
> For each of the Patriarchs owned a big brand.
> Abraham immigrated in search of a range,
> When water was scarce, he wanted a change.
> Old Isaac owned cattle in charge of Esau,
> And Jacob punched cows for his father-in-law.
> (Lomax & Curdy, n.d.)

What kinds of links between time and agency enable these conflations to make any sense at all? And why does the Old Testament figure so prominently? Is it a matter of narrative correspondences, or is there a deeper import?

The major ontological disjunctive moment for Christians consists of the birth, life, death and resurrection of Christ – a disjunction that transfigured the conditions of human life on earth for believers. Ricoeur (1999: 237) calls this the 'Christian pattern'; it claims universality for its 'history of salvation'. My argument is that western colonising practice replicates this pattern as the foundational template for frontier time, space and action.

The term 'Year Zero' comes from the Christian calendar; we are familiar with the characterisation of our time-constructs as linear, so it is important to examine the specific structure of this calendar. In fact, its structure is palindromic and thus involves both linearity and mirroring. A verbal palindrome can be read from left to right – MADAM IM ADAM – or from right to left without loss of meaning. The letter 'I' in this palindrome is the central point, and moving out from the centre there is an identical structure in each direction. In the Christian calendar, moving forward and backward from the notional Year Zero, each side is the numerical counterpart to the other. This structure is also an ancient and persistent narrative structure. Joel Rosenberg (1986) shows that many of the stories in the Hebrew Bible are palindromically structured, and Northrop Frye's (1982) literary study demonstrates that this structure articulates the message of divine purpose in the Christian Bible.

A verbal palindrome is a word game. A palindromic narrative structure, however, is not a game: in biblical narrative it articulates the design and purpose of history. The difference between the two lies in the centre, for in narrative that is a site of transfiguration. Thus each side is both related to and differentiated from the other. In diagram form it is represented: A - B - C - /D/ - C' - B' - A' (Rosenberg 1986: 205). This structure underlies the Christian calendar, where the life of Jesus is positioned as the transformative event. The same structure holds in the Christian Bible. An event on the older side (the Hebrew section) can be understood to correspond with an event on the newer side (the Christian section), and from a Christian perspective the newer event is the realised form of that which is foreshadowed in an older event. For example, Adam prefigures Jesus; virtually every passage in the New Testament can be interpreted to reference the Old. In Frye's (1982: 81) words, 'The New Testament, in short, claims to be, among other things, the key to the Old Testament, the explanation of what the Old Testament really means.'

Palindromic narrative thus articulates the view that a plan of history exists, that history moves from an early (proto- or pre-) configuration through disjunction/transfiguration to the realised or fulfilled configuration. This mirror effect connects past and future in relational differentiation based on sequence and replacement. Frye finds here a theory of historical process based on 'an assumption that there is some meaning and point to history'. He suggests: 'Our modern confidence in historical process, our belief that despite apparent confusion, even chaos, in human events, nevertheless those events are going somewhere and indicating something, is probably a legacy of biblical typology [correspondences]' (Frye 1982: 81).

Disjunction signals the shift from before to after. The concept of fulfilment depends on precisely this shift. There is a relationship between 'pre-' and 'post-' in that the prefiguring type (the prototype) enables that which is to come, and is replaced by that which comes after. The historic destiny of the 'pre' is completed when it is superseded by the 'post'. Fulfilment is thus embedded in an irreversible sequence which has a moral dimension: the fulfilment is assumed to be the good and right outcome, and the process in which the new replaces and fulfils the old is the destiny of history.

Biblical orientation to divine agency, and the easy secularisation of this structure of time, history, agency and destiny, ought not to blind us to its violence. Year Zero is in practice a declaration of war. One aspect is the mode of totalising monologue. Christian typological exegesis validated Judaism, but only in Christian terms. Hatley tells us that Levinas equates this totalising/silencing/assimilating project with warfare: 'one sees the other as a mode of resistance to one's own ideas about her or him, ideas the other must be pressed to embrace' (Hatley 2000: 180). Violence pervades the process, since the past is deemed only to have value to the extent that it justifies and makes way for the present; the present, of course is a step on the way to the future.

On the frontier, discursive and physical violence are steeped in a dynamic of destruction and creation. Taking the Bible as a template for history in the palindromic mode, we see that the old continues to exist ambivalently: its presence is superseded even as its shadow articulates the contours of transfiguration. In textual terms, the New Testament shows how to read the Old Testament, and thus the Old Testament exists only as a text for the future. From being a text in and for itself and its people, it is twisted into a text for others. Frontier narratives in the palindromic mode define what exists on the 'other' side of the frontier as awaiting transfiguration. The violence proceeds from here: the 'other' side is appropriated – from being people who live among and for themselves, they are forced into being people whose lives and deaths are for others.

Cleaning up the Country

Indigenous survivors of conquest offer privileged insight into the unmaking of life in frontier zones. Victoria River people emphasise massacres and the brutally enforced confinement of survivors. Hobbles Danaiyarri, for example, explained how Captain Cook, the emblematic invader, came looking for country, 'cleaning it up' for occupation by his own people: 'Captain Cook reckoned, "I been want to clean that people right up. That's good country. I like to put my building there. I like to put my horses there. I like to put my cattle there ..."' (quoted in Rose 2001b: 64).

The violence by which those on the pre-zero side of the frontier are forced to give way to those arriving from the post-zero side is asserted to exist within a moment that is about to be overcome. The metaphor of right and left hands is useful for describing life during this explosive moment. The right hand of conquest can be conceptualised as beneficent in its claims: productivity, growth, and civilisation are announced as beneficial actions in places where these purportedly had not existed before. The left hand, by contrast, has the task of erasing specific life. Indigenous peoples, their cultures, their practices of time, their sources of power, and their systems of ecological knowledge and responsibility will all be wiped out, and most of the erasure will be literal, not metaphorical. The left hand creates the *tabula rasa* upon which the right hand will inscribe its civilisation.

The frontier is thus a cauldron of modernity, a time and place where modern culture simultaneously reveals its capacity for destruction and reinvents its own myth of creation. The hand of destruction and the hand of civilisation mutually shape a chronotope focused on Year Zero.

Consider Frederick Jackson Turner's classic analysis of the American frontier:

> The United States lies like a huge page in the history of society. Line by line as we read this continental page from West to East we find the record of social evolution. It begins with the Indian and the hunter; it goes on to tell of the disintegration of savagery by the entrance of the trader, the pathfinder of civilisation; we read the annals of the pastoral stage in ranch life; the exploitation of the soil by the raising of unrotated crops of corn and wheat in sparsely settled farming communities; the intensive culture of the denser farm settlement, and finally the manufacturing organisation with city and factory system . . . Particularly in the eastern States this page is a palimpsest. What is now a manufacturing State was in an earlier decade an area of intensive farming. Earlier yet it had been a wheat area, and still earlier the 'range' had attracted the cattleherder. (Turner 1994: 38)

The story is about stages: from the frontier moment which makes the break between before and after, to settlement, followed by intensive cultivation, followed by industry and cities. Turner's palindromic structure mirrors pre- and post- in the overall narrative, while focusing most specifically on the stages of colonising development. In Australia, the explorer John Stokes made a similar statement of replacement. He sailed up the Victoria River in 1839, and subsequently wrote:

> I would fain hope that ere the sand of my life-glass has run out other feet than mine will have trod this distant shore, that colonisation will, ere many years have past [sic], have extended itself in this quarter; that cities and hamlets will have risen on the shore of the new-found river, that commerce will have directed her track thither, and that smoke may rise from Christian hearths where now alone the prowling heathen lights his fire. (Stokes 1846: 46)

This self-conscious and mannered passage positions the White man as time-lord. It claims the country as newly found, and defines the country (and the people) as without history, situating it (and them) in a narrative structure of disjunctive change. This is a country that is about to be transfigured: from wilderness to civilisation, from heathen to Christian, from unused space to sedentary cities and hamlets.

Rereading Stokes's little memento concerning the Victoria River, we see these Year Zero features: the construction of paired type and anti-type, or as we should read them using more familiar terminology: prototype and developed type. Thus the fires of the 'prowling heathen' are paired with the anticipated Christian hearths. Other contrasts invoke absence: cities and hamlets will fill in what must be 'empty' space, commerce will fill in what must be 'unused' wealth. In Stokes's (1846: 83) words, his explorations open the ground for 'the gradual but certain progression of civilisation and Christianity'. The medial point in Stokes's articulation of time is himself as he claims the land for civilisation. On the frontier, the coloniser establishes his right to play God and destroy the world in order to fulfil his vision of creation.

We can now see how it is possible for conquerors to equate themselves variously with God or with God's chosen people. As agents of the Year Zero they occupy the position of transformation. Pastoralists (discussed further in chapter 4) link themselves with Old Testament figures, I would suggest, not only because of the pastoralist parallels but also because the Old Testament gives way to the new. They quite consciously see themselves as agents of changes through which they themselves will one day be superseded. Mary Durack made the point explicitly in reference to her grandfather:

> He [fore]saw the roads pushing out to the little bush towns and station settlements on the rivers. He heard the rattle and rumble of the coaches, the noise of the big house parties, the sound of music and dancing and the merry laughter that he had missed in this great quiet land. (Durack 1986: 307)

Jay Arthur (1997) offers another perspective on the relationship between settlers and God in her study of terms that have been used to describe Lake Argyle in the Kimberley, and the process of proposing and constructing a dam. She finds that settler Australians describe the Ord River prior to the dam with words that indicate a state of incompletion, and then describe the dam as the fulfilment of the destiny of the river. She writes: 'The colonist stands in relation to the colonised space as creator and re-creator' (Arthur 2003: 112). Truly a biblical moment! Arthur concludes her study of the dam by saying: 'what was lost is [deemed to be] irrelevant as a function of the deficient and unfinished past. The country under Lake Argyle is not drowned but saved. Colonisation is not occupation but the eighth day of creation' (1997: 46).

For Indigenous people, the Year Zero of colonisation was and remains a violent thrust into Indigenous space and time. From the settlers' perspective, however, especially the perspective developed after the first decade or two of settlement, the colonising frontier is a place where something is going to happen, where nothing has quite happened (yet), where everything is in transition. Looking at the frontier in the transitive mode of the conqueror, we see a moment in which history is about to begin, an unchanging moment, in effect, when 'nothing' is happening.

In Australia this disjunctive frontier is stretched across the range lands and deserts, waiting, so to speak, for the rest of the story to catch up. About 80 per cent of Australia is hot and dusty outback where the frontier has arrived in the form of the left hand, and where the right hand of industry and cultivation has not yet arrived. A disjunction is stretched across space and through calendrical time, a Year Zero sustained through the past century as a more or less suspended moment awaiting transfiguration. This Australian outback can be understood as a stretched time-space, managed through a regime of violence within which is enacted again and again the deaths, the damage, and the promise of fulfilment.

As an example of a practice that stretches time, I quote the words of 'Young Bill' Lavender, a White Australian who travelled into the Victoria River region as a young man and worked on Victoria River Downs Station (VRD) for a few months in 1913:

> It seemed, at least outwardly, that nobody was expected to have any feelings but contempt for the niggers, including mixed

bloods also for the most part, and the minority (and of course there were a few whites who felt keenly about the very raw deal the 'nigs' were getting generally), but kept their dinkum opinion to themselves ... But all this was some of the dark side of the early Territory and the tail end of these customs were still dying hard. (Lavender n.d. 207)

According to Young Bill, the 'raw deal' included 'wholesale and individual shooting of the blacks . . . and the ruthless acquiring of their [sic] women'. The tail-end of these hard customs continued to die slowly for decades. Not until the Aboriginal people went on strike between 1965 and 1972 did they begin to break out of the silence that surrounded the 'raw deal'. Citizenship, the implementation of the *Aboriginal Land Rights* (NT) *Act 1976*, and other beneficial legislation began to bring a measure of justice into Black–White relations.

This stretched time-space is a moment into which is consigned all the destruction, damage, and indifference that modernity generates in its rush for wealth, power, progress, and whatever other desiderata are subsumed within the overall narrative of fulfilment. When this moment is stretched, damage proceeds apace and indifference, or a constrained silence, reigns. It is a very long moment of violence, suffering, and insulation. I see a vision of progress continuously wrested from this country through torture and crucifixion. Indigenous people and the land, waters, soils, plants and animals are sacrificed to the shadowy promise of fulfilment.

Looking at frontier practices of 'now', we see a long transitive moment that neutralises the present. The coloniser celebrates his pre-presence in glorifying 'wilderness' as a place where he can encounter his own absence. On another side of the frame, the coloniser celebrates his post-presence in mourning the Aborigine whose living presence has been erased. Knowledge of brutality is concealed, both because it was covered over in the past, and because the punctuation of time disassociates present consequences from past action. The record of warfare is located in all the unmarked places where the bones and blood, or ashes, of Aboriginal victims are washed into the soil, as well as in the bruised bodies and broken families of the survivors. Violence can be discerned in fragmented Dreaming tracks, lost species, ruined places, and devastated ecosystems.

Report from Mistake Creek

Both John Stokes and Patsy Durack would be disappointed with the Vic River and Kimberley regions today. The vision of progress has not come about as they imagined. Commerce, hamlets and Christian hearths are relatively minimal, and although the occasional heathen (White and Black) prowls the backblocks, the vision of progress is still beyond the horizon. Furthermore, Aboriginal people have refused to fade away or assimilate or just die, and their numbers are growing. And in spite of the harsh histories of labour on cattle stations, citizenship and the decolonising work of land rights legislation have seriously destabilised the power relations which seemed so certain for so long. Not only has the rest of the story not caught up, but new stories are coming into being.

The long transitive moment poses problems for settlers as well as for Aboriginal people. The redemptive purpose, let us say, of all this violence is the creation of a new civilisation. One of the ways in which we would know that civilisation has been successfully established is that White people will have replaced Aboriginal people. The pre- will have given way to the post-, and fulfilment, if not achieved, must be near at hand. Public declarations of Indigenous survival challenge complacency about the completion of conquest.

Christian narrative time stretched out the return of the Messiah. From death to resurrection took three days; from ascension to return has thus far occupied two millennia. Colonisation alters this structure. During the past 200 years Aboriginal people have been declared dead repeatedly, and have again and again refused to die. And again and again living people's pain is amplified through denial.

From the perspective of conquest it becomes a matter of some urgency to ensure that Aboriginal people really are dead. Anthropologists have been favoured purveyors of the news of the death of Aborigines. In examining the books and articles in which anthropologists have decreed the imminent or recently accomplished death of groups, languages, social relations, and modes of behaviour, one concludes that anthropologists have been the necrologists of the nation. For example, A.P. Elkin wrote in his 1970 article 'Before it is too late':

> 'Before it is too late' has been a recurrent challenge to research in Australian Aboriginal Anthropology. Faced by the sure and certain dying out of tribes and by the even quicker breakdown

of their culture, George Taplin ... [and numerous others] recognized and responded to the challenge. With the help of correspondents near and far, they observed, gleaned and garnered what and where they could ... As with search in the mineral and oil fields, so, too, the Institute [of Aboriginal Studies] is observing, surveying, probing, sounding, drilling and extracting. The dividends will be high, though probably not in every project. Some fields are poor. (Elkin 1970: 19, 21)

This scientific practice is itself a form of death work as it values the living precisely to the extent that they can offer up information concerning a past that the anthropologists seem to have assumed in advance would be discontinuous with their future. The 'salvage' in these practices is directed towards information, not people. Some of the writing shows this utilitarian focus in detail; it is the more pitiless for being the more personal. For example, in 1953 Mervyn Meggitt conducted a short survey of the Malngin and Gurindji people of Limbunya Station on the headwaters of the Victoria River. He found that their numbers were diminishing radically, and he foresaw the death of the Malngin and Gurindji people on the station. When he asked people about the lack of offspring, he was told that the country was too poor. Rather than understanding this as a statement of lack of food, which is what is being said in Aboriginal Pastoral English, he understood it as a statement of lack of Dreamings. He concluded the article by calling for urgent attention to be dedicated to the Malngin in order to document them more completely before they died out (Meggitt 1955).

Meggitt was not alone in predicting imminent death for Malngin and other people in the Vic River district. Anthropologists Ronald and Catherine Berndt (1987) had visited Limbunya in 1945. Malngin people then attributed their small numbers to a massacre in the early days from which their people never recovered (p. 84). In respect to food, the Berndts formed the view that there was probably enough bush tucker in the region but that the people were worked so hard on the station that there was not adequate time to supply their nutritional needs through their own hunting; they noted that the area around the homestead was barren (p. 88).

The Berndts too noted the small number of children – only 6 per cent of the total Aboriginal population. They, or perhaps Catherine alone, asked women about this fact, and they learned that abortion was also a factor. They state that the women's attitude could be summed up as: 'Why should we have children? ... Why should we breed more people for kadia, or kardiya [Europeans] to use the way they use us?' (pp. 90–91).

The situation at Limbunya was dire and complex, but probably no worse than any of the other cattle stations the Berndts visited (Wave Hill, Waterloo, Birindudu). Unfortunately they chose not to make their findings public, thus forestalling any possible public effort to press for better conditions for Aboriginal people. The title of their book, *End of an Era*, refers to the period they documented in the 1940s. The forty-year gap between research and publication suggests that the Berndts were experiencing some time-stretching themselves. This gap produces for me an extremely disheartening stretch between the life and death urgency of the situation they encountered, and the forty years it took for them to decide to make the information public. (The Berndts prepared a short report in 1948 that was circulated but not published. Their original report has not been made available.) Their role as anthropologists investigating working conditions and morbidity, and their desire to document 'traditional' culture, were never fully resolved, in fact probably could not be resolved, as Gray (2001) discusses in an ethically sensitive analysis of this portion of their research.

The Berndts' use of the phrase 'end of an era' forces the question: has the Year Zero ended? Has some new sociality replaced the violence of the frontier? If we were to follow a strictly linear progression, then we would have to answer in the negative. The story was that White people would replace Black people, that farmers and then industrialists would replace pastoralists, and so on; these replacements have not happened. If we take a more twisty non-linear approach to the question, then we see substantial changes from an era of violence and desperation to citizenship and, in the Northern Territory, to land rights, protection of sacred sites, provision of education, and other social measures that benefit Aboriginal people without demanding that they completely abandon their own ways of being in the world.

The Malngin people, whose demise Meggitt and the Berndts thought they were witnessing, refused to die out, and lived to see a day when colonisation was overtaken by and intermingled with decolonising action. Under the NT land rights legislation they were able to make a claim for Mistake Creek Station, and as the claim was successful they have regained a portion of their former homeland (Aboriginal Land Commissioner 1996). Many of the Malngin families had lived and worked on Mistake Creek, Limbunya, and other stations in the area. The changes they experienced in their lives are almost impossible to imagine. Consider the late Jimmy Manngayarri. He was a wonderful teacher, an interesting and unpredictable thinker, and had a huge knowledge of country, having walked a vast portion of the region between the Victoria and Ord rivers in his long and eventful life.

Manngayarri knew the violence of frontier station life at first hand, having seen his mother's mother's brother shot to death, and seen many other people punished. He was a child on Limbunya long before the Berndts or Meggitt got there. He said of violence:

> Oh, they've been doing that in my time. I saw it. When I was a big one now, I saw that. Same thing when I was [a] very little boy, he was doing that for my mother. Harry Reid was kicking my mother here on the kidney. He kicked her in the kidney till she dropped dead. I was only a little boy, that big [about four years old].

Harry Reid was on Limbunya as manager in 1920, so the event probably occurred around this time. I asked Jimmy why Reid had kicked his mother, and he said that he, Jimmy, had been crying, as kids will, and Reid told his mother to shut him up. Jimmy didn't stop crying, so Reid kicked her to her death. The old man related this violence to a broader pattern:

> Well, still I remember that yet. You know, what I was seeing when I was big now. I remember that now, everything. That's the way what I came to think now. Oh, yeah. Yeah! People been do the wrong thing. And policemen tied them up like a dog. No good tie them up on the tree, and tie his fucking arm like that. Take the pants off, and tie it [him] on the tree. Belt him with the bloody big chain. Mmmm. No good at all. All that. Oh, bad things. They did the bad thing. (quotes taken from Rose 1991: 90–91)

Jimmy Manngayarri lived and worked on Limbunya and Wave Hill stations, and after the strike he remained in Daguragu, the community formed in the course of the strike, where he was one of the stalwart Lawmen of the region. He gave evidence in two land claims – one for a portion of his mother's country and one for a portion of his father's country, and he assisted many people because he was so old and held so much knowledge. From a time of violence and death to a time of land rights, land ownership, and citizenship, he kept faith with received wisdom and adapted to new knowledges. He died in 2001, respected by a large number of people in addition to his own countrymen and women, including scholars and lawyers who worked with him and judges who heard him give evidence (for example, see Hokari 2002).

As I have written elsewhere, a land claim hearing is an extraordinary procedure. History, Dreaming sites and actions, continued use of and care and concern for the country, and aspirations for the future all come together for a few days. Evidence is oral, the setting face to face, and Aboriginal people have the right to explain, to a person whose understanding could make a genuine difference to their lives, something of who they are, why they appear as claimants, what their relationship to the country is, and their hopes for the future.

The many peculiarities and disjunctions in the procedure have been critically analysed by Merlan (1998), Povinelli (1993, 2002) and to a lesser extent in my own work (Rose in press [b]). The core peculiarity lies in the paradoxical injunction that Aboriginal claimants must authentically produce a cultural presence 'in a way that just so happens, in an uncanny convergence of interests, to fit the national imaginary of the traditional Aboriginal person' (Povinelli 2002: 189). Povinelli's extended analyses display the seeming impossibilities of the claim process, and, like Merlan's, are extremely perceptive. Nevertheless, my experience of the claim process has also included moments when Aboriginal Law has spoken to European Law and produced results which honoured both. In addition, it does return to Indigenous people portions of their homelands (see chapter 6).

The land claim procedure places a high value on Aboriginal people's memory. The connectivities of the past in the present, sustained under dire circumstances for decades, or a century, or more, are brought into the hearing. Remembrance and contemporary knowledge constitute the evidence, supported with written material wherever possible, and tested by the opposing parties. People's knowledge is put to work to help them overcome some injustices, to gain some power in social and land relations, and to recuperate from a past marked most strongly by death some possibilities for a living and thriving future.

The Year Zero has been overtaken, but it is not overcome. A discursive war is still being waged by some. In contrast to the decolonising work of land claims, a few public figures seek to construct histories that aim towards comfort. La Capra (1998: 26) cites Friedlander (1993) as the author of the phrase 'homeland history', a term coined in reference to Germany but equally applicable to Australia. Homeland histories are the 'type of history that mitigates or evades threats to identity and a desired self-image'. In Australia homeland histories work like sieves to strain out Aboriginal remembrance and hold only narratives of comfortable triumph. They are, in consequence, highly contested, not only by settler historians but also by the Indigenous people whose remembrance is at issue.

Over to the west of Mistake Creek and Limbunya Stations, Bedford Downs Station straddles the Durack Range in the Kimberley region of Western Australia. There is a creek there called Mistake Creek where some Aboriginal people, a group that included women and children, were killed in 1915. Governor-General Sir William Deane made a speech there 'on the occasion of the Ceremony of Reconciliation with the Kiji [Kija] people' in June 2001.[4]

Sir William stated his personal regret that 'such events defaced our land, this beautiful land'. Keith Windschuttle and other public commentators took an offensive approach to this modest statement. Their attack targeted not only the Governor-General, but also Kija people and Kerry O'Brien of the ABC. Cathie Clement, an experienced historian of the Kimberley region of Western Australia, has written an even-handed account of the controversy, and readers who wish to know more of the details can consult her excellent article (Clement 2003).

The point I want to draw out is the connection between Indigenous people's remembrance, the strong determination on the part of some White people to reject that remembrance, and the ongoing structure of violence. In this attack on Kija people and the Governor-General, we see the Year Zero being stretched into the 21st century to promote a totalising history. We see our Australian nation still unmaking and remaking itself in its tortured struggle to temporalise and spatialise its own moral presence.

Peggy Patrick, a Kija woman whose mother's mother was killed in the event at Mistake Creek, has generously shared her response to the attack. Like Jimmy Manngaiyarri, she shows resilient strength and dignity, and a willingness to make peace. In part, she says:

> Bad enough this terrible thing bin happen before. That Windschuttle hurt my family feeling and it make us feel bad for all the relation bin get killed at Mistake Creek...
>
> After that first lot of gardiya [Europeans] come here people were forced to go sit down la station and work for them. Policeman bin riding everywhere got a horse bringing people in. They work for tea, flour, sugar and tobacco, no money. We were treated like dog in we own country, just like a slave. Government mob never even think about we human being. We had no vote and no citizenship. We know people bin get killed all over the country. Now people like this Windschuttle try to say nobody bin get killed because gardiya never write 'em down what they bin do...
>
> He rubbish my name and he rubbish all my relation that bin get kill. He make big shame for me all over. Make me and all my family real upset.
>
> We bin bring out hard story what bin happen to blackfella. We talk about bad story so black and white can be friend when we look at true thing together. Look like nothing change. Gardiya killed blackfella with gun and poison and now look like he killing our life making fun of my word. Not worth. (Patrick 2003: 216–17)

4

CATTLE KINGS AND SACRED COWS

> Counter-modernity ... would connote at the very least, no absolute breaks with the past and the traditional. It would make space for questioning the revolutionary fervour that wills the past to be dead ... It would also ... mark the processes by which the pastness of the past is made present so that human possibilities for living could begin to be visualized in terms of a braiding together of discrete temporalities that resist a linear, empty, homogenous ordering of time. (Ganguly 2001: 36)

One of the problems with linear time narratives is that the world often fails to conform. Harold Kaplan (2000: 74) reminds us that 'in the long run redemptive violence didn't work for the communists any more than it did for the Nazis'. In the frontier region of North Australia, as in the United States as Slotkin (1992) shows us, a lot of work goes into maintaining the hope that sustains linear narratives. A significant part of the dynamic of the Year Zero is people's efforts to try to force the social and environmental world to conform to the story. In the last chapter I looked at the Year Zero primarily in its destructive aspect, only pointing briefly to another potential: that it is a space that may harbour numerous and contradictory possibilities. Now I want to examine that other potential in richer detail. One side of the story is that of White people who have battled to hold on to cattle stations and do not want to become superseded. Another twist is that many aspects of cattle culture are now shared among Indigenous and settler peoples (McGrath 1987). Furthermore, some cattle stations are now owned by Indigenous people. In the last part of this chapter I will argue that rodeo and camp draft events are arenas of performance in which the unfinished quality of the Year Zero is enacted in its plenitude of possibilities. My focus is on the dense entanglements of violence, peril, extractive industries, and the celebration of resistance and countermodern alternatives. But first, let us consider the long history of cattle culture.

Cowboy Diaspora

The history of colonisation is a history of cattle and horses as well as people. Some of the Aboriginal people who taught me were baffled by the fact that White people took the lives of cattle to be of greater value than the lives of the Indigenous people. Others were bitter that White people had used Aboriginal labour for the really hard jobs in preference to the labour of animals, because they did not want to wear out their animals. Hobbles Danaiyarri suggested that White people had been doing this kind of cruel conquest for a very long time. A few years ago I came across a description of the ancient God Indra, and it struck me that he and his mates sounded a lot like some of the Northern Territory cattlemen I have known. My encounter with Indra prompted me to follow up Hobbles's suggestion.

I now suggest, provocatively, that the conquest of Australia did not begin in 1788. It began about 10 000 years ago when our ancestors domesticated cattle and began a long and intermittent career of cattle herding and raiding. My proposal is that from the *Rig Veda* and Zarathustra to Hercules and Captain Starlight, from the Mithraic rituals to the bullfight ring and the rodeo, from the Olympic races to outback picnic races, Indo-European people's relationships with cattle and horses are enmeshed in an ethos which turns out, not coincidentally, to be ideally suited to conquest.

The ancestors referred to here are the Indo-European peoples from whom most of the non-Indigenous settlers in Australia are descended. Historically, we Indo-Europeans include the Indic, Iranian, Tocharian, Anatolian, Armenian, Greek, Italic, Celtic, Germanic, Baltic and Slavic language groups (Puhvel 1988: 33, 37). We appear to have come into existence at least 7000 years ago, probably earlier. A recent and extremely thorough study by two Russian scholars places the Proto-Indo-European (PIE) homeland in the region of what is now eastern Turkey and northern Iran. It seems probable that our ancestors were involved in domesticating cattle, although that is not proved. We know, for example, that the PIE term for cow is *k'ou (Gamkrelidze & Ivanov 1995: 482). This word in its many cognate forms is found right across the Indo-European languages and appears as a loan word in languages as distant from us as ancient Chinese (p. 491).

At about 6000 BP (before the present) the Proto-Indo-European group began to branch out linguistically and spatially (p. 791). With the domestication of the horse at about the same time, people increased their range and amplified their capacity for warfare (Anthony 1986: 295). Archaeological strata dated to about 6100 BP in the area around the Dnieper and Don Rivers on the edge of the great steppes show clear evidence of horse-riding. A horse increases the human range by a factor of five; the capacity to ride expanded people's subsistence range, giving them a competitive edge against pedestrian hunter-gatherers of the steppe. This shift in relative mobility destabilised boundaries and was marked by rapidly increasing warfare (Anthony 1986: 295). It was to be repeated in other zones of conquest including Australia.

From about 4400 BP these people initiated what was to become a succession of expansions westward into Europe and south into the Middle East and India, conquering local agriculturalists, many of whom, it should be noted, kept cattle and engaged in mixed farming, and many of whom already had bovine cults. Jeremy Rifkin (1992: 26) describes these Indo-European pastoralists this way: 'Like the cowboys of nineteenth century America, their military superiority lay in the mounted steed, their wealth was measured in cattle, and their territory was the arid grasslands of the temperate zone.'

According to David Anthony (1986), the most successful strategy of these people was the combination of two sets of technologies. Four thousand years ago horses provided high-speed, low-volume transport, while ox-drawn carts provided low-speed, high-volume transport. The pastoralists of the steppes used both, and when they turned their attention to conquest they were devastatingly successful. In almost exactly the same way, the pastoralists of inland Australia with their horses and bullock teams used both strategies and were devastatingly successful.

Once we invented the war chariot (about 3500 BP, Gamkrelidze & Ivanov 1995: 465) we gained a huge conquering advantage and turned our forces towards the great agricultural civilisations (Drews 1988: 111, 57–60). Indo-European cultures of warfare, horses and cattle probably reached a peak in the period around 3550 BP. According to Robert Drews, this was the period when chariot technology was perfected for warfare, and gave fantastic advantage to those who had it. As Drews puts it in his study of the Greeks: 'The "coming of the Greeks" ... was essentially a takeover of a relatively large alien population by a relatively small group of PIE speakers whose advantage lay in their chariotry' (p. 225).

In addition to the Indo- and Iranian branches, people of various tribes moved into Europe over the millennia. There were Celts; later there were the great exotic tribes of antiquity: Illyrians, Scythians, Tocharians, and so on. Then there were the Germanic Ostrogoths, Visigoths, Anglo-Saxons, Franks, and later, the Slavs (Puhvel 1988: 35). In about AD 800 the Vikings took to the seas, conquering and settling, or raiding and trading from North America to Byzantium (Oxenstierna 1967).

In about AD 1400, Western Europe again launched a series of explorations, and migrations: the Americas, parts of Africa, India (which had already been invaded by Indo-Europeans several thousand years before), Asia, and Australia all received the force of this most recent expansion. Some of the invaders stayed to form the settler societies whose dilemmas we now live and work with.

Our best knowledge of the ancient world is of the Indo-Iranian peoples because we can tap into written records. I offer a brief discussion of Indo-Iranian cattle culture, taking note as I go along of some of the parallels with outback Australian cattle culture.

Proto-Indo-European languages classed domesticated animals together with humans, differentiating all of us from the wild animals. Bruce Lincoln (1981) takes this collaborative classification further and proposes that in cattle cultures, the cattle are regarded as the non-human members of the conquering society. One form of evidence is the mutability between people and bovines.

'The Bovine's Lament' (Lincoln 1981: 140–42) is a classic piece in Indo-Iranian liturgies. It demonstrates the mutability or transformability between people and their cattle by humanising the bovine and allowing him or her to comment on society. The *Rig*

Veda, the *Ramayana*, the hymns of Zarathustra, and other texts all contain forms of the bovine's lament (I am using a broad definition of the lament in my discussion). The basic plot is that the bovine bemoans the cruel behaviour of certain humans. Here is a brief example from a long lament in the *Ramayana*:

> Unhappy, weeping, and pained by sorrow, [Sabala the cow] reflected thus:
> 'Why am I abandoned by the good and great-souled Vasistha?
> Why am I, who am most unhappy, shamed and afflicted by the king's soldiers?'
> (Lincoln 1981: 145)

A contemporary Australian parallel of the bovine's lament is written on a water tank at the No. 11 bore on the Murranji track. This droving track is a section of a much longer track connecting the Northern Territory and some Western Australian cattle stations with the railhead in Queensland. It was used from about 1900 to 1956 by drovers taking large herds of cattle east for sale. The water tanks record the thoughts of the working people, many of whom never recorded their views in lasting form in any other medium. When Darrell Lewis and I first started documenting the tanks, we were impressed by the stories they told, and sympathised with the anonymous writer who mourned the stories that must be lost:[5]

> If this tank could only talk mannys the tale it would tell of mad men & mongrel horses & fucked out bullacks

78 Part One: Here and Now

The men's thoughts are expressed in these brief and poignant jottings, and in poetry, art, vilification, signatures (including numbers of cattle), and the seemingly inevitable desire for women. The tanks constitute an irreplaceable record, and some of them now have heritage listing (see Lewis 1992 for a full report). Typically the men recorded the passage of themselves and their mobs of cattle. Thus, for example: 'Slip Prendergast mustered the rushing Newrys on 26/6/[1]955 and passed on'. Prendergast is the drover and the rushing (stampeding) Newrys are cattle from Newry Station.

Slip Prendergast mustered the rushing newrys on 26/6/955 and passed on

The drovers' ephemeral record includes their own version of the bovine's lament. The best example concerns Slippery Prendergast's brother Splinter:

> Come Drover men and shed a tear
> For I am just a bald face steer
> And now at last my bones you've seen
> For I was just a flamin queen
> I'm sorry boys you've come too late
> Splinter Prendergast shot me with his .38
> Although I knew my end was near
> For I had a canker on the nearside ear.

> Come Dogies mourn and shed a tear
> For I am just a bald face steer
> And now at last my bones you've seen
> For I ever just a flamin' queer
>
> I'm sorry boys you've come too late
> Splinter Prendergast shot me with his 38
> Although I knew my end was near
> For I had a earber on the near side ear.

An even more poignant form of the lament was set in the style of a two-line verse, and was written or scratched directly onto the skull of a dead cow:

> Here I lie, my name was Toby,
> Flogged to death by old Dick Scoby.

The laments show a humanisation of cattle, and thus a reversal of the more usual human–domestic animal relationship in which the human speaks and the animal responds. Here the animal tells the story of people's actions.

There is also a delightful inversion of this genre: the representation of humans in bovine form. *The Book of Enoch* has an example:

Of Adam:	And behold, a cow sprung forth from the earth; And this cow was white.
Of Eve:	Afterwards a female heifer sprung forth.
Of Cain:	The black heifer then struck the red one [Abel], and pursued it over the earth. (Conrad 1959: 112)

The North Australian parallels run along two dimensions. The first is that Aboriginal people referred to equines as a kind of secret code for talking about White people. A grey horse was a White man, for example. And cattlemen themselves were not above referring to themselves in terms of equines and bovines, as the following poem, again taken from a Murranji water tank, makes clear. The language is droving vernacular. Stag means bullock; pluro means pleuro-pneumonia:

> The pluro stag
> Stepped out of bed
> He coughed and farted
> And shook his head
> Now listen boys
> I am getting old
> I cannot stand this fucking cold
> With rushing stock
> I get no rest
> I think I give this droving best

The ancient epics tell of cattle raids, praising the joys of warfare and the gaining of cattle. Indra's place in mythology is as the warrior in the first cattle raid. In the description of him that first caught my eye, Indra is the apotheosis of the ancient cattle warrior, but I felt that I knew him well because his type also shows up regularly at rodeos and camp drafts: 'strong armed, colossal, tawny-bearded, pot-bellied from drinking. He wields the thunderbolt in his more godlike moments, but fights like a hero from his chariot ... He is a cattle raider, and above all he is the destroyer of the strongholds of the enemy' (Piggott, quoted in Drews 1988: 156).

I grant that some imagination is required. For chariot, read bull catcher, ute, or pick-up; for thunderbolt read branding iron. The well-to-do pastoralists of outback Australia knew this cattle-raiding character all too well. He is immortalised in a bush ballad written by Billy Linklatter that purports to represent the point of view of the well-to-do cattleman of the Ord River region of the Kimberley. According to legend this poem was first carved onto a boab tree. The reader will realise that Linklatter himself was not a member of the landed elite. Duffers, in this vernacular, are equivalent to the

American rustlers, but somehow the term 'duffer' seems to invite a greater sense of affection.

> Oh Heavenly Father, if you please,
> I pray to You on bended knees,
> That You and your blessed Son, our Lord,
> Will keep the duffers from the Ord.
> O, paralyse Dick Thompson's hand
> When he picks up his duffing brand.
> Keep Skinner and Simpson from the Osmand Glen
> For Jesus Christ's sake. Amen.
> And now, O Lord, forgive my sins
> And may every cow on Ord have twins
> (Linklatter & Tapp 1997: 64)

In both Indo-Iranian culture and in the cattle culture of outback Australia, cattle raids are represented not only, or even principally, as theft, but rather as a liberation for both the duffer and the beast. A superb Australian example is the traditional song 'The Eumerella Shore':

> There's a happy little valley on the Eumerella shore,
> Where I've lingered many happy hours away,
> On my little free selection I have acres by the score
> Where I unyoke the bullocks from the dray.
>
> To my bullocks then I say
> No matter where you stray,
> You will never be impounded any more;
> For you're running, running, running on the duffer's
>   piece of land,
> Free selected on the Eumerella shore.
>
> When the moon has climbed the mountains and the stars are
>   shining bright,
> Then we saddle up our horses and away,
> And we steal the squatters' cattle in the darkness of the night,
> And we brand em at the dawning of the day.
>
> Oh, my little poddy calf,
> At the squatter you may laugh,

> For he'll never be your owner any more;
> For you're running, running, running on the duffer's
>   piece of land
> Free selected on the Eumerella shore.
> (trad.)

What I find so enjoyable in this song is that the selector's joy is represented as the poddy calf's joy; it addresses social injustice and delights in retribution through cattle raids. It links subversion of authority with spatial freedom and freedom from servitude. However, its carefree joyfulness conceals an underlying dynamic. In pastoral societies generally, ancient and modern, people have to negotiate a particular problematic: that the animals are both their productive resource and their subsistence. To kill and eat one's own beasts is to foreclose on long-term productivity, whether that be milk, dung, blood, and other products of living beasts, or, under capitalism, money. To kill and eat one's neighbour's beasts allows one to escape this dilemma (Lincoln 1981: 157), and according to Denoon (1983: 35), on the frontiers of capitalism cattle are more easily stolen than purchased. In Australia one thinks immediately of the bush dictum that you never eat your own beef. In short, the little poddy calf, whose freedom expresses that of its owner, is still, in the long run, somebody's dinner.

The ancient epics speak to the hero status accorded to the successful warrior/raider. The epics are known in Indian and Iranian sources, but they confront us everywhere. The tenth labour of Hercules, one recalls, was to go to what is now Spain and steal some red cattle that had been stolen from his people in the first place (Walcot 1979: 333). In Irish literature the greatest and most popular epic is 'The Cattle Raid of Cooley'. There are two prize beasts: the white bull and the red bull. Queen Maeve sets out to steal the red one, and the epic tells of feats of valour, treachery, deceit, and incredible daring. In the end, the bulls fight, the red bull wins, and goes back to his own home and dies there. Maeve is ruined, brought down by the intractability of men, gods and the red bull (Kinsella 1969).

These stories show astonishing similarities to Australian outback culture. The legendary 'Captain Starlight', the white bull, and the Roma jury are key images in glamorising cattle theft. Jeff Carter (1968: 106), in his popular account of the pastoralists' way of life, describes Harry Redford, aka Captain Starlight, as having 'pulled off the greatest cattle duffing feat in history' (it is unclear whether he means Australian history or world history). In 1859 Starlight stole 1000 head, including a pure-bred imported white bull. He drove them for over 1000 kilometres through deserts without tracks, indeed through country where the explorers Burke and Wills had perished only ten years earlier, and he finally sold the mob for $11 000. It was the readily identifiable white bull that brought Redford down (who says life doesn't imitate art?). He was arrested and tried in the outback Queensland town of Roma. The prosecution brought conclusive evidence against him, and the jury acquitted him, thereby proving the importance of being tried by a jury of one's peers! His legendary status was consolidated with the acquittal, and the term 'Roma jury' entered the Australian lexicon (Carter 1968: 106–108).

The Redford example is classically characteristic of Australian outback culture and, like all good legends, it conceals as well as reveals. It is situated in the outback, on the frontier, where settled society had not yet imposed its standards. Redford stole the cattle, but he did so according to a set of rules which was accepted by his peers. Think, for example, what would have happened if Redford had killed the prize bull in order to avoid being captured. Would the Roma jury have been so accommodating? And what would have happened if he had stolen horses instead of cattle? Remember that Ned Kelly was accused of stealing a horse (no worthwhile evidence was ever adduced) and ended up with three years' jail (Molony 1980: 64).

These stories belong to settlers. A Roma jury defines who is and who is not within the social order. At the same time that cattle duffers were practising their trade with relative impunity, cattle men in newly occupied country were killing Aborigines because of their alleged predations on cattle. This, too, is an old pattern. According to Lincoln, who proposed that cattle were part of society, the Indo-Iranian social order was divided into two main groups: on one side were the people themselves and their cattle, and on the other side were the people whom they had conquered. He writes that Indo-Iranian warriors went out aggressively defending their own 'zealously and with a sense of supreme confidence and self-righteousness' (Lincoln 1981: 132).

On the frontier Aborigines were assumed in advance to be cattle killers, so that even if there was no evidence of killing there was a presumption of guilt. Further, Aborigines were said to harry and disturb cattle, so that some cattlemen claimed it was not possible to have Aborigines and cattle occupying the same country without detriment to the cattle. A slightly more modest assessment was made by the Inspector of Police of the Northern Territory in 1922: 'Natives and stock will not thrive in one place. The squatter wants the water for his cattle, and the natives cannot do without it.' The Inspector recommended that Melville Island be made into a prison island for the inevitable Aboriginal offenders (Report of the Inspector of Police 1922: 14).

In her study of the violent legacy of monotheism, *The Curse of Cain*, Regina Schwartz makes a compelling case for the tenacity of biblical thought. She deals with the model of replacement that I analysed in terms of time in chapter 3, and she situates the model in reported history and divine commandment. As a template, the delivery of the chosen people into Canaan, and the annihilation of the Canaanites, models the idea of one people, one land, one God. This is the story about 'creating a people through the massive displacement and destruction of other peoples, of laying claim to a land that had belonged to others, and of conducting this bloody conquest under the banner of divine will'. The violent legacy of this myth, Schwartz (1997: 62) contends, is that it 'advocates the wholesale annihilation of indigenous peoples to take their land'.

Australian conquest seems to accord with this analysis over the long term, as settlers expected Aborigines to die out or to be assimilated, and thus did not expect to have to share land, politics and history with them. In the shorter term, however, it was said to be the cattle that could not coexist with Aborigines, and the problem people were said to be the 'wild blacks', in contrast to the 'station blacks'.

Across North Australia, settlers coming out of Queensland and New South Wales had experience of limited coexistence with Aboriginal people. Many of them, like the Duracks, brought Aboriginal workers with them, and most if not all expected to acquire a local Aboriginal labour force in due course. The phrase 'cleaning up the country' or 'clearing the land' in the context of colonising pastoralism meant eradicating or subduing the natives in order to make room for cattle. Subsequently confined to stations, the survivors were denied absolutely the freedom that is celebrated in 'The Eumerella Shore'. In no way were they running free. The point of subduing them, and effectively imprisoning them, was to ensure that the cattle could run free and that the people could not.

These brutal practices are more comprehensible if cattle and horses are understood to be the non-human members of these conquering societies. In addition, cattle become agents of colonisation in their own right as they impact on the ecologies they encounter. As Milton (1997: 200) writes in his study of settler pastoralism in the Transvaal, cattle are the 'shock troops' of Empire. Throughout the continent, cattle, horses, sheep, goats, and other hoofed mammals brought rapid and irreversible changes. Eric Rolls (1984: 84) writes about the process brilliantly: 'In Australia thousands of years of grass and soil changed forever in a few years.'

Holding Country/Holding Time

Frederick Jackson Turner's landmark essay on the frontier, discussed in chapter 3, articulated a myth of national character and purpose formed through the encounter between the colonising settler and the land he conquers. Nation formation in frontier theory and narrative is a story of progress from wilderness to civilisation. I argued that the Year Zero is a transitional moment between timeless land and history, and between empty or unconquered land and the civilisation that is destined to follow. From both Indigenous and settler perspectives, Year Zero is a moment of uncertainty, a site of incomplete conquest, a place where people's deepest commitments are in peril. On the settler side, it is a place where ruthless self-interest is legitimated as a matter of survival. The Year Zero is a moment in which everything is up for grabs and almost anything is sanctioned because the stakes are so high: not only is the survival of the nation in peril, but the individuals, and their civilisation and history and destiny, all hang in the balance in this crucial moment when conquest has begun but has not yet been achieved.

In the Year Zero control of country is deemed to be minimally secured, and extractive industries such as mining and pastoralism attract immunity from regulation and also secure government backing. They represent themselves as essential to ensuring the future for the nationhood that is to follow. The matrix of incompletion is thus immensely favourable to certain forms of personal and corporate freedom. In the ancient world and now today in the Americas and in Australia, the pastoralist ethos is extended across a range of private and corporate interests: 'don't fence me in!'

Cattle and human cattle culture work to hold in place this stretched and transitive moment. Conquerors claim the land, clear out or subdue the natives, and use their cattle to fill the country with settler presence even when there is only a handful of settler humans. Victoria River Downs is a good example. When the station was taken up it covered 13 060 square miles (33 825 square kilometres). As I have discussed elsewhere, in calculating the Aboriginal population in about 1880 one arrives at a figure of at least 3000 people, depending on one's assessment of population densities before conquest. By 1939 the Aboriginal population had dropped to 139 recorded individuals, meaning that in all probability there was more than a 90 per cent loss (discussed further in Rose 2000a: 7). During this same period, the number of settler Australians increased from zero to about twenty-five (ranging generally between twenty and thirty). James Michener visited in the 1950s, by which time the size of VRD had been reduced to about 5494 square miles (14 229 square kilometres). He reported that 'it is said that "20 white men and 12 windmills run VRD"' (Michener 1956: 64). He clearly was not counting the labour of the Aboriginal workers, whose population had increased slightly since 1939. The number of cattle, in contrast, was at least 100 000. In truth, the station personnel had no idea how many head were on the property and it is possible that there were as many as 200 000 head.

The cattle themselves, four-legged soldiers in the army of conquest, occupy the country, and through their own reproduction make possible the production of wealth on the frontier. Cattle enable this social paradox: country is conquered and fully occupied by settlers, while at the same time it is almost empty of human settlers.

From Transition to Tradition

Until recently, cattle culture was regarded as almost sacred because it held the country and time in a suspended state. Its sacred status provided a protective shield for extractive industries, and elites. But, as discussed in chapter 3, in that long transitive moment other social processes have overtaken the master story. Patsy Durack expected to be superseded, but today many settler cattlemen and women intend their cattle (or sheep) properties to be sustainable, and they do not want to be squeezed out or overtaken. In fact their own peril and uncertainty now far outweigh the peril and uncertainty of the nation on the frontier. Nick Gill's study of pastoralism in Central Australia (for example, Gill 1997) shows that today pastoralism is 'a contested domain' in that area. Pastoralists are, in their view, under threat from the conservation movement, Aboriginal land rights, and 'questions regarding the economic return from pastoralism relative to benefits from alternative uses and tenure regimes' (p. 50). In addition, many pastoralists now see themselves to be working knowledgeably with the country, not against it (p. 63), and thus to be working in a mode of collaboration rather than conquest. This proposition can be challenged along numerous dimensions, but for my purposes here the pertinent point is the worldview, not environmental practice.

The shift is from a transitive moment that would be superseded, leading to a more permanent way of life. That way of life is now represented as a 'tradition' and it is finding new alliances as it seeks to defend itself from replacement by more intrusive industries, particularly irrigation agriculture. A pertinent example is the Cooper Creek story. The great rivers of the Channel Country on the eastern side of the Lake Eyre Basin are among the few unregulated dryland lowland rivers in Australia. Their flow is best described by the flood pulse concept: episodic flooding fills the rivers and thousands of kilometres of channels, spilling over into floodplains and bringing life to exceedingly arid land. In this region, floods are erratic; Walker and colleagues (1997) compare the dynamics of inland floodplain rivers to the boom-and-bust model of the economy. Native plant and animal species are adapted to booms and busts, and the Channel Country floodplains become moving wetlands that are significant breeding sites for many species of birds as well as home to a great variety of non-migratory species.

In 1995 a group of farmers sought permission from the Queensland government to draw water from the upper reaches of the Cooper system in order to establish an irrigated cotton industry. Their proposal was opposed by the region's pastoralists who believed that, if implemented, the scheme would undercut their own livelihoods. Pastoralists were joined by environmentalists, who took the view that introducing irrigation into our few remaining unregulated rivers is ecological malpractice. It was also opposed by ecologists who were concerned about the regulation of rivers whose ecosystems are wholly adapted to an erratic system of flood events. The government did not accede to this proposal, but other irrigation proposals are currently being put forward (summarised from Walker et al. 1997 and Fullerton 2001).

Out of this experience a new Australian identity is taking shape: the green grazier (see also Goodall 2000). According to Griffiths (2001: 58), 'In the face of corporate cotton, pastoralists mobilised in defence of their social as well as natural environment ... Many of [them] talk of ... planning for drought and accepting flood as a bonus, going with the flow.' Rather than maximum extraction, they are seeking ways to ensure permanence for their way of life, and rather than conquering Nature, they are seeking to work with it. As the mayor of Barcoo Shire (one of the main areas of resistance to dam proposals) said recently in a speech in Canberra, 'we don't manage nature, nature manages us.'

This now threatened way of life has secured a place in national imagery. The romance of the outback and cattle, like the American romance of ranching life, speaks to the nation through film and television, and through events such as rodeo (discussed below). Kimberly Hedrick writes of ranchers in the Eastern Sierras that:

> They have an intense emotional attachment to their landscape and their way of life, and so they fight furiously to retain their rights to graze public lands and freedom to manage their private lands as they see fit, not only to maintain their economic viability, but also to preserve their sense of self. (Hedrick n.d.)

Cattle culture can be seen to shelter and support a transitive moment, but as I now want to show, it also shelters and supports those who resist being superseded. Cattle events such as rodeo and camp draft provide complex imagery of both danger and glamour, of both violence and certain forms of passion, freedom, and possibility. They are meticulously organised and rule-governed, and are supported by a large set of industries; at the same time, they perform unpredictability and subversion, and assert the value of cattle culture as an end in itself. I will suggest that they perform a meta-narrative that asserts a vivid and enticing countermodernity, and that this particular countermodernity is best expressed within this chronotope of uncertainty.

Into the Arena

In recent years we have seen an analysis that lines up a set of hierarchical dualisms, as discussed in chapter 1. Thus, culture: nature; human: animal; mind: matter; man: woman; civilisation: savagery. My argument works against the monolithic quality of these analogies. If humans, horses, and bovines share a social order, then they occupy a conceptual and social arena which cannot properly be reduced to a monolithic binary that separates humans from animals or culture from Nature.

My analysis takes a turn away from Elizabeth Lawrence's excellent study of rodeo, while also drawing inspiration from her study. The basic thesis Lawrence pursues is that in rodeo men (in particular) re-enact the ethos of the frontier, again and again conquering and taming the wild. 'It supports the value of subjugating nature, and reenacts the "taming" process whereby the wild is brought under control. This can be thought of in terms of the force of "culture" reaching out to dominate "nature"' (Lawrence 1982: 7).

In contrast, I am suggesting that cattle events, rather than performing triumph, actually perform uncertainty, and thus contribute to the ongoing life of the Year Zero as a manifold of possibilities. So I also want to explore the idea that cattle events perform subversions or alternatives to civilisation, and here my work engages with ideas developed by Richard Davis (in press) in his work on Aboriginal stockmen in rodeo. Davis analyses rodeo in the Kimberley, and his focus is on Aboriginal cowboys. His work contrasts to some degree with that of Elizabeth Furniss's (1999) work on First Nations people in Canadian rodeo. There, and in some of the US rodeos, Indians are important participants specifically as Indians, not first and foremost as cowboys. However, it is also the case that in Canada and the United States rodeo is immensely popular among Indigenous people. There, as in Australia, the Indigenous people are cowboys. Their entry into cattle events builds on their lifelong work with cattle and offers contexts for competition and achievement (Iverson 1999).

Davis notes that the frontier is a site of crisis, replacement, and transfer: 'the frontier rests on the maintenance of fundamental differences between colonists and indigenous inhabitants in which there is transfer of creative energy from indigene to colonist.' He argues that rodeo performatively resolves national crisis, and asks, reasonably, how Aboriginal men fit in. His research with Aboriginal stockmen shows that their knowledge and sense of belonging to country is part of their cowboy identity, and he argues that when they express their skill with cattle they are also expressing their relationships to and knowledge of the land. In this way, competing in rodeo brings country, memory, knowledge, and a sense of superiority to White cowboys into a competitive sphere where Aboriginal men are (or should be) equally rated and have fair opportunities to win. Their competition is not against Nature but against the colonisers.

My interest in rodeo and similar events is incited by this extreme openness to numerous meanings, all being performed in the one arena. In addition, there are other cattle events outside rodeo, and the larger repertoire bears an even larger set of possibilities. Camp draft is a good place to start. This Australian event is roughly equivalent to the American and Canadian penning events. It tests the communicative and partnership skills of horse and rider. It does not promote the view that human culture is separate from Nature; rather it promotes inter-species relationships that are based on trust, the ability to think separately, to communicate with each other, and to work together.

In camp draft a small herd of cattle is penned in. Rider and horse enter the pen and pick out the beast they will work with. They run it around a clover-leaf circuit making sure that it does not touch the rails, and they take it through a final set of posts, making sure that it goes through in the right direction. In contrast to a number of rodeo events, camp draft is open both to women and men, and neither has any particular advantage. Indeed, in team draft families often work together, and some members of the team are children. Camp draft horse and rider work together to effect control over a third species, the bovine. The horse has to out-think the cow, as well as communicate with and respond to the rider. In team camp draft four riders and four horses cooperate; the team includes human and horse members.

In contrast to the cooperation that characterises camp draft, many rodeo events look extremely competitive. The bucking bronco events exemplify an extreme differentiation from camp draft and are the emblem of rodeo. We do well to remember that rodeo 'sports', like camp draft, are based on the real working lives of cattlemen and women. A Murranji water tank artist reminds us of this:

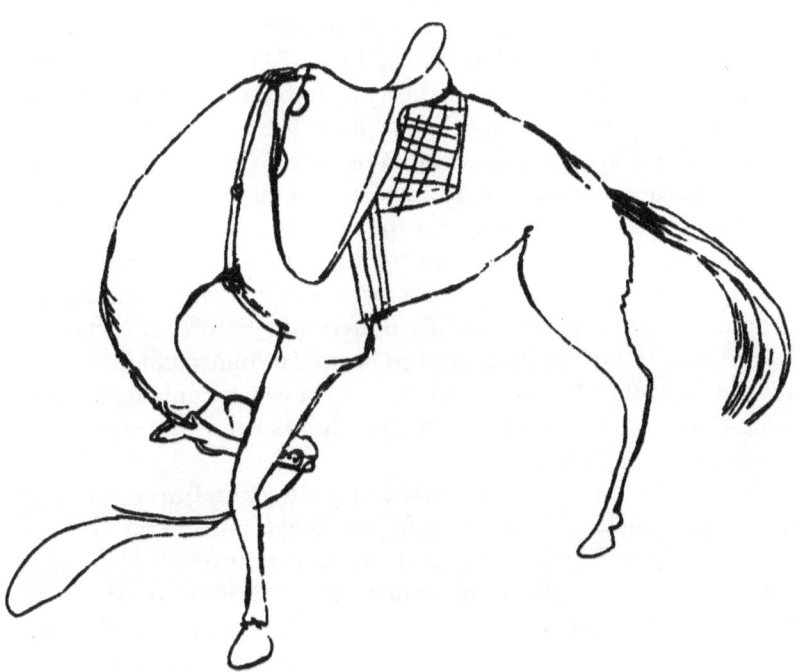

On the face of it this event looks like a great example of human mastery over wild Nature, as if one were replicating the conquest of wilderness again and again. If one follows this line of analysis, though, one must note that as often as not the horse 'wins'. In a recent interview with a man whose family breeds horses specifically as bucking broncos I asked if they were breeding the wild back into the horses. 'Not at all', he said. They are breeding them for a capacity for performance. According to this man, the horses are gentle and lovely; they are horses who know that when they come out of the chute their job is to 'buck like hell'. There is a discipline here in which humans and horses work both competitively and collaboratively to produce a particular performance. The human seeks to stay on, the horse seeks to buck like the devil, and, significantly, both horse and rider are rated on their performance. What appears to be a contest for control may also be a collaboration towards performance. The intensity of the collaboration is captured in a cowboy poem called 'Rodeo Hand' by Peter LaFarge (1991). One line of it reads: 'Horse and man moving together as though they had traded souls in some prairie night …'

Let us recollect that the western master narrative is a story of progress characterised as the triumph of civilisation over savagery and culture over Nature (Plumwood 1994: 74). Plumwood's excellent analysis of this system of thought and action emphasises the qualities of hyperseparation (humans from Nature) and mastery (of humans over Nature). This story values the work of man over the work of Nature, of men over women, and of mind over body. Camp draft and rodeo offer possibilities for subversion by giving us a different set-up. Here we see human nature and animal nature being disciplined towards each other. Humans have to understand animal communication; animals have to understand human communication; horse and human both need to be able to understand the body language of cattle. This is an ancient story in which humans and their domesticable animals move closer to each other through learning to communicate and cooperate.

But, while unsettling the master narrative, and doing so very delightfully, these events also perform the foundational chronotope – the Year Zero. They perform uncertainty; they perform danger; and they perform incompletion. They thus contribute to the reproduction of awareness of uncertainty and peril that has been so supportive of untrammelled extraction and immunity from regulation, and that is now a characteristic of pastoralism itself.

Taking the cattle and horse events together, I suggest that they can be understood as a meta-narrative that is at heart countermodern in its capacity not only for opposition but for alternatives. Opposition to the major dualisms of modernity is most evident in camp draft where men and women and horses work together. Their success is achieved through cooperation, not hyperseparation; without eradicating difference, they work productively with it.

Alternatives are performed across all types of events. Not only do men and women (settler and Indigenous[6]) perform peril, they also perform value. They assert the beauty, danger, companionship, hard work, and uncertainty of their own way of life with cattle. I would go further and suggest that in these events other binaries are destabilised and that subtly both audience and participants are invited to reject civilisation's subjectivity and to embrace an alternative way of being. I do not intend to lose sight of the fact that rodeo, in particular, is deeply embedded in capitalism, and is not pre-modern by any stretch of the imagination. My point is that while there is so much going on in these events, their capacity for subversion remains awesome.

We have seen how Aboriginal rodeo contestants destabilise the master narrative. The mind/matter binary is also vividly brought into destabilisation. Western denigration of the body, as matter to be dominated by mind, is well attested. Jay's (1993) analysis of 20th-century western philosophers' defence of the body's knowledge is an excellent study of both denigration and defence. Feminist studies of gendered bodies in the western world take the analysis further. They have required us to consider that the body is not a homogeneous site of denigration, but is also the corporeal repository of particular kinds of subjectivity (Grosz 1994). Thus western liberal democracies rest on a concept of subjecthood, or subjectivity, which is implicitly male and individuated. The individual subject is a body with clearly and cleanly demarcated boundaries (Kristeva 1982; Rosengarten 1996: 16–27). Grosz (1994) makes the further point that the good subject is in control of the body – that is, the body is fully enclosed, and the boundaries are under the will of the person. The hyperseparation of mind and body denigrates the knowledges of the body, and all those aspects – sounds, smells, leaks of one sort or another – that draw attention to the materiality of our physical being.

Rodeo and camp draft can be seen to perform an alternative that directly affirms the physicality, and thus a subjectivity, that modern civilisation wishes to deny. In rodeo and other events, matter and mind, like nature and culture, are extravagantly entangled. It is possible that civilisation's own self-loathing is being performed here even as conquest, in some contexts, is being promised as well. We get skills, communication, and knowledge intermingled with dust, sweat, shit, pain, and blood, perhaps even death. We get exhilaration to the max. Speaking from a position in the grandstands, we can enjoy seeing skilled and trusting relationships between people and animals as well as dangerous and uncertain relationships. We can slip into the frontier thinking that despises authority, and maybe we can kid ourselves into thinking that we enjoy that kind of freedom.

These performances thus invite multiple and inter-braided forms of desire. We can take pleasure in imagining that collaborations between humans and other species might be part of our own repertoire. More deeply, perhaps, we can vicariously experience an earthy, dynamic, and engaged life in a space that performs the possibility that civilisation has not yet won. We can imagine a non-linear twist to the whole oppressive story: perhaps the battle today is not for control of civilisation but for defence against it. In that mode, it may not matter whether horse or man wins, or whether the man is settler or Indigenous; what matters is that they perform together their intersubjective, countermodern, embodied and dangerous collaboration. As we hold our breath and clench our hands we can find ourselves increasingly excited at the thought that maybe, perhaps, civilisation will not win, ever.

PART TWO

BATTLEFIELDS

Many forms of violence were amplified in conquest. People died of new diseases, fertility was curtailed through new sexually transmitted diseases and malnutrition, and children were taken from families so that future generations were disappeared. Then there were the issues of who had the right to survive, and would not Indigenous people be better off if they could somehow cease to be themselves (see Povinelli 2002).

For more than two decades now, historians have been attempting to quantify the approximate number of Aboriginal people directly killed by White people in the course of settlement (for example, Reynolds 1981; Broome 1982; see Broome 2003 for an overview of methods and results). The figure of 20 000 people seems likely to be an accurate estimate using available evidence, but given that in so many areas the figures for population loss run at about 90 per cent or more, and given that the original population was probably 750 000 or more people, one may wonder what purpose the figure 20 000 really serves.

In Part Two I examine a few aspects of this wider battlefield, focusing on the future in the present along the Victoria and Daly Rivers. These chapters examine battlefields of body and soul, allegiances and claims. Struggles for agency and power in a field of violence and dishonour bring us face to face with the past in the present in ways that numbers simply cannot do. Even more significantly, they show the violence of settlers' efforts to lay claim to the future.

5
GENDER OF THE GUN

Now come all ye sports that want a bit of fun,
Roll up your swags and throw on a gun,
Get a bit of flour and sugar and tea,
And don't forget a gallon of Gordon's O.P.;[7]
Crank up your lizzy and come away with me,
And I'll show you some sights as you never did see
Down on the Daly River Oh! ...

You are awoke in the morn,
And your heart is filled with glee
By a little dark maid with a pannikin of tea,
She'll give you such a welcome, you won't wish to go
Away from the Daly River Oh! ...

While the buffalo kicked, we poured in the lead;
We killed him ten times to make sure he was dead;
Then we sharpened up our knives and we all hopped in –
Three whites, two Chows, four bucks and a gin.
We tore off his hide and ripped him up the guts,
Took his little tit-bits, his fancy funny cuts,
Then we cranked up the lizzy, shouted 'Right oh!
All aboard for the Daly River' – Oh.
(Burgoyne, quoted in Harney 1946: 218–20)

The Daly River, south of Darwin by about 200 kilometres, has had the reputation of being a very tough place from earliest colonisation and continuing to the present. This poem, only part of which is quoted here, was written by Jim Bourgoyne and is sung by Ted

Egan. It tells of life along the Daly River in the 1930s. Egan (1979: 22) writes: 'I like to be reminded of the good old days ... on the Daly ... The country has always been an Aboriginal paradise in terms of "bush tucker" and wildlife generally...' Anthropologist W.E.H. Stanner carried out fieldwork along the Daly in the same period. His elegant description of the Daly River region offers a fundamentally dissimilar sense of place in the 1930s: 'The river seemed to me a barbarous frontier – more, a rotted frontier, with a smell of old failure, vice, and decadence' (Stanner 1979b: 80).

In this chapter I examine the links settlers were making between Nature, natives, and gender in two moments in the frontier: at the point of conquest, and in the stretched period of settlement. Each speaks to peril for White people, each speaks to a different kind of peril, and each is silent (in different ways) about the man-made catastrophe being inflicted upon Aboriginal people.

Speaking Guns

European settlers arrived in the Victoria River country in 1883; they brought violence and they encountered it. Before long they requested police assistance in subduing the area. Mounted Constable Willshire was in the Victoria River District from May 1894 to September 1895. Willshire is the only person in the early years of the Vic River frontier to have left us thorough accounts. His book *Land of the Dawning; being facts gleaned from cannibals in the Australian stone age* (1896) was written while he was in the district. His account directly concerns the people with whom I have studied; most of them are descendants of the peoples Willshire encountered.

According to Kimber's even-handed biography, Willshire was a first generation Australian from a professional background. His father had been a journalist before turning to school teaching, and later to the public service. Willshire himself received a reasonable education before going off as a young man to become a drover (Kimber 1990: 317–20). We may suspect here some romance with the outback, and his later literary works display a sense of the romantic coupled with a certain literary flair.

Willshire entered the South Australian police force (at that time the Northern Territory did not exist, being the northern portion of South Australia) and in 1891 he was brought to law by Magistrate

Gillen, then Protector of Aborigines, for massacring Aboriginal people in Central Australia (see Povinelli 2002: 93 for a vividly contextualised account). He was acquitted, and two years later was posted to the Vic River where, according to one source, he was 'able to commit mayhem at will' (Kimber 1990: 319).

He and his Black trackers set up a small camp on Victoria River Downs Station, and from there they went out on patrol in search of 'cattle killers' and other desperadoes. Willshire had available to him the two standard myth-images of savagery: the Bloodthirsty Savage and the Childlike Savage. He drew on both in a wildly cacophonous fashion. A few examples can stand for the dozens that could be offered:

> What savages they are, to be sure! ... nothing but lead from a rifle can steady the cannibals. (Willshire 1896: 34)
> They are innocent children, and very susceptible to kindness. (p. 72)
> They watch for you, they lie in ambush, and the treacherous beings crawl stealthily upon the weary white traveler at nighttime. They cannot understand friendship, and will not appreciate kindness. (p. 25-6)
> ... a wild and timid lot that want softening to subjection by firm and kind treatment. (p. 69)

Willshire's description of the land shows a similar bi-polar imagery. Along with the soothing breast of Nature, we find alligator-infested waters, sombre landscape scenes, and numerous references to impenetrable growth which greatly impeded his pursuit of the wild savages. Most vividly, however, the contrast is between the fertility and beauty of the land and the non-productivity and savagery of the inhabitants. There is also ample evidence of imperial imagery. The Victoria had previously been named by Stokes (chapter 3), who was impressed with the 'nobility' of the river (Stokes 1846: 40). Willshire applies the royal image to the Wickham River; here he writes about VRD Station:

> ... one of the largest stations in Australasia, magnificently watered, containing prolific Mitchell grass plains and flooded coolibah country, extravagant in fertility ... The Wickham, the queen of beautiful rivers, whose banks sparkle with flowers, presents its soothing breast to the untutored children of the forest, who in their undisturbed liberty and ignorance are not qualified to appreciate the land of wealth and beauty in which

> their lot is cast. It is obvious to anyone with practical knowledge who wanders through this bright and wonderful *terra incognita* that her resources will in the future be practically limitless. (1896: 37)

Aborigines, Willshire tells us, are not capable of comprehending the fertility of their environment: he also advises us that with their 'primitive weapons' they are also not capable of exploiting it (pp. 49–50). In numerous passages the contrast between country and people evokes a sense of sullied sublime:

> Next morning the pure white clouds were just unfurling their snowy folds over the high basaltic ranges when a blackfellow and I ascended Mount Bynde to get a view of the surrounding country ... On looking down I saw a native village in a secluded dell, but not the domain of a gentle race of savages, but that of a fierce and bloodthirsty horde who will kill and eat white men whenever they get an opportunity. (p. 48)

Some of his most powerful descriptions are attempts to convey the grandeur of the country. He struggles to represent the sublime, that essential feature of the romantic imagination of landscape (Bishop 1989: 42). Most of these passages form the context or counterpoint to his descriptions of killings, and seem to invoke the land as witness. I read these as attempts to endow his own actions with an exalted purpose, as if by foregrounding the land he could evoke eternity as an ally in claiming the moral ground of action. Here is an encounter with some 'cattle killers':

> They scattered in all directions, setting fire to the grass on each side of us, throwing occasional spears, and yelling at us. It's no use mincing matters – the Martini-Henry carbines at this critical moment were talking English in the silent majesty of these great eternal rocks. The mountain was swathed in a regal robe of fiery grandeur, and its ominous roar was close upon us. The weird, awful beauty of the scene held us spellbound for a few seconds. (p. 41)

Willshire never admits to killing anyone. Perhaps his Central Australian experience had indicated the advisability of circumlocution. As William McGregor (1990) points out, in this statement Willshire does not shoot, and the Martini-Henrys are not loaded with bullets – they appear to speak of their own volition. Their 'words' are the story that could not be told.

Willshire's invocation of the language of the sublime seems to signal his sense of feeling overwhelmed by the situation he had precipitated, the actions he had undertaken, and the monumental excess of it all. There is a huge literature on the sublime in relation to trauma (for example, La Capra 1998), and in relation to Australian landscapes (Gibson 1992; Tumarkin 2002). I do not follow the path into this literature, as my focus is on Willshire's actions and sense of peril, but one cannot read his work without being struck by his use of the sublime in two main contexts: as a context and site of displacement for his own actions, and as a means of heightening the contrast between Nature and the natives. In the first instance he displaces his own agency ('the mountains' ominous roar', p. 41); in the second he seems to justify his work ('fierce and bloodthirsty horde', p. 48).

Willshire's actions depend on the contrast between degraded and childlike savages. For the most part, it is the men who are degraded and the women who are childlike. This undoubtedly derives in part from his experience of men as warriors and of women (frequently) as terrified survivors. He was certainly clear about the difference: 'The women are good and the men are bad', he wrote in the dedication of the book (p. 6). Willshire also saw the hand of God on the frontier: 'Men would not remain so many years in a country like this if there were no women, and perhaps the Almighty meant them for use as He has placed them wherever the pioneers go' (p. 18). Willshire seems to have deployed his forces to exterminate men and capture young women. Children and old women seem to hold little interest for him, and it is difficult to ascertain what happens to them; Aborigines say that he killed them, but it is impossible to know with certainty. Deprived of family to care for them, it is probable that they died in consequence of the violence either directly or indirectly. One passage characteristically mixes his views on men and women; he is advising police to pay particular attention to young adult men:

> When I first endeavoured to decrease their raids on the squatters' property I was checkmated in every movement by their vigilance and adroitness. It is quite different now, since I have brought them to their bearings. There are those who would be shocked to hear of hundreds of black virgins all nude and in the full tide of youthful enjoyment ... but this is how they are in their wild state, free from the vices of civilisation. (p. 71)

Just as Willshire never states that he killed people, so he also never states that he captured women, although he did manage to rescue a good number. Equally, he never states that he engaged in sexual activity with Aboriginal women, although the narrative makes best sense if one assumes such liaisons. Willshire and his three trackers had about twelve local women at the police station. They obtained many of them through terror. One example, chosen from several, indicates the process:

> We were flanked on either side by great walls of stone, and the bucks will fight like demons where there is no 'get away.' Then we all rose to show ourselves, and there was a furious stampede of powerfully built niggers, some climbing the cliffs, some running back to us with spears, some diving in the water, several climbing into the rocky fissures, and the women and children huddling together in a cave, the rude interior of which fairly glowed with girlish beauty. The imagination cannot conceive the terrors of that dreadful time ...
>
> Out from their flower-festooned alcoves came the brilliant bevy of blushing maidens, all timorous and coy. (p. 61)

After this, as well as other similar events, Willshire's trackers (never himself!) spent the night with the women, 'perfecting themselves in the art of love' (p. 32). I read this type of event as massacre and capture followed by what appears to be gang rape. The coercive terror of these acts is invisible to Willshire. He says, with no apparent irony: 'Black girls, as a rule, will come to white men of their own accord' (p. 36). Like most other commentators, he says that Black women can be seduced by trinkets – a dress or a mirror will appeal to their innate femininity and bind them to the donor.

Willshire's frontier work is making a space in which civilisation can flourish. Nature is conceptualised in two attitudes, one of which is domesticable, and one of which is hostile to civilisation. Aboriginal men and impenetrable growth will be cleared out to make way for civilisation. Aboriginal women and rich fertile land are capable of responding to the bushman and becoming civilised, although they will, of course, always be women and land.

Taking Nature as a constant, Black men are situated far lower on the scale of humanity than Black women, and Black women, while identified with Nature, are closer to civilisation than are Black men. The implication, quite clear in Willshire as in many other writers of later decades, is that not only are Aboriginal men less human than women, but that they treat women very badly. Their alleged lack of respect for women marks their inferiority both to White men and to Aboriginal women. Aboriginal women are centred with Nature through their innate femininity. It is understood that they will naturally seek out White men, for their femininity seeks civilised treatment. White men thus appear as the chivalrous protectors of Black women, even in the most violent contexts.

We have seen that Willshire was blind to the coercion he exercised. Another woman who was captured after a massacre resisted, and in doing so aroused Willshire's passion to an extent that is noticeable even in a book already filled with dusky virgins and heaving bosoms. During the night this woman tried to escape. One of Willshire's trackers (although the story makes better sense if we hypothesise that Willshire is the actor) gave chase and grabbed her by the hair just as she was about to throw herself into 'crocodile-infested' waters. According to Willshire, she proceeded instantly to fall in love with her captor. Taken back to the police station, she became 'a paragon of gentleness, and her animal passions subsided into tranquillity' (p. 47). Willshire's experience with women is summed up this way: 'as a rule these lubras [Aboriginal women] become domesticated, and attend to the requirements of their lord and master with the same attention as a good white woman would' (p. 35).

If miscegenation were not an issue the future would be clear. As it is, Willshire's intentions are baffling. His absolute hatred of 'half-caste' people (pp. 18, 35) suggests that a Black woman's labour and sexuality can be worked by White men to benefit White men, but that anything she produces herself will be flawed.

Willshire's frontier is a White man's world; one could easily conclude that there were no White women in that part of the world. In fact the Durack women were on the west side of the watershed (Durack 1986); to the east was Jeannie Gunn (1954). Some women battled through the area on their way to the goldfields of the Kimberley region, and others settled in the Victoria River valley itself (see James 1989 for more detail on outback women). Their absence in Willshire's imagery may be logically necessary to his lone hero figure, but it does not accurately reflect the frontier situation.

In sum, Willshire's project was to do the work of the left hand – to clear away impediments to civilisation. The peril in Willshire's writing is twofold. The peril for individuals was that they might be killed in combat. Aboriginal people were fighting for their land, and some White men were killed. Willshire occasionally expresses his own fear of being overcome by Aborigines (for example, pp. 25–26). The further peril is that the project of settlement might fail. This peril led Willshire (p. 71) to remonstrate that: 'It has been my duty for many years to protect the property of the settlers who pay the Government good rentals, and if there is one virtue I possess greater than another it is in my dealings with wild savages.' It was truly a time of uncertainty.

Romancing the Bush

Ernestine Hill (1955) is my major representative for a later period of settled life. Meagan Morris (1988) provides an excellent analysis of Hill's work as a whole; I take up her work in the North, drawing mainly on her classic *The Territory*, first published in 1951. A great deal had changed from Willshire's time to the time Hill was travelling around the Territory in the 1930s and 1940s, and writing about it in the 1940s and 1950s. She speaks to and from a moderately settled region. She was constructing a White Australian identity through which Australians have sought to free themselves from the derivative identity as Mother England's uncouth children (chapter 2). During her lifetime she was an enormously popular author; by the 1950s, however, her work was about to become outdated and her enthusiastic audience was on the verge of disappearing. Since the 1960s interest in her work has virtually died (Morris 1988).

Willshire was unable, and probably had no intention of trying, to conceal absolutely the way in which the North was conquered. By Hill's time, however, settlement had overtaken conquest, and while she discusses violence, it is always in one of two contexts: that of the occasional act of necessity which she regrets, or that of individual idiosyncrasy, which she regrets or condemns. In Hill's narrative, Willshire's Winchesters have been replaced by a commercial transaction. The pioneers, she says, had 'bought a kingdom for a billy of sweet tea and a stick of tobacco' (Hill 1955: 2).

Compared to Willshire, Hill defines Aborigines in a much more positive light; the Bloodthirsty Savage imagery is long gone. Subdued Aborigines were not threatening both because they were controllable and because according to the ideas of the day they were about to become extinct. In Hill's myth-making, Aborigines are still close to Nature, and this is a virtue which for the most part she will extol. She seems reluctant to grant full and equal humanity to Aborigines, and she does so mainly in the context of noting that they are dying out. Aborigines, she says, have 'a history, tradition, law and religion far older on earth' than the English. They are intelligent, and they have mastered the art of enjoying life; they are far more Christian than Europeans. Finally, and central to her imagery, is this statement: 'They covered and used the whole continent far more equably than we have done without one blemish of nature, without wreaking the vengeance of erosion' (pp. 345-6). All of these highly positive attributes are followed by the statement that they have been hurled into oblivion.

Hill's bushman is most definitely a man, as was Willshire's. But in contrast to the practicality which Willshire extols, Hill's bushman is a romantic. His endeavours, many of them, are failures, but he still has his dream. Beyond that the parallels cease. The bushman is a new type in the history of humanity, according to Hill: 'something new in the rank and file of mankind, civilised man with no need of civilisation. He could live like the blacks in a black man's country, and build a white man's empire' (p. 422). For the most part he is single and nomadic: 'They were married to [the land] for better or worse, in the acquired taste of their own solitary life and the joys of eternal roaming' (p. 260). She suggests that in the outback a new type of civilisation is evolving; it traces its ancestry to Empire, its education to Indigenous people and Nature, and it transcends both. Landscape is thus crucial to her construction. In describing country she has shifted from regal metaphors to kinship or local metaphors. The Victoria River, which Stokes found so 'noble' that he named it after the Queen, is described very differently in Hill: 'Granddad of all Territory streams is the Victoria' (p. 228). Hill goes for the exotic, and she finds most to interest her in the lower Victoria. The area around Victoria River Downs Station she defines as 'conventional' beauty:

> forests of grey box and gracefully drooping nutwood and bauhinia hung with scarlet mistletoe and alight with movement of parakeets and painted finches. On either side is an infinite realm of grassy Plains and rolling downs, guarded by the broken forts of hazy red ranges, jeweled with pandanus springs and a hundred singing creeks. (p. 229)

In this passage Hill has gone about constructing a most enticing image of the conventional. Whatever else the outback may be, it is nothing like the Australian or British metropoles; Hill subverts any possibility of proposing the outback as a reflection of a settled landscape. At the same time, city readers will find that this landscape is by no means conventional, so Hill is also constructing the possibility of people who are so at home in this landscape that they actually do find it conventional.

There is no space in Hill's scheme for the proposition that Aborigines might become a new type, or that Black and White together might become something new in the history of humanity. Aborigines cannot evolve, to use Hill's terminology, because they are dying out. That White and Black might evolve together would involve miscegenation, and here Hill retreats into near silence. She tells us very little about the bushman's sexuality. As an imaginary type he is a loner, married only to the land. Throughout the book she discusses some individual bushmen who had permanent liaisons with Aboriginal women. She characterises these as marked by loyalty, devotion, and love. This reading is by no means without foundation, but it is also extremely selective.

Hill gives us an Australian outback which epitomises all that is unique and best in the continent as a whole. Most strikingly, it is, for the moment, indomitable. Settlement has taken place, the Aborigines are subdued, but the *land* is not conquered. The stretching of frontier time in Hill's work is attributed to Nature, and Nature is the other main hero of Hill's work. Nature refuses civilisation, tearing it down even as White people work to construct it. This imagery is signalled repeatedly by reference to insects, and there is a chapter titled 'White ants'. Hill's dramatic prose captures her myth-image of unconquerable Nature with perfect precision. Writing of attempts at agriculture along the Daly River, she says:

> For the Government farms were doomed to shabby failure. They came to nothing in the first year, and were mercifully drowned in the next monsoon ... Crops withered in hot winds, then rotted in wet ground. They were riddled with pests and smothered in weeds. Science could not save them ... Everything useful was overrun by everything noxious ... (p. 279)

The Territory is a lament for the passing of the Aborigines, as are most popular and scholarly stories of the period. Equally significantly, it is an elegy to White outback society and, most stunningly, to Nature itself. The plot of Hill's narrative is that eventually civilisation will triumph. In her scenario, that triumph requires the death of Nature as she constructs it (cf. Merchant 1980). With Nature's death the people who were at home and at peace in that environment must also be eclipsed. And thus a range of relationships among people and between people and ecological place will also be destroyed.

The peril in Hill's elegiac work is that the project of civilisation will succeed. Like Willshire, she works with a theory of replacement, but fifty years later she is in a mood of regrets. The Aborigines are nearly gone, and one day the land will be transformed and the White pastoralists will be displaced, ultimately to be lost to the contemporary world. Hill dramatically gives voice to White people's imminent disappearance, a loss she represents as inescapable.

Words and Silence

Constable Willshire's guns spoke English; the sounds of battle were reduced to conversation, and the conversation was presided over by Nature – either in the mode of 'silent majesty' or in the mode of 'ominous roar' (Willshire 1896: 41). In Hill's work one of the main silences is the sexuality; her quintessential bushman is married to the land.

Willshire implied that Black women's femininity would lead them to White men. He mentions their gratitude at being rescued and their fascination with womanly trinkets. The whole context is defined as ordained by the Almighty to meet the natural needs of White men. During subsequent decades the language changes slightly, but the terms of reference remain the same. At issue are the natural drives of White men and the alluring femininity of Black women. Ann McGrath (1987) provides an overview of the many different types of White male–Black female transactions and relationships in the North; my purpose is not to reiterate the survey but rather to focus on the relationships in which transactions were embedded. In this I follow the lead of Hobbles Danayairri and others (in Rose 1991: 179–88). Briefly, my supposition, and theirs, is that if coercive relations were possible, and if Aboriginal people had no legitimate defence against such relations, then the fact that some relations were not coerced cannot serve to deny the power supporting the whole set of interactions and obligations.

In Willshire's time the gun was used to eradicate and terrify. In relation to Black women, the power of the gun was invisible, and a relationship established through terror was ascribed to femininity. In the 1920s, 1930s and 1940s most of the Aboriginal people in the Vic River valley were working on cattle stations (a few worked for the police). Each station had a White management, and White and Black workers. Aboriginal labour was the mainstay of the pastoral industry, and, in contrast to White labour, wages were not required. On some stations (not all) overheads were kept even lower by underfeeding people and undersupplying items such as clothing. The result for many people over long periods was socially induced starvation. Prostitution was a structured mechanism through which food and other goods were transferred from White to Black (Rowley 1974: 262–63). Guns remained essential gear for White men.

The other tool of conquest, which I will label the cock, was also wielded with impunity. Tom Cole (1990: 26–27), in *Hell, West and Crooked*, tells a story from Lake Nash Station (eastern Northern Territory) about a group of White and Black stockmen joking about the numbers of testicles the Black men were eating as they were branding and castrating cattle:

> The talk ... switched to the food value, and not only muscle building. It seemed that Jabiru, in addition to a couple of wives, also had a girlfriend or two. 'That Jabiru properly greedy bugger,' said little Jacky, 'He like eatem plenty ball, try make 'im strong long girl friend.' Everybody laughed, enjoying Jabiru's discomfiture. He said, 'Me tink you fella jealous.' I thought maybe he wasn't far out there. It's the same old thing wherever you are.

In this story White men are the amused onlookers. Their own involvement in securing sexual access to Aboriginal women is entirely missing, although we would do well to be suspicious of the casual construction of an image of a superabundance of Black women. We might imagine that sexuality was only problematic to Aboriginal men, that they suffered a surplus of women and a deficit of virility. We would also have to imagine that this was a relatively free play of masculinity in an open market of testosterone.

As VRD Aboriginal men and women tell of these times, they assert that both European men and Aboriginal men believed they had some rights to Aboriginal women. Men describe their own rights and duties towards woman as being founded in the complexities of kinship and alliance: women were sisters, mothers, daughters, wives, potential wives, and so on. These men also recognise the less formal but no less pertinent play of desire directed towards lovers and potential spouses. But it was never the case for them, as Willshire claimed it to be (1896: 14), that sex was 'only natural', or that 'women of all ages and sizes are running at large' (p. 14; see Povinelli 2002: 71–110 for a superb analysis of these issues in Willshire's time and in subsequent analysis).

European men's rights were founded in and inseparable from the pastoral economy itself. According to Bill Harney (1945), a patrol officer for the NT Native Affairs Branch, on stations in the Vic River District, 'young women are regarded as part of the wages paid to keep [European] men on the stations'. Cole (1990: 119) himself recalls that he recruited a cook to a station with the inducement that 'the lubras [Aboriginal women] are the sweetest little girls in the Territory ...' In this context, the image of Australia as the working man's paradise takes on a highly charged meaning.

On some stations (VRD and Wave Hill in particular) and continuing for decades (on those two stations), White men deliberately contravened the rules which existed within their own society and which applied to their dealings with White people. Marriage was not only virtually unthinkable but also illegal (those men who established permanent liaisons with Black women were ostracised, and are not the men discussed here). Men took as of right immature girls (Berndt & Berndt 1948: 48); they took as of right other men's wives; they required that the husbands acquiesce, and then ridiculed them for acquiescing; they paraded their sexual relations with women to the women's fathers, brothers and others who were their protectors within Aboriginal law; they engaged in gang rape, and they beat women and men unmercifully; they required Black men to beat each other and they exercised their imaginations in developing other ways to hurt and humiliate men and women (see Berndt & Berndt 1987; Rose 1991).

The relationship between guns and masculinity has received ample attention in other contexts, but not, I think, in the outback. In a competitive field, differential access to firearms (and the right to use them relatively freely) skews relationships of power in particularly loaded ways. I would suggest that in this context the cock is a displaced gun. It may not be that a man totes his pistols as a symbolic penis, as popular psychology indicates, but rather that a man totes his penis as a symbolic gun. Tom Cole's reported good-natured joking with Aboriginal men intimates and obscures a multitude of unwritten rules about men and power. Most particularly it obscures the power that underwrote European dominance, representing as a sufficiency of testosterone what was equally likely to be a Colt, a Mauser, or a Webley.

Sex of the Bullet

Under colonising regimes, Indigenous children have been separated from their parents right from the start, but in the early years of the 20th century Australian states developed legislation that enabled them forcibly to remove children from their families. In the Northern Territory, removed children were consigned to institutions where, it was expected, they would be educated enough to work for White people and would start to assimilate into White society. The particular concern was with children of mixed ancestry. 'Full-blood' Aboriginals were expected to become extinct, and their mixed offspring would be disappeared into a homogeneous White settler world. The legal basis for this work was dissolved at different times in different places, and by about 1967 the demand for assimilation was dropped (summarised from the National Inquiry 1997). These are matters of extreme significance in their own right, and are discussed in excellent, and often excruciatingly painful detail, in the *Bringing Them Home* report (National Inquiry 1997).

Only recently has systematic sexual abuse come to be included within the United Nations definitions of crimes against humanity. The issue first arose in international law in the case of Jean-Paul Akayesu, who was tried for crimes against humanity by the International Criminal Tribunal for Rwanda (ICTR 1998, para. 417, p. 94). In order for rape to count as a crime against humanity, it has to be part of an intentional and systematic attempt to destroy a group (ICTR para. 598, p. 130).

The connection between rape and destruction rests primarily in the disposition of the children. The ICTR judges took a broad view of this definition, noting that where group membership is determined by parentage, then rape may be used to force women to give birth to children who will not belong to their group. The judges imagined a case of patriliny such that the children would be rejected by their mother's group. They also noted that these criminal practices might have the effect of discouraging women from procreation.

Both aspects are pertinent in the pastoral world of Australia. As in Rwanda, Aboriginal women were discouraged from bearing children (discussed in chapter 3). More importantly, perhaps, mixed-descent children in Australia were not usually rejected by their mother's group, but rather were claimed and taken by the state. The common practice of White men's sexual use and abuse of Aboriginal women can be assessed in this light. The removal of children ensured that sexual activity promoted the disappearance of Aborigines.

This is a graphically cruel matrix: the hand of the Almighty, and the naturalising discourse of bovine testicles and human sexual prowess, an economy of starvation and sex, and policies of removal. This matrix works towards more appalling facts. By mid-century the Martini-Henrys were no longer speaking English to kill and terrify in the present moment of encounter. Now the cock shot its bullets off into future generations of people who would be taken and never returned. Under these policies and practices, White men killed the future while still making use of living people in the present.

The future, as I have been discussing in previous chapters, is not empty homogeneous space. In relation to generations of people, the experience of time is the experience of connectivities sustained as gifts across the generations (Hatley 2000: 61–64). White men's bullets were invading the future, claiming it and killing it without having to take responsibility for it.

Many of the bullets carried diseases that made women infertile, and there is evidence to suggest that venereal disease 'wrought the greatest havoc' of all introduced diseases (Watson 1998: 90). Watson's painstaking research in south-western Queensland indicates that some bushmen knowingly transmitted venereal diseases to Aboriginal people (p. 92), and that the effects of disease were drastic – sudden and massive loss of life, and widespread loss of fertility and fecundity (pp. 90–44). Even without disease, however, the loss of future generations was also ensured through removals.

Furthermore, these bullets had the potential to destroy the past as well as the present, as they unmade the continuities that held generations of people together through time (discussed in greater detail in chapter 10). This dreadful matrix of violence disguised as playful fun and state benevolence amplified catastrophe, causing multiple waves of pain and loss across time, through social relations, and within the corporeal and consubstantive relations between people, other living beings, and country.

Aenocide was practised over decades and decades, and the result for many women was that survival became a curiously empty proposition. To live as the utilitarian object of others meant being physically invaded by bullets that ripped right into one's own selfhood, taking the future and starting to unmake the past.

Report for Judy

> Dear Judy,
> You acted for others to witness, and I find your life to be incredibly powerful. As best as I can offer, this is for you.
> Sincerely, Debbie.

I wrote in the Introduction that Daly saw the wild closing in around him. Along with that Whitefella-induced wild there was the loss of his wildly passionate forebears, among them a woman named Judy who was a countrywoman of Daly and the other Wickham River people.

Judy was an associate ('stud') of a Whitefella cattle duffer named Brigalow Bill (aka W.J.J. Ward). In 1907 he took up a small block in an area of sandstone that was unwanted by the larger companies, and would later become Humbert River Station. He complained about the rent almost from the beginning:

> I came here and stocked the lower end with my stock and after sivilizing [sic] the country and getting half my stock killed with Blacks and stand a chance of being driven off it witch aught [sic] to be mine by the rights of stocking. (*TCPJ*, 6 July 1908)

Brigalow Bill's problems continued. In 1909 he came to the notice of police because of a dispute over his woman Judy. Two other men, also described as 'ruffians', Nye and Webb, spent Christmas 1908 with Brigalow Bill. Webb grabbed Judy and rode off to Borroloola. Brigalow followed them across the Murranji track and the Barkly Tableland. The police account is surprisingly vivid:

The M.C. ascertained that W.J.J. Ward (Brigalow Bill) of Humbert River was in pursuit of one Webb across Murangi [sic] track because Webb had enticed away, while he and a ruffian named Nye were Ward's guests, Ward's lubra [Judy]. Nye, later, offered to get the lubra for Ward for a number of heifers. Ward abandoned his own horses at Longreach and took away Nye's horses, of course without permission. It was feared a tragedy might be the end of the affair so the M.C. awaited the arrival at V. R. Downs of Drover Phillips, daily expected, for news of the affair. On Phillips' arrival the M.C. learnt that Ward had passed Newcastle still in pursuit of Webb and that Nye – riding Ward's abandoned horses – and a ruffian known as 'Rackarock' were on Murangi track going in same direction. (*TCPJ*, 14-3-09)

We do not know how Judy made it back to her own country, but in March 1910 the police were called into the area again, this time to investigate reports that Brigalow Bill had been murdered. They found his hut splashed with blood and had no doubt concerning his death, but the body was not located. Eye witnesses told them that he had been killed by Aboriginal men who surrounded him, and that he had been tricked by Judy, who had hidden his gun (*TCPJ*, 25-03-10).

The resulting police chase after one or another possible suspect was a lesson in chaos and is discussed in detail elsewhere (Rose 1991: 119–29). While men were tracked, captured, interrogated, and taken to gaol, Judy appears to have weathered the whole thing extremely well. Constable Holland, who had been a key figure in the search for the killers, wrote up a summary from eyewitness accounts and he reports that Judy organised the killing. She told the Aboriginal men to hide in the creek bed, and she either hid Brigalow's gun or stole it and gave it to the Aboriginal men. These witnesses say that once Brigalow was speared a man named Gordon cut his throat with a tomahawk. Judy, it was reported, stood over him and pulled out his whiskers, saying 'good job him dead. Me fellow no more like him' (*TCPJ*, 15-06-10; *TCPJ*, 17-04-10, reprinted in Read & Read 1991: 31).

I imagine her standing over Brigalow Bill and I wonder if he was even dead when she ripped his beard off and made her speech of defiance. Local knowledge adds even more power to this intense moment. Brigalow Bill was down and dying. Judy stood over him declaring her pleasure, and she pissed on his face.

Judy was being grabbed back and forth, making her way in an extremely dangerous field of conflicting demands which were resolved in part through murder. I imagine Judy hitching up with Gordon, the man who was accused of the murder. I wonder, in fact, if she may already have been one of his wives. Gordon was one of the regional Lawmen, and a leader of the local war against Whitefellas. He was Daly's father's brother and further along in that same violent year, he was murdered by his own relations. If Judy was with him, then she, too, may have been killed in the wild violence of that time. Several of Gordon's wives were killed, and in retaliation Gordon attacked a VRD Aboriginal man whom he thought had killed the women. Following this attack, the station manager sent local Aboriginal men out to track and kill Gordon. They did so, and returned with his severed hands (see Rose 1991: 119–29).

Judy probably died young; the genealogies show that she was childless. Her bones will be there in the country, and people today know the bones are there even as the names are being forgotten. In Daly's words: 'Humbert River Station [Lingara]. That's the way we're living there ... now. We know our father dead there, mother dead there. We're going to go the same way' (in Rose 1991: 128).

6

THE FELLOWSHIP OF MATES

> Out of control (again), as in our semi-genocidal history of conquest and settlement. What to do? Maybe we want to live inside a new story, but how do we define it, how do we choose it, how can we make it come to be? (Kittredge 1996: 98)

In 1986 an American journalist named Tony Horowitz hitchhiked around Australia; like many travellers, he was particularly drawn to the outback. Subsequently he wrote about his travels in a book called *One for the Road*, and there he draws an analogy between the Inuit (Eskimo) elaboration of words for snow and the Australian elaboration of words for the outback: woop woop, back of Bourke, beyond the black stump (Horowitz 1987: 22); to which I would add: never-never, no man's land, and god's own.

The provocative aspect of these terms is not that there are so many of them, but rather that they refuse to specify time-space co-ordinates. We do not know where or when the outback is or was; the terminology points us away from the now and the here, and then dumps us.

The outback is part of a colonising conceptual domain that resonates with the frontier. It thus signals time, space and history in their most contentious as well as most formative and vital moments. For Australians there is an implicit notion that the frontier has not fully passed; known as the outback, it is imagined to be just over the horizon. Indeed, the social and cultural co-ordinates are likely to be far more explicit than the time-space co-ordinates. I am suggesting that the lack of specificity in time and space enables Australians to hold the outback vividly in their hearts and minds, and to sustain its significance as a formative and transformative site.

Max's Tour

In this chapter I analyse a tour organised explicitly towards themes of outback history and Australian identity. Max's Tour, operating out of Timber Creek (NT), was the winner of a 1993 Northern Territory Brolga Award for excellence in tourism, and when I took the tour for research purposes in 1991 it was a remarkable event no matter how one analyses it. I must add that Max Sharman has sold the business, and the current owner, Geoff Pike, has reworked the tour. Much of what I say here does not apply to the current tour experience, although it is still called Max's Tour.

Timber Creek is an extremely small town located on the Victoria Highway, which is now a two-lane bitumen highway. It is the major connecting road between the Top End of the Territory and Western Australia; Timber Creek is halfway between Katherine in the Territory and Kununurra in Western Australia. It is a regional centre – there are two pubs, two shops, a caravan park, police, a medical centre, a small government suburb, and, most visibly of all, Max's Tour. The town is physically and socially dispersed. To quote Max, 'there are thirty whites and fifty blacks, just enough to give the place a bit of colour'.

Max ran two tours daily, a four-hour morning tour and an hour and a half evening tour which was a condensed version of the morning trip. He accommodated thirty persons per tour, and the longer trip cost $25 per person in 1991. Max's brochure described the event in these terms:

> Max will take you on a voyage through nature, history and wildlife, back to the days when Timber Creek was a remote outpost and the river the lifeline of the biggest cattle stations in the world. Here you will find the real Territory.

I will suggest that Max played with liminal time and space to make his tour a ritual event which constituted an initiation of the tourist into an Australian identity that was raced, sexed, and authenticated. I use the word 'authenticity' in this context to denote the possibility of transfer between two statuses, that of settler and that of autochthon or native, in a way that enables the settler to belong to the country he has invaded. A crucial feature of this transfer, as I suggested in chapter 3, is that it is linear and requires replacement. The settler is the successor to the Aborigine, and there is only a brief moment of concurrence. The Max's tour initiation depended on the unspoken proposition that settlers, as conquerors, were strangers in their 'own' country. Max enabled his daily groups of tourists to participate in a ritual transformation that linked them to the resolution of the contradictions inherent in making peace without having declared war, and in being a stranger in the only country one can call one's own.

The basic scenario is already familiar through Hollywood westerns, western novels, and television, and is summarised most succinctly in the phrase (and title) 'the Last of the Mohicans' (see Fiedler 1986). In brief: settler (male) encounters Aboriginal (male) in a moment of recognition as the Aboriginal dies and the settler flourishes. In that moment the Aboriginal passes the mantle of belonging to the land (autochthony) to the settler. A new relationship is established as the settler inherits the world of the Aboriginal. In this elementary relationship of the colonising frontier two men, one White and one Black, encounter each other. The White man knows that he belongs to the future, and that the Aboriginal man belongs to the past. The dynamic between them is an act of conferral, perhaps best expressed as the relationship between initiate and master. Treating whole groups of people as if they were generations, the relationship is linear: the ancient autochthon passes away and the settler takes his place as the new (and superior) indigene.

Max generated a ritual space in which this moment of conferral was re-enacted and the tourists were given an opportunity to link their own lives with the lives of the settlers on whom was conferred the authenticity of the Aborigine. As I am analysing ritual action, repeated regularly in a liminal space, I will shift to the present tense.

Into the Circle

Tourist ventures are embedded in a paradoxical dilemma: everybody knows that the outback is remote and that it is not a tourist venture. A tourist venture is designed to make money, and so it relies on people. If tens or hundreds of thousands of people can get there annually, then it cannot be that remote. And if its drawing power is tourism, then can it really be the outback? On the other hand, if it is not the outback, there is no point in going. So tour ventures must say that the outback is both: both then and now, both here and just over the horizon; here both for those who live here and, however briefly, for those who are just passing through.

It is precisely this paradox that underpins Max's construction of liminal time/space. In the four hours of the morning tour, Max constructs the time-space co-ordinates which outback terminology nullifies. He promises a trip through time and space; what he delivers is even more complex than the promise. He is not promoting the concept of the changeless so much as the possibility of continuities with the past: he emphasises change in order to dramatise that which has not changed. As the relationship of succession indicates, change must be shown to exist to account for the conqueror, and it must be incorporated within a narrative of continuity in order to indigenise him.

The establishment of continuities enables Max to develop what I take to be the most significant portion of the tour. He constructs social and cultural co-ordinates which effectively say: this is the real Australia, and the settlers in these parts are the real Australians. Real Australians are defined as outback mates, and Max asserts in numerous ways that he is one of them. On his tour Max offers brief honorary membership in the fellowship. He verifies the authenticity of bush mates, defines the limits of the community, and asserts the quality of the values appropriate both within and beyond this community.

The tour is spectacularly popular and, in contrast to many tourist-oriented events, remarkably memorable. I say this from my own experience and from informal interviews conducted at Timber Creek and elsewhere. The key to this success is that the tour is terrifically entertaining. Max makes jokes and keeps people laughing, he personalises the relationships between himself and his tourists; he tells bits of gossip that facilitate a sense of insidership. His antics with crocodiles and other wildlife are unusual, and the people who bring video cameras keep them running for long periods. My informal surveying indicates that many people remember Max's Tour as one of the highlights of their trip around Australia, primarily because it was such good fun. Of the many moments of the four-hour tour, the most memorable seems to be the time in the circle when Max requires each tourist to have a go at playing the didgeridoo.

Max is a showman; his spiel is very well thought out and highly structured. It owes many debts to Ernestine Hill (1955). Within his memorised routine there are spaces for spontaneity, and while it is clear that he is reciting a lot of his information, he undercuts the boundary between performer and audience through a variety of dialogic strategies, including the continuing jokes which draw people into the tour as participants rather than simply audience.

There is an implication in much of what he says (overtly stated in a couple of contexts) that he is offering the tourists a set of understandings which give them a privileged position among the Australian populace. These tourists, he implies, are special people, deserving of special information which he, as a remarkable bushman and 'a legend in his time', is in a position to share with them. Max is described as a legend in his time in a song about himself, from a tape of songs about tourist sites throughout Australia, which he plays on the homeward journey. As a final feature of the tour it verifies a representation of himself which he begins well before the tour gets under way, and is crucial to his subsequent moves in which, I suggest, he makes of himself the initiator of the tourists.

Max promises a voyage through history back to the days when Timber Creek was remote and the Vic River was a lifeline, and tourist jokes provide an important medium for nullifying the temporal gap between past and present. Recall that this gap has to be there because if you are here as a tourist then this cannot be the frontier you've read about in books and ballads. The gap has to be there to account for your presence; a good entrepreneur like Max will close that gap.

We stop at a bottle tree, and we all pile out and walk around to the far side of the tree where there is a plaque dedicated to the memory of John Lawler. Max describes him briefly as one of the dregs of society who washed up in the outback. He goes into a sing-song eulogy, saying 'Just a ringer and a drifter'. And then with a complete change of cadence and intonation: 'Bet he didn't expect to become a tourist attraction!'

The gaze of the tourist is imaginatively reversed, and the tourists become the object of John Lawler's gaze. Laughter greets this quip, but along with laughter there is a bit of foot shuffling and sideways looks which I understand to be signs of self-consciousness. Most analysts seem certain that the tourist gaze is appropriative; it certainly seems often to be one way (for example, Fiske et al. 1987). Max's imaginative reversal of gaze and subjectivity has a powerful effect in two dimensions. It closes the gap between past and present, providing the dead man with a consciousness which interacts with the tourist. It reduces the intersubjective distance produced by the appropriative gaze by briefly positioning the tourist as object.

Spatial themes are constructed around the proposition that this place, the outback, is and was remote. I use the term 'constructed' quite deliberately. Max discusses the medical service, for example, saying that there are two bush nurses, one male and one female. They go on patrol to stations and Aboriginal communities. The doctor comes once a month for a general check-up. If there's a real emergency they'll fly you out, but it takes four hours for the plane to get here, so 'you'll either get better or die. There're not too many hypochondriacs around Timber Creek.' The construct is remoteness, the imagery is enjoyable, but the facts are dubious. Timber Creek is on a bitumen highway, and at a pinch it takes two hours to get to the nearest hospital by motor vehicle except on the rare occasions when the Vic River floods over the bridge, at which point a plane would be required.

The more important theme is Max's use of liminal space. The region is constructed as remote, and within this remote area he will play with space. His tour takes you from town to highway, and from highway to river. Along the river he pays due attention to crocodiles, which are the Top End emblems of wilderness and danger. The river becomes liminal space: it is the flowing link between past and present, between the tourist and the outback. You drift along through wilderness, danger, and history, and you end up on an island, itself a liminal place. Max closes off this liminal space and makes himself completely central by reminding you that you are on an island surrounded by man-eating crocodiles, and that there is only one boat – his. You walk to the centre of the little island, and sit in a circle while Max boils a billy and tells you stories. Here in this inner circle of multiple liminalities you participate in the ritual which is the heart of the tour.

Max presents himself as a true bushman. As discussed in chapter 5, Hill's (1955: 422) scenario is that the bushman is a natural man in an unnatural country; 'something new in the rank and file of mankind ... He could live like the Blacks in a Black man's country, and build a white man's empire ...'. In Max's updated version of this myth, nationalism replaces Empire. Max will show us that it is still the case that he can live like a Black in a Black man's country and build a White man's nation.

Positioning the White man in the Aboriginal domain has the dangerous potential of blurring the binary on which replacement depends. Max's performance will repeatedly assert the boundary between Black and White, while also asserting a continuity between the two. Characteristically for this frontier imagery, the White male is central and women are absent.

The issue of living like a Black in a Black man's country rests on the proposition that Whites can effectively *become like* natives and belong to the place without *going* native and losing either identity or their superordinate position. Max explores this theme in a highly complex fashion. For Max, White belonging requires verification; the badge of authentic belonging is bestowed by the authentic native himself – the Aboriginal. Native verification of White authenticity is expressed in this story about Nat Buchanan:

> He was a restless soul, old Nat Buchanan. He was always searching, further out and further out – to the other side of sundown. He came back to Wave Hill once after many many years. There was only the book keeper there. He introduced himself as Mr Buchanan. Well, it didn't register with the book keeper. He thought it was another old city bloke wandering around in the bush. Because Nat rode a camel, with a big bright green umbrella over the top to keep the sun off. They didn't call him 'Bluey' for nothing. His pack was on another one, and an old blackfellow for a mate. What a sight. And when he told the book keeper that he was going right down through the desert country to the South Australian border, the book keeper said 'You're mad,' he said, 'you'll perish. There's no water down there. Men don't come back from that country.'
>
> 'Ahh, we usually find it,' said Nat.
>
> Well, he tried to persuade him not to go but to no avail. And when he woke in the morning the old man had gone. So when the boss came back from the stock camp the book keeper told him about this old man who'd gone off into the desert.
>
> The boss said: 'Ahh, blast it. We'll have to go out and rescue him now. Better to find him alive than dead.'
>
> So they set out. There they found him, way down in desert country, a hundred miles south ... sitting under a beautiful big shady gum tree, water all around him, happy as Larry.

> Well the boss was going to go crook on him for causing too much trouble, and one of the old Aboriginal stockmen who'd been on the station for years, spotted him. And he said, 'Whoa, I been tink dat old fella been properly pinish, dat old Paraway, old Bluey Buchanan. Him know all this country. Him belong this country.'
>
> Oh, Bluey said, 'I forgot to tell him I was Bluey Buchanan.'
>
> You can imagine the reunion then. Shake hands all around, everybody giving a big smile. They reckon even the camels had a bit of a grin.
>
> But old Nat, he was still wandering around this country until he was a fair age. Finally, they persuaded him to settle down on a little farm just north of Tamworth, NSW. But settling down and leaving his beloved Territory must have broke the old man's heart for he didn't last long.
>
> Oh, but I've got a feeling, and I would like to think so. Somewhere today old Bluey's spirit is wandering along the Victoria. For it is men like Buchanan who shaped Australia and make you proud to be an Aussie.
>
> A great bushman. One of those men who are born with an innate sense of direction. Few men have it. You know, they reckon he could track the holy ghost through a thunder cloud.

There are several points to which I want to draw attention:

- Nat Buchanan is defined as a great bushman, the kind of man who makes you 'proud to be an Aussie'.
- The emblem of this definition is that because of Nat's sense of direction, he can live in this country.
- While the fact of an 'innate sense of direction' would seem to indicate a biological factor over which one has no control, the more compelling theme that Max draws from this is that Nat Buchanan can traverse the outback and thrive; his thriving is an indication of his authentic belonging.
- Verification of his authenticity is offered by an old Aboriginal man: 'old Bluey Buchanan. Him know all this country. Him belong this country.'

Max is addressing the question of whether White Australians can authentically belong to the country they have conquered. His answer, of course, is yes. The outback is the site where belonging can appropriately happen and where it can properly be verified. The bushman who can live like a Black in a Black man's country needs Blacks for two purposes which taken together form a paradox of settler identity. First, the Black man verifies the White man's authenticity, thus establishing continuity. Second, the Black man remains subordinate to the White man's superiority, and thus does not threaten the boundary between them.

I want to linger for a few minutes on the relationship between White men and Aboriginal skills. Knowledge of Aborigines and competence at skills which are generally defined as Aboriginal are crucial to the definition of the bushman. He can be thoroughly competent at both Black and White skills without losing his white identity and status and is thus forever superior to the Black, who can never be fully competent in both worlds. There is a zone of danger here which contains the possibility of the White man going native. Ernestine Hill implies that in the outback there are evolutionary dead ends as well as opportunities, and that White men can descend as well as ascend the evolutionary ladder (Hill 1955: 3). Black women can be understood as a devolutionary temptation, and within this logic miscegenation signals the loss not only of supremacy, but also of conquest in so far as conquest is understood to be a lineal replacement of native by conqueror.

In line with Max's presentation of himself as the superior bushman, he takes this time in the centre of the island to demonstrate his mastery of a number of Aboriginal skills. He makes smoke (not fire) by rubbing two sticks together. This display, in spite of (or perhaps because of) its boy scout qualities, indicates the competence of the bushman which is so central throughout the whole tour. Max displays his dual set of capabilities along several lines: he makes smoke but not fire because it would be irresponsible to make fires at this time of year (the unstated implication is that Blacks use fire irresponsibly); he uses the right woods as he had been taught by Aborigines, and he gives the wood its English name (Sesbania pea) which is, of course, based on its Linnean label.

Throughout all of this, Max maintains his White man's superiority. The most compelling example was offered in the context of his storytelling. Max told how he got his didgeridoo:

> Made by a very famous Aborigine, a fellow by the name of David Blanazi. Some of you've heard of David. He's the fellow who taught Rolf Harris how to play the didgeridoo. He's from

a little settlement halfway between Katherine and Mataranka called Barunga. But David, he's been all over the world, he's been to London, Paris, New York, Timber Creek.

He's not a Jawoyn, he's a Buntang. Now they're a similar skin or clan. He'd often come up to the corroborees, and when he did I'd get him to play as a guest artist because he's an excellent player. He could do the call of the plover or the dingo or the kookaburra. It'd just reverberate down this hollow limb, barely missing a beat in the haunting sound of the didgeridoo.

Very clever. But he wasn't too clever the night I got this didgeridoo. He was as full as forty monkeys – drunk, dirty, swearing, spitting all over the customers. I went over to hunt him, and I said 'what do you think you're doing David?'

'Want this didgeridoo boss? I want to sell him and get more grog.'

I said, 'well, give us a look at it.'

It was painted up something terrible. No one would have known ... but to me it was a good stick. And so I bought it off him and had it stripped down and repainted by a member of the Jawoyn tribe, a fellow by the name of Kurritjar ...

Here we see the White man's superiority demonstrated through his many competences, and we see the Black man's inferiority: he is a world-renowned musician but he can't handle alcohol. Listening to this with attention to discourses of Empire, we hear the familiar story of the gifted native who cannot handle civilisation and ends up destroyed by it.

Max's tour is about Australia, and he is initiating his tourists into the outback (implicitly defined as the real Australia) and enabling them briefly to become bush mates (implicitly defined as the real Australians). Max positions himself as a descendant of men like Bluey Buchanan, a true bushman, and he positions himself as the possessor of those boundary-threatening and boundary-sustaining qualities of Aboriginal knowledge and White male superiority. He plays the didgeridoo, sings a bit of song, dances very briefly, and accompanies himself with clapsticks. He also presents himself as an expert on Aboriginal culture in something of an anthropological mode.

The story of his didgeridoo signals superiority, and in his playing, which is very good, he also signals danger. For example, a piece that involves making the didgeridoo howl like a dingo is introduced as: 'Azaria Chamberlain's theme song, or *The Dingo's Lament*. Hang on to your babies, ladies!' Immediately after this display of skill and knowledge, danger and superiority, he passes the didgeridoo around and each of us tourists has to take a turn blowing. He dips it in a bucket of water after each person, saying he doesn't want anybody to get AIDS.

For many people this was the highlight of their tour. Max walked around the group handing the didge to each person in turn. He made jokes with most people either before or after they played. Many of the jokes had to do with rude sounds – there were references to farts and laxatives in particular. But they also had to do with one of the dangerous topics of the bush: miscegenation and the consequent blurring of boundaries between Black and White.

Anyone who played the didge well received a comment implying Aboriginality:

> Hey look at this! What colour was your mother, eh?

Or:

> Ah, no problem, here you go, splash of the old tar brush here somewhere.

The colour jokes depend on the assumption that there is no splash of the tar brush. We were all being well and truly defined as White here, and it is in that context of whiteness that people laugh. In short, they are on their way to becoming Whites who can master Black skills without losing their whiteness; proof of their progress is that they can joke about the possibility of a less than pure whiteness.

For me, this event conveyed a compelling sense of bonding. I felt that I was being drawn into complicity with a set of values which I oppose. Further, I think that every person who put their mouth to the didgeridoo became an accomplice to a particular set of relations between Black and White.

The apparent purchase of the didgeridoo from a man who was drunk and dead keen to sell it at any price is too low to be tolerated among White mates, but thoroughly appropriate, even clever, in the Black–White context. I would suggest that this 'theft' may be seen as emblematic of the relations between White and Black in many other domains of life, most notably the conquest of the continent. Recall Hill's statement that White people 'bought a kingdom for a billy of sweet tea and a stick of tobacco' (Hill 1955: 2).

I felt that to blow the didge was to give implicit assent to White supremacy, to dual standards, and to the proposition that there are contexts in which these stories and these jokes are appropriate. It was also implicit assent to the proposition that, like farts and other bodily functions, this conquest and those relationships are all natural.

The naturalness of Max's discursive strategies is reinforced also by the many resonances with conventional Territory discourse as encountered in pubs and anywhere else where White people, men especially, gather and socialise. Their near obsessive conversations run to familiar themes of Blacks and the bush: the gullibility of Blacks and the smart moves of Whites, the four-wheel drive tracks they have traversed and the difficulties they have overcome, the fish they have caught, and the Blacks they have seen broken down in the same bush they claim to travel so successfully (Cowlishaw [1997] gives these themes excellent analysis). Every tourist will have heard this talk. Max does not present new ways of thinking; he elevates and validates the conventional by positioning it within a symbolic and mythic structure of legitimacy.

Max does not say much about women. His silence develops a significant theme. His very few comments are directed towards contemporary women: 'hold on to your babies, ladies'. More specifically he targets us, not surprisingly, for our bodies. After everyone has blown the didge, Max makes this extraordinary statement:

> Oh my god, I forgot to tell you girls, holy bloody hell, too late now. You've never seen a gin [Aboriginal woman] playing a didgeridoo, have you?
>
> And you know why? There is an ancient Aboriginal legend that within the didgeridoo there are child spirits, and any woman that plays it has a piccaninny!

Then, turning to a woman close to where he was positioned in the circle:

What are you laughing at? You had two goes!

For me this statement, made after we had all participated, came as a series of direct hits. He indicates the phallic aspect of the didge, an aspect which had been submerged through references to the gastrointestinal tract, although perhaps hinted at with the reference to AIDS. This phallic gesture, hinting at some *unspeakable savage ritual*, seemed to verify that we were mutually implicated in an experience so bizarre that it would have to have extraordinary significance.

Max made a hit in the direction of gender relations, marking an inequity which had been submerged in the relatively egalitarian circle. He hinted at White women's superiority over Black women through our assumed freedom from superstition and our greater control over our reproductive capacity. Prior to this statement, we had been accomplices in White supremacist relationships, but our complicity was mediated by men because the relationship had been constructed only between men. Now, it seemed, we were given the status of White supremacists in our own right. Further, we were initiated into this status by Max himself. His pretence of having forgotten to tell us the crucial fact that Aboriginal women do not play the didgeridoo was expressed as self-conscious 'forgetting' designed to indicate to us that we had been tricked. That the trick was a joke indicated, I think, that none of us need seriously expect to get pregnant. Our superiority to Aboriginal women was thus verified by Max himself.

The identification of didge and phallus, and the fact that we had all had our mouths on it, seemed further to separate men and women out. The jokes about pregnancy clearly indicated that the phallus would act on men and women differently. However we responded, it seems unlikely that we were identically affected by having come into intimate contact with the White man's Black phallus. It may be, too, that we women were being given a marginal position as honorary males. Like men, we could encounter the phallus and not become pregnant. But if we were honorary males we were definitely peripheral: in so far as this ritual speaks to the verification of an authentic belonging, then it seems to pinpoint and validate maleness as a key feature of belonging. Black is authentic, and Black women do not play the didge; ergo, authentic belonging is a male prerogative.

The last anecdote Max told while we were still on the island broke up the circle of mates, I felt, and repositioned women well and truly on the outside. The context is a rather complicated story Max told about some of the Borroloola characters. (Borroloola is at least 1000 kilometres east of Timber Creek, but in this outback ritual space such considerations become entirely pedantic.) Max reported what he said had been a recent interview with an old timer named Wagga Darcy and a woman interviewer:

She said, 'why don't you go down and live on the gold coast where the climate's not so hot, spend the rest of your days in comfort?'

'I'm not going down there and live with all them people. Anyway, who'd be looking after all me old mates up here?'

'Got a few friends, have you Wagga? Who would they be?'

'Ah, I got plenty. I got me horse and me dog and me pig and me goat and me donkeys and me chooks.'

She said, 'you never got married, Wagga, did you? Why didn't you get married?'

'Ahh, not too late yet. Anyway, what would I want to get married for? Anytime I want one, I just run one down on the flat.'

And up to a couple of years ago he was still catching them!

Max's earlier phallic gesture differentiated between White and Black women, constructing us as superordinate in our own right. This subsequent story does not specify whether the 'ones' Wagga Darcy runs down are White or Black, or for that matter, even if they are human. The point is that it doesn't matter. Let us assume that he is not talking about animals. What he is saying is that White or Black, differentiated though we may be among ourselves, women are essentially resources to be run down. Sexual violence, one concludes, is integral to mateship and authenticity, and White men can extend and withdraw their invitation to women to enter into the circle of mates. Women, then, do not become irrevocably transformed through initiation; we are granted, rather, a conditional status which signals the underlying possibility that all women really are undifferentiated and that none of us fully belongs with the mates.

I felt pushed out of the circle of mates, but Jay Arthur (personal communication) suggested this atrocious anecdote might also be understood to confirm our positioning as honorary White men. The gender logic would seem to be that there is no autonomous female position from which this joke could be funny; a woman is either excluded from the circle or included as a type of male.

Entrée into the circle of White mates, then, can be understood to be gendered and conditional. The conditions, for both men and women, include an assent to White supremacy and an assent to sexual violence. White women, I suggest, have the possibility available to them of being marginally included but not ultimately transformed. We are positioned ambiguously – potentially both outside and inside the circle. The fact that Max does not tell us what colour or what species Wagga Darcy runs down is coercive. It is because we do not know that we are exempt that we are faced with this injurious proposition: that our access to the protective circle requires our assent to the violence from which we require protection.

But on the other hand, if we knew that Wagga only ran down Black women, would we feel safe? Would we want to trust the security of such a boundary? And would we want to be part of the inner circle of such mates? The Wagga Darcy anecdote hinted at the possibility of women going feral. The spectre or fantasy of women running at large in the bush is familiar already from Willshire's writings more than a century previously. Rather than joining the White men, could we not join the Black women? I am pondering the concept that the White phallus thinks (pardon the personification) it can control this boundary, keeping White and Black women separate. This thought suggests that a significant challenge to the phallus is the feral quality of women, a quality which might also be understood, in light of the Wagga Darcy anecdote, as a possibility of female bonding. All women have the potential to run in the bush, it seems, and if from a position in the bush we were to establish our own circle of mates, we could do so without regard to race. We could thus challenge the injurious hierarchies I have discussed: racial distinctions and the superordinate position; maleness as the essential condition of belonging to the country; the impossibility of concurrent Indigenous and settler relationships to land.

The possibility enabled through the logic I am pursuing here is that female–female relationships can challenge the cultural logic of White male supremacy in conquest. In this light, it is worth considering Fiedler's view that the peculiar alliance of the Mohican and his White successor includes the fear that White women will fulfil their potential to castrate males. Nothing in Max's tour suggested to me that Freudian fears were implicated in this logic of conquest, although the relational logic he constructs between men and women certainly offers a motive for castration. Female bonding in the bush, it seems to me, can be imagined as a prospect pregnant with possibilities, the least enticing of which would be a reversal of gender relations marked by domination through violence.

I hasten to add that I recuperate the possibility of women's bonding outside the circle of mates as a supplement, in the sense that it is evident in the logic of the story, but is also buried within or circling around the edges of the story.

We tourists know that we do not leave the island transformed into authentic bushmen, but I think it is fair to say that through our participation we tacitly assented to conditions of authenticity. Within that liminal circle of mates Max laid claim to an Australian future based on these foundations: conquest as an accomplished fact, Aboriginal conferral of legitimacy, the linear relationship of succession from Black to White, White supremacy and racial contempt, sexual violence, and maleness as the primary condition for genuine belonging to society and to the land.

Report from Timber Creek

At the same time that Max was representing Timber Creek as a frontier town, local people were implementing real changes. In 1992 Timber Creek became the first (and only) Town Council to have equal numbers of Black and White Town Councillors. To honour their achievement, the Council applied for and received a grant from the Reconciliation Council, and they commissioned Darrell Lewis (1997) to write a book called *A Shared History*. This book uses photographs from the region and draws on historical archives to tell the story of the entanglements of the lives of Aborigines and settlers over the past 120 years. Against the narrative of replacement and exclusion, *A Shared History* recuperates a narrative of shared time and place. It was commissioned by, and depicts, a town in which people work to make their lives with others rather than against others. Much of the history contained in the book is not a pretty story, but it is a very true one. The other very true story is that not all of the Town Councillors were men. Black and White women served on the Council.

This startling situation is a direct result of the *Aboriginal Land Rights (NT) Act 1976*. In spite of its many limitations, the Act has the potential to put a positive value on coexistence. Successful claims have forced the redistribution of land, and power relations are adjusting too. Timber Creek was once a place of racial separation and considerable oppression; land rights have changed the power dynamics, and the story is not over.

Timber Creek proves in real time and place ideas that I have been expressing in more abstract ways. Ethics of decolonisation reverse or sidestep temporal and spatial forms of punctuation, replacement, and exclusion. This means they embrace the coexistence of the peoples who share this place, and embrace the present moment as the time in which all of us share our lives. These ethics expand the present, enabling it to become a real domain of moral action.

7

BATTLES, BETRAYALS AND RESILIENCE

> The moniker 'Big Sunday' provided an uncanny clue to the origin of the ceremony for those who dared read it. Stanner confirmed a nation's worst nightmares – the 'fertility Mother cult' sprouted up, like the flu and venereal disease, in response to European settlement. (Povinelli 2002: 142)

In 1886 a group of Jesuit missionaries trekked out to what they thought was a wild place, specifically the Daly River of North Australia, to make contact with wild savages (Indigenous people). They intended to bring to the place the civilising influence of the cultivated garden, and to the savage the civilising influences of agricultural labour, Christian marriage, and salvation. Central to their thinking was the view that savages were open either to corruption or to salvation, and that once corrupted they were no longer suitable material for civilisation. They were thus in search of a particular type: the pristine savage (Alroe 1988 is insightful). They imagined this type as an absence – not only the absence of their own European civilisation, but an absence of all civilisation: a veritable *tabula rasa* on which they would inscribe redemption through their own cultural and colonising practices and through the spiritual authority of Jesus Christ. The missionaries were to become completely disheartened. One of them went a bit mad, others were accused of sexual relations with Indigenous women, and one was sent away in disgrace; many of their most promising converts died, and after starting afresh in three different locations over a fourteen-year period the mission was closed precipitously because of a decision made overseas.

In this chapter my interest is with battlefields of the soul and the claims on the future that the Jesuit missionaries were making. The Jesuits acted vigorously within their faith right up to the moment of leaving. Aboriginal people who were caught up in their schemes, whether by choice or by happenstance, experienced both the vigour and the abandonment. White people's claims on Aboriginal people's future were, it seems, provisional. Betrayal hits people with the knowledge that somehow they never really mattered; it is thus deeply implicated in the ethics I am exploring.

In examining some fragments of religious thought that are available in the records, while avoiding matters that are not to be discussed in public, I chart a careful course with a particular aim: to consider some of the ways in which the rough abrasions of conquest have pressed Aboriginal people to formulate new claims to their own future. I want to ask what kinds of storied theological connections people may bring to bear in considering their situation in relation to the future. A further aspect of the story is that Daly River Aboriginal people were blocked in almost every direction. They were offered Christianity and then abandoned by the missionaries. They incorporated aspects of Christianity into their own religious practice, and subsequently lost confidence in it as they experienced the decline of country and life optimism. A new religious movement ('Big Sunday') offered hope of revitalisation, and then was outlawed. That any religious vitality could spring from this long period, during which the wild kept putting on new guises in which to invade people's spiritual life, is itself quite astonishing.

I do not engage with the rough and abrasive situations in which Whitefellas also found themselves to be enmeshed as they tried to extend tolerance across cultural difference, and to understand Aboriginal people without having to acknowledge their own implicated violence. This is another story, now analysed in excellent detail by Povinelli (2002, especially chapter 3).

Reductions

The Jesuits' intention was to establish a centre to which people would come in order to settle permanently. They followed the model of missionisation which had been developed in South America: that of developing self-sufficient agricultural settlements called reductions. The Norwegian naturalist Knut Dahl stayed at the mission while collecting specimens in the region and subsequently wrote about his experiences in North Australia (1926). He described the Jesuits' goal of introducing agriculture to Daly River Aborigines:

> Let us, the Jesuit argues, first of all persuade these savages to give up their roving life, let us teach them to cultivate the soil, and let us make them understand that their work in this way brings them greater happiness, makes them more care-free than their old life. Then possibly their progeny, the new tribes of settled agriculturalists, may be more susceptible to our religious propaganda. (Dahl 1926: 36)

The regulations were strict, and could not be enforced. They required people to ask for permission to leave, and they called for agricultural permanence, for families to live in small huts, and for monogamy. In addition, they required the renunciation of 'walkabout', of all connection with Indigenous rites, and segregation from pagan natives (O'Kelly 1967: 99). In the words of Fr MacKillop (brother of the recently beatified Mary MacKillop), the Superior for much of the time, it was necessary to civilise in order to Christianise (in O'Kelly 1967: 42, footnote 128).

Their efforts to establish cultivation were truly remarkable. O'Kelly summed up the last few years, and they were, actually, the better years:

> In '92 a plague of caterpillars necessitated a double sowing of maize; in '93 a visitation of rats made it necessary to plant the African Corn four times and reduced the harvest to six tons (destroying an estimated seven tons); in '94 the ravages of field mice meant that some fields had to be sown three times, and then reeds sprang up and ruined many acres; in '96 birds reduced the corn harvest to three tons (though ten tons of sweet potatoes and yams were grown this year); in '97 intense heat defeated their irrigation and reduced an expected six ton crop of corn to two; in '98 the first flood devastated all crops and gardens and the same occurred in '99. (O'Kelly 1967: 59, note 60)

The missionaries' fluctuating ability to support Aboriginal people constitutes one of the most contradictory aspects of their endeavour, and one of the main reasons why the rules were unenforceable. When they were flush with food they attempted to bring people in, impose Christian morality on them, and induce them to give up their own way of life in favour of an agricultural mode of subsistence. Dependence on agriculture was, however, unsustainable. It was simply not possible for them to prove to Aboriginal people that settled life was more carefree. For part of almost every year of the whole fourteen years, the missionaries had to send people away because of lack of food. Aboriginal people were thrown back on regional subsistence and social networks because the mission could not support them. In addition, local reliance on bush tucker meant that the country around the mission became over-used and depleted (see Rose 2000b for more detail).

The mission was brought to an abrupt and unexpected end in 1899 by a decision made by the European Jesuit superiors. There had been concern over the years that the mission might be closed, but shortly before closure the Jesuits had received reassurance that they would be able to continue. Then came another flood, and then a visitation by a superior, and then instructions to leave. Over a period of a few days in July 1899 the Aborigines were dismissed, some of the buildings they had helped to construct were dismantled, the irrigation was turned off, their gardens fell out of fertility, and the livestock they had helped herd were sold off. Absence came full circle, from *terra nullius* and *tabula rasa*, through a recursion of ecological practices which devastated the land and failed to provide a living, and a spiritual offer of mediation between God and humanity that was summarily withdrawn.

The glimpses we have of the life of Daly, one of the senior Aboriginal men of the region, illuminate the exchanges, reciprocities, failures of reciprocity, and, from a missionary perspective, final expendability of Aboriginal people. Daly was one of the Lawmen of the region. He had been arrested and tried for murder in conjunction with the Coppermine killings of 1884, and had been acquitted (discussed in Alford 1989: 52). A few years later he became one of the missionaries' great allies. Daly recruited people, built huts and planted gardens, and like the others he came and went. Although he had promised one of the missionaries to refrain from participating in his own religious rituals, he must have continued his Law work because the missionaries took a set against him. In January 1890 (wet season) he came to the mission very ill and seeking admission. According to the diarist:

> Daly is in a wretched state, we have judged it better not to admit him to the station because of his hard obstinacy and deceitful character, on the other hand we cannot reject him and expel him by force. He now lies sick out in the open, with his whole family, with no food except what his wife Jinny brings him every day. He has asked whether he is soon going to die. (10/1/1890)[8]

On the thirteenth of the month the issue was decided: 'The wondrous Providence of God intervened to remove a great impediment to our work by taking Daly from this life' (13/1/1890). The missionaries refused him a Christian burial, so his own people were free to take his body back to his own country, to the swamp called Woenelen where he was buried in traditional fashion. Today Woenelen, like other swamps, is rooted up by pigs.

The Jesuits staked out a claim for a future of agriculture and Christianity for Daly River people and their homelands. They urged people to join them, and punished those who, in their view, impeded their work. The lands were devastated, and some people felt torn, with no clear prospects in any direction. The promises now look more like damage, and the unflinching idea that somehow future salvation would redeem current sufferings was radically enfeebled by the fact that the Church itself lost faith.

Taming the Cross

The Jesuit missionaries vigorously opposed Indigenous religious practice. Down on the Daly between 1886 and 1899 Aboriginal people were punished for participation in ceremony. They were not allowed to observe taboos or other markers of ritual status at the mission. The diaries are full of references to punishment, and threats of the punishment of God are also indicated. In this entry concerning the death of a senior man named Bede we see both threat and response:

> 'Nine weeks ago Fr Conrath told this man not to go to the "Karamala", which is a pagan festival, threatening him with the punishment of the Almighty God if he did go. "I shall go", said the native, "let God punish me".' (3/8/1898)

The quirky manuscript that Fr Kristen wrote while he was recovering from nervous exhaustion also offers glimpses of how Aborigines perceived Christian teachings. He informs us that the Aborigines had formed a punitive view of the crucifixion:

> Of course Fr Conrath spoke mostly on divine mysteries under the cross, the great mysterious sign on the hill. Some Blacks thought that cross was for hanging them up if they would not yield to his counsels ... (Kristen 1899: 197)

This interpretation of the cross seems certainly drawn from the missionaries' threats of punishment as well as from the crucifixion. In addition, of course, random violence and the punitive expeditions and dispersals by other settlers and police contributed to people's understandings of colonisation. The quality of mercy was never conspicuous on the frontier; images of a punitive god were given flesh by people's own experiences. Along with people's own experience, however, are the religious 'facts' of the case. God, so the theology went, did allow his only son to be sacrificed. Missionaries taught about God, used the same language of kinship (Father, Brother), and meted out punishments. Recall the man named Daly who was left to die in the rain.

The missionaries attempted, early and late, to prevent their converts and potential converts from participating in the ceremonies of which they were aware, with the exception of circumcision, towards which they were ambivalent (O'Kelly 1967: 92). The restrictions were extensive. In 1895 four young men left the station because they did not want to break with the Law that forbids young men to eat certain foods (25/2/1895).

Knut Dahl gives us another, more vigorous, perspective. When the 'Great Corroboree' of 1894 was on, Dahl tells us, although the missionaries do not, the mission was deserted. The corroboree was held nearby, perhaps to make it easier for the mission people to attend. But while the mission was deserted, there was constant activity. Before the ceremony there were the fights to resolve disputes. This year a Chinese gardener had sold or given guns and grog to the Aboriginal people, and the fighting apparently got out of hand. Fr MacKillop and Dahl intervened at the request of one of the mission men who came running to them in alarm. Dahl describes the event:

I gave my mount his head, and before long the hot air was whizzing past my ears. I have a vague recollection of riding through a maze of fallen logs, the horse jumping them one by one, never slackening his mad career until we reached the wide plain bordering on the lagoon. Here I met Dominik [the Aboriginal man who had raised the alarm, and with whom Dahl had become friendly], who told me that the blacks had fled for the lagoon, the man with the blunderbuss among them. Presently I saw a small party of blacks running at top speed for the thickets of the swampy lagoon and Father McKillop in hot pursuit of them, the tail of his black cassock flapping in the air like a flag in a storm. I came pounding into the swamp on the edge of the jungle-covered lagoon at the moment when Father MacKillop's revolver flew out, forcing a mob of squealing women and children to stop ... The reverend father was reading the sinner and all the spectators a lesson, the points of which he emphasized with his revolver. I am rather afraid that the sum total of his eloquence was that they were all, and the fellow with the gun especially, a lot of ne'er-do-wells, who had better remove themselves to their own country, and the sooner the better. Otherwise we would shoot every mother's son of them. (Dahl 1926: 106–107)

In this case, as in others, the issues were resolved and the ceremony went on.

The missionaries were extremely alert to the existence of a ritual which appeared to them to be exceptionally evil. The ritual was called Tyaboi, and Fr MacKillop wrote:

I am about to make a strong assertion; but I believe it to be true. I believe they have human sacrifices, that from time to time one man, with his own knowledge and consent, is offered in sacrifice for the good of his people – offered to the evil spirit whom they so fear. This is the leading feature in the great religious and highly immoral ceremony, which they celebrate every few years. They call it Jaboi. (MacKillop 1892–93: 261)

MacKillop is incorrect. There are absolutely no reports of human sacrifice among the Aboriginal people of Australia, nor are there, to my knowledge, any practices that could reasonably be misinterpreted as human sacrifice. Fr MacKillop's account of Tyaboi is so clearly an account of Christianity that I feel stunned that he did not see it. One man, with consent, sacrificing himself for the good of his people – who is this if not Jesus? It follows from the plain facts that the 'evil spirit' is likely to be God himself: the Father who killed his own son and who, through the missionaries, threatened to kill other men as well. In short, the evidence suggests that the missionaries introduced to the Aborigines of the Daly the concept of human sacrifice to a punitive God. It is highly doubtful, however, that human sacrifice was ever practised. The far more likely scenario is that it was mimicked.

Fr Kristen recorded in the diary:

> '"Tyaboi" begins, and the fight of the devil with Christ for the blacks. Benbenyaga (blacks), Chinese garden, Chinese, Coppermines, all mixed up in it – so we have heard from a Christian boy sufficiently grown up to know ...' (17/10/1893)

On this evidence Tyaboi (Jaboi) can be recognised as a contact cult. It incorporates what is new and relatively unknown within an Indigenous cosmology. The purpose is to tame, socialise and perhaps to gain power from what is wild, unpredictable, and unmanageable. In colonising contexts contact cults have an unruly and imaginative capacity to mirror, mimic, transform, destabilise, deconstruct, parody and politicise the colonisers and the worlds of ideas and material goods they drag along with them (cf. Fabian 1979; Fernandez 1979; Wagner 1979; Koepping 1988 provides an overview of the Australian literature to date; Swain [1993: 114–58] takes up these issues).

Fr Kristen's translation of the word 'benbenyaga' is at odds with his understanding expressed in his manuscript. There he explicitly equates the term with the ritual sex that was part of Tyaboi (Kristen 1899: 193). Ritual sex appears to have been part of Indigenous rituals in many parts of Australia and it played upon settlers' imagination in ways that range from pornographic to apologetic, as Povinelli (2002) explores in detail. The missionaries sought to keep women away from ceremony entirely, and it is likely that in their own view they were protecting them. In 1890, for example, the diarist writes:

> 'The men when going away wished to take with them for a few days the elder girls. Fr Superior would not allow this owing to danger from those blacks who are now engaged in carrying out their diabolical practices called "Tyaboi".' (7/9/90)

The purposes of Tyaboi would have included that of bringing the new people, places and experiences of colonisation into Indigenous religious practice. Fr Kristen tells us that the Chinese, the gardens, the Coppermines and the Aboriginal people were all incorporated into the ceremony. What he does not tell us, but what an anthropological reading assures us, is that the missionaries too would have been included. We can infer this through comparison with other such religious practices, and we can rest the inference locally on a fact that the Jesuits noted: Aboriginal people enjoyed the pomp of the more solemn ceremonies, and found the occasion of a person's first mass deeply impressive. The diarists noted that vestments, candles, bells and deep silences had a strong impact on those who attended mass (O'Kelly 1967: 84). We can thus infer that the ritual would have included vestments, and mumbo-jumbo in pidgin Latin or Malak Malak. There would have been crosses and bells, and a variety of gestures to mimic communion and other Christian rituals. There would, in short, have been evidence which would have confirmed the fear that Satan was alive and well right there on the Daly.

In sum, Tyaboi seems to have been a ritual designed to tame the punitive practices of the cross – to appease the punitive Father (or missionary) who was willing to sacrifice his son(s) in order to achieve the goal of salvation. Tyaboi would have sought to socialise the missionaries within a regional Aboriginal sociality, and to bring into being the reciprocities which the missionaries and all the other newcomers on the Daly so constantly refused.

Fr Kristen's manuscript expresses in wild profligacy his view that many White men, including the Government Resident (Dashwood), the Chief of Police (Faulsch), and Constable Willshire, were Freemasons, and thus parties to a global conspiracy. In his view, they were recruiting and corrupting Aboriginal men. He offers a discussion of Freemasonry in which he links Canaanite sacrifices to Molloch (in which children were sacrificed) with the name of one of the local tribes and languages, Malak Malak; he further claims that this language is a corruption of Hebrew. He goes on to analyse Malak Malak language use as leading directly to moral perversity, concealment, and error. In his view, this is the influence of Freemasonry, and he forgives the 'wild ignorant Black' for going astray, claiming that they were taught the use of secret codes ('deliberate unopenness') by White Freemasons (Kristen 1899: 195-99).

Fr Kristen, like all good conspiracy theorists, is never without an explanation. He shoots all his critique back to the Freemasons, and so he also must ask: did Aborigines learn Freemasonry from White settlers, or did Aborigines themselves export it to Europe in earlier centuries? He concludes that the latter hypothesis is probably correct, and thereby seems to confirm his own marginal wackiness. But conspiracies, remnants and codes of hidden meanings find their power in contexts in which people are struggling to figure out what is going on, and this was the situation both for the Jesuits and for the Aboriginal people.

Aboriginal people were engaging in intellectual work that sought to find connections between Indigenous Law and the Gospel. Fr Kristen tells us that Aboriginal people were querying the social and theological implications of the Christian story:

> In the year 1893 after the usual Sunday instruction ... when I had read and explained the parable of Our Lord, if I remember well, it was the 7th Sunday after Pent. an old man ... came to me and inquired earnestly whether that Master Jesus was a Mallac [Malak], one of their own brown race? The question startled me so much, that I asked him why? The man pronounced the only word: *yoloc jimin* ... (Kristen 1899: 198)

His discussion reverts to Freemasonry, and the questions we would most like to learn about are dropped. Fr Kristen understood *yoloc jimin* (or *ngoloc jimin*) to refer to a speech style, and his immediate concern was with varieties of speech and the use of secret words which he interpreted as defiling holy words (the deliberate lack of openness, moral perversion, etc. discussed earlier). He was compiling a set of defiling words, and his attention had been particularly grabbed by *jin-man* and *jinja*, which he seems to identify as secret and blasphemous words for Jehovah. In his transcript he establishes links between the Malak Malak Jesus, secret language, and a set of words – *jinja, jin-man, jahjin* – which he claims 'blaspheme' (p. 195) or refer to an evil master (p. 204).

The word *Jin-man* resonates with Chinaman, as well as with terms for sin. It seems certain that the missionaries preached against the Chinese, as they would have been excellent local non-Aboriginal representatives of paganism. O'Kelly tells us that Frs Kristen and Conrath held the view that the Chinese were corrupt people and were abusing women, and they were praying for their removal from the region. Fr MacKillop took a strong anti-Asian stance, and in his view the Chinese vices were the worst in the region (O'Kelly 1967: 53). Whether *Jin-man* derives from Chinaman, or from sin, of from other sources entirely, the term has a long and disruptive history, as we will see.

Remembrance

The missionaries packed up and left in 1899. The place was bought by Mr and Mrs Niemann, and Mrs Niemann has given us a lovely description of it:

> In the sixteen years of their occupation the missionaries had made their Daly river station a veritable earthly paradise. Situated on one of the most beautiful stretches of the river and only about a hundred yards from its bank, the roomy house, with its wide verandahs and lofty rooms, gave an instant impression of cool spaciousness ... In front stretched the garden, fragrant and aglow with unfamiliar flowers and shrubs, and a flight of steps cut in the steep bank led from the garden gate to the water 40 feet below. On either side lay well-kept orchards, and beyond were crops of all descriptions, for the missionaries had been firm believers in the magic properties of territory soil and climate, and had devoted much time and money to experimental planting. The whole place, protected from straying blacks and animals by a fence of six foot wire netting, covered some 50 acres, of which eight were given up to the homestead and its gardens and orchards. Saw mills and pumping plants (the whole place was irrigated), a fish-curing room and all appliances for curing and pressing tobacco ... while in the garden a swimming pool, fringed with pomegranates, mangoes and guava, and emptied by a waste pipe into the river, guaranteed bathing undisturbed by crocodiles and water snakes. (Niemann 1920: 49)

She notes that the Blacks' camp was 400 yards from the house, and she describes the pleasure of hearing people singing at night.

The Jesuits, it will be recalled, had embarked on a long-term project to teach the natives the meaning of industry and property; the station was built from the labour of Aborigines as much as that of the brothers. When it was sold, however, the Aborigines were left with absolutely nothing. The new owners seem to have 'inherited' an Aboriginal workforce made up of former mission people whose country was there, or nearby, and whose lives had been dedicated, at least in part, to learning more about Christianity and to making a living from agriculture and animal husbandry.

The secular press in Darwin was quick to label the mission a failure, implying that it had had little impact on the Aboriginal people. Subsequent discussions tended to reinforce this position. And yet missionaries attempted to suppress initiation and other ceremonies, they intervened in mortuary rites, they altered marriages, attempted to take over authority relations, and had large impacts on the environments on which they depended. The environments so depleted were people's countries, and so they had large impacts on people's long-term relationships with place. To sum up all this as a failure to have an impact, or to assume that the impacts had only been superficial, is to gaze across a field of violence, to overlook a multitude of harms and deaths, and to declare that nothing happened. It is to record an event as if those who were harmed never mattered. Denial of impact was thus also a denial of accountability and responsibility. The missionaries and everyone else could rest assured that their departure was morally acceptable because their presence had had no effects. The easy and comfortable shrugging off of impacts is a perfect example of the unethical position I have been exploring: to write the past as if those who were enmeshed in the colonising project never actually mattered.

Yet some Aboriginal people took the Jesuit teachings seriously, seeking to engage with them on a spiritual or theological level. I turn now to this engagement. When Stanner got to the Daly in the early 1930s he encountered a people who were in a state of spiritual despondency. The story of how that came to happen occupied his mind and heart, and his best writings come from his attempt to understand the pain, anger, and emptiness which he felt his close friends to be experiencing, as well as their exhilaration at encountering a new revitalising religious practice (Stanner 1979a, 1979b). My focus on the missionaries leads me to emphasise their impacts, but I must also be clear that the social conditions Stanner described were brought about by a full set of regimes of frontier violence of which the missionaries were only a part.

According to Stanner, in 1932 local Aboriginal people had a cultural myth that was in its heart an inversion of the Christian Father and Son. He noted that the two traditions (Christian and local Aboriginal) were 'remarkably parallel institutions about man and his whole situation'. He held the view that there was 'no historical connexion whatever' (Stanner 1979a: 56). I will suggest, of course, that there was an historical connection; one story may be about 'man' in the abstract, but the other story is about the Jesuit presence and absence, and thus about local Aboriginal people's prior experience of colonising Christianity and betrayal.

The myth tells of a great man, Angamunggi, who was killed by his son. The son was named Tjinimin, a term evocatively close to those we have heard from the Jesuits (particularly *Jin-man*). Tjinimin seduced his sisters, and then speared his father, while Angamunggi (the Father) 'sat unsuspectingly, surrounded by his many children, at song and music during a festive gathering of all the clans.' The father lived long enough to generate sources of life – permanent fresh water pools: 'And in his death agonies, Angamunggi gave men perennial waters. They were life-giving waters, for it was in them that, somehow, he also placed the spirits of all children who have been born since then' (Stanner 1979a: 55–56).

The name 'Tjinimin' seems clearly related to Fr Kristen's *Jin-man*. The Father–Son myth tells of the son named Tjinimin who creates absence: it speaks of a failure to nurture, a failure to reciprocate, a failure to observe sexual rules. These characteristics clearly mark the missionary endeavours as they are likely to have been perceived by those Aboriginal people who cared enough to take them seriously.

We can read this terrible myth of patricide as the missionaries' attack on Indigenous religious Law: 'Angamunggi sat ... at song and music during a festive gathering of all the clans' – he could have been Daly, who died in the rain, or Bede, or any of the Aboriginal Law people who worked so hard to hold life together in the face of invasion. The missionaries, as we have seen, did their best to 'kill' the Law by prohibiting the work of Lawmen and Lawwomen. Tjinimin had incestuous relationships with his sisters: does he also incorporate the Brothers who were having sex with Aboriginal women?

In identifying Law with fertility, the story speaks to the crisis of both. Stanner tells us something of what had befallen:

> In the 1920s a widespread conviction had grown up on the Daly River that their own culture-hero, Angamunggi ... had deserted them. Before I had heard a word of Kunabibi [a religious movement referred to by some as 'Big Sunday' or the All-Mother] I had been told that Angamunggi had 'gone away'. Many evidences were cited that he no longer 'looked after' the people: the infertility of the women ... the spread of sickness, the dwindling of game among them. (Stanner 1979b: 84)

An ontological negation had erupted on this barbarous frontier. An emptiness lurked in the country itself, and in the hearts and minds of its people. Stanner's words suggest that Daly River people had examined their situation, as if in a looking glass, and had come to the theological conclusion that their life-giving Father (Angamunggi) had truly been killed. Double death confronts us here – Angamunggi was killed by his son Tjinimin, but left his life-giving capacities in the water of the country. Now that capacity too was being killed. The evidence was the loss of life: human life, animal life, and life support systems. Signs of such loss were already visible in the Jesuit diaries. Life, one might say, was trickling out of the country, and the waters of life no longer seemed perennial.[9]

Ronald and Catherine Berndt assessed the long-term impact of the mission in 1946 when they spent a few months on the Daly. In their view the mission endeavour had had very little impact 'on traditional institutions', and they noted that people who had been at the mission had not handed the Christian teachings on to new generations (Berndt 1952: 2–3). They seem to have taken an extraordinarily narrow view of what might count as impact, and the idea that lack of transmission equates with lack of impact is particularly dubious. It is at least possible that people did not hand on the teachings because they felt betrayed by them. The Berndts collected some stories that speak far more to betrayal than to lack of impact. Their main research colleague was a man named Mathew Melbyerk who had been with the mission when he was young. He had been one of Stanner's main colleagues as well, and Stanner (1979b: 88) described him as 'the most intelligent and detached Aboriginal I have known'.

Mathew Melbyerk's account of 'The Allocation of Food by Jesus' tells a pitiless story of Christianity. It begins with an account of Jesus feeding his Apostles apples (in never-ending abundance), after which they made and ate other foods:

> So they returned to their garden. Later they grew wheat, and made flour. Then Jesus made a big damper. When it was ready, they all sat down at the long table and they ate of this damper until they were full. But they did not finish it: Jesus put it away, as he had done with the apple.
>
> And the Father talked to Jesus: 'All of this is for white men – they will have iron, houses and everything.' Thus the Baijang [Father] put motorcars, aeroplanes, houses, horses and so on

for all the white people; he also made rifles, guns, pannikins and knives; and Baijang spoke to Christ, 'That is the Dreaming for all of you lot.'

Jesus Christ was on the side of the white people – he gave all that food to them.

Adam had only native food, for Adam and Riva [Eve] were Aborigines. They had nothing when they left the garden owned by God.

Chinamen grew rice and made grass houses: white men saw these, and the Chinamen saw the iron houses: the white men saw the rice, and the Chinamen saw the flour: each bought from the other. Only the Aborigines had nothing. (Berndt 1952: 8–9)

Australian Aboriginal people's stories of this type (generally classed under the label 'cargo cult') search for moral relationships between settlers and Indigenous peoples (Swain 1993; Rose 1994; see Burridge 1960 for a classic study). The story of Jesus' Allocation of Food vividly conveys a people's sense of looking at themselves from afar, objectifying themselves as a set of absences and losses. It also conveys with brutal force the exclusion of Aborigines: 'each bought from the other. Only the Aborigines had nothing.' The attempt to transform the wild place and the wild person into civilised place and civilised person was an attempt to fill an emptiness with culture; it resulted in the creation of emptiness. The truthfulness of the story is wrenching. The missionaries and other settlers flourished to some degree over the decades, but when Adam and Riva left the 'garden owned by God' (the mission) 'they had nothing'.

New Business

Stanner recounts men's enthusiasm when they were introduced to, and inducted into, a new religious form of practice called 'Big Sunday'. It seemed in that time and place to overcome the perception of abandonment and amplifying loss. It was not long, however, before White people were intervening. The problems surrounding Whitefellas' perceptions of Big Sunday concern ritual sex, and Povinelli analyses these issues in excellent multifaceted detail. She is interested in the problems that ritual sex poses for the liberal state, and for the liberal administrator, and she brings the issues together around White male sexuality on the frontier. In her words:

> *Settler* sexuality and *settler* immorality erased the clean line between the 'horrible rites' of native society and the quotidian practices of settler society. Settlers did not just think, look, imagine, and feel implicated in indigenous sex acts as critical judges, but they did this also as critical actors: they knew it, they were the condition of it, they did it no differently. (Povinelli 2002: 146)

The quandary for White administrators was: should they prohibit something they deemed to be unacceptable in a liberal state, or should they allow a form of Indigenous authority to continue to sustain those Aboriginal people who were beyond the reach of daily outside administration? The quandary was not so much resolved as sustained. Aboriginal men along the Daly were told that they could no longer practise the ceremony, and yet, somehow, they did.

The move against the business around Darwin and on the Daly appears to have been prompted by reports of deaths having been caused by ceremony. Povinelli (2002) discusses the events and provides excellent and detailed analysis of the complexity of Whitefella thinking. The bare bones are as follows. According to Elkin (1950: 77, note 9):

> It is said that the Government told the old men not to hold the ceremony any more, because natives from other parts working in Darwin blamed this ceremony, performed by the almost local natives, for any sickness or other ills which befell them. Many fights were thus caused.

A letter from E.W.P. Chinnery, Director of Native Affairs, to Police Constable Turner (a Protector of Aborigines) at Daly River in 1940 is explicit:

> I attach a statement made to Mr Harney to the effect that the ... [term deleted] ceremony is taking place at the Daly River under the direction of a native called 'Old Djongman'.
>
> I would be glad if you would inquire into this matter and if confirmed see the natives concerned and tell them that the practice is not favoured by the Administration and must be discontinued ... (Chinnery to Turner 1940)

Turner's reply indicates, to me, the contempt in which Aboriginal people and their culture were held:

I produced one of the Meteorological Rain Maps, let them all see same, and informed that the 'Government' said that 'ALL SUNDAY GROUND BUSINESS' had to be stopped, it was 'Finished'. I pointed to different parts of the Maps, informed them that 'All that Sunday Ground Finished, and they cannot make any more'. Of course showing this Map was all 'Bluff' but they did not know any different. (Turner to Chinnery 1940)

Aboriginal men kept 'Sunday business' and other business alive, although it is possible that women's roles in the business may have dropped out in this region. The prohibition was not enforceable, and decades later, in Aboriginal claims to land and in disputes in the region, people who had been able to sustain living traditions in spite of prohibitions were in a favoured position for gaining title to land.

Travelling

The missionaries denied that their actions had enduring effects. Spiritual traces tell another story. Quite provocatively, Jin-man or Tjinimin seems not only to have survived along the Daly for decades, but also to have been carried to other parts of Australia, perhaps through transformations and exchanges of Tyaboi and other rituals. It is possible that Fr Kristen's teachings were later to arise, transmogrified but still wildly appropriate, in other frontier situations. The anthropologists Petri and Petri-Odermann (1970, 1988) were in Western Australia in the 1960s, and they report the rise of a new cult centred on 'Jinimin-Jesus'. According to what they were told, Jinimin revealed himself to the Aborigines in the east. He had both black and white skin colour, but his message was for Aboriginal people: 'Jinimin had proclaimed that all the land had from the beginning belonged to the Aborigines and that in the future there would be no differences between Aborigines and other Australians – all would share equally in that land' (1970: 258).

Petri & Petri-Odermann call this ritual complex the Jinimin religion, and they report that Jinimin was said to have stated that Aborigines could only bring about this desired state of affairs by adhering to their own traditional Law. He was said to have revealed himself while people were singing song cycles of the Law known as Worgaia, also known as Gadjeri (1970: 266). This Law is the same as the 'Big Sunday' which Stanner (1979b) encountered in the 1930s and which the administration prohibited.

I hear this echo: Angamunggi can sing again, and the land can be restored.

Jinimin, I suggest, is a transformation of Tjinimin/Jin-man, metamorphosed through successive exchanges. Western Australian revitalisation cults probably have their roots in numerous missionary sites (the Daly Jesuits were not, of course, the only missionaries), but the term Jinimin, signifying Jesus, links the Daly of the 1890s with Western Australia in the 1960s through a path we cannot properly detect (see Swain 1993 for extensive discussion of paths of portions of the cult and its relation to other cults). Aboriginal people in Western Australia spoke of restoration through Dreamtime action:

> The return of the Dreamtime beings ... to their original territories took place expressly on the orders of Jinimin-Jesus (or Our Lord Himself). They march on the underground routes, using camels which carry their belongings including the cult objects. (Petri & Petri-Odermann 1970: 263)

These Dreamtime Magi on their underground tracks – towards what devastated homelands do they trek? And will they regenerate life, land and Law?

The missionaries offered a promise of life, and delivered a punitive god who demanded human sacrifices. They delivered a blow to Indigenous Law, along with an objectifying awareness of loss, deception and failure. From my western perspective, most of the signs of the passage of their lives are places where the waters of life are drying up – a wilderness of invading settlers, pigs, and weeds. But from an Aboriginal perspective it seems that wounded space is not so empty. Stories of Jinimin and the Dreaming speak of an imagination sharpened and expanded by the experience of the most barbarous of frontiers. They offer evidence of a continuing spiritual presence and an Indigenous promise of life.

8

THE TRANSFORMATION OF CULTURE INTO HISTORY

> Christian missionaries were among the shock troops of the modernization process, quick to point out the barbarous and unprogressive consequences of traditional religious beliefs and practices. (Robert Bellah, quoted in Cuddihy 1974: 167)

Hobbles Danaiyarri was one of the Yarralin leaders who kept asking the missionaries to go away and stay away, and he became bitterly angered by their persistent returns. On one notable occasion he strode out into the middle of camp with a Bible in one hand and a butcher knife in the other. He struck at the Bible, and shouted: 'Strike me dead, God: if this is your book, strike me dead.' He chopped up the Bible, shouting the whole time, and then he turned to the crowd of people who had watched him and exhorted them to follow their own Law.[10]

Hobbles was driven to swings of despair and fury at the prospect that his people had survived Captain Cook only to fall prey to Jesus. Assemblies of God missionaries in the Victoria River District also treat conversion as a matter of life and death. Their message goes like this: the end of the world is at hand, those who have given their souls to Jesus will attain eternal life, and those who have not given their souls to Jesus will be thrown into the fiery pit. Two major forces are at work in the world: God and the Devil. Aboriginal culture is the work of the Devil, and most activities and beliefs which can be classed as Aboriginal culture are manifestations of the Devil and will doom people to eternal suffering. The only way to avoid eternal suffering is conversion to Christianity, and this requires a radical rejection of the society, culture, and religion in which Aboriginal people were raised, which they share with other Aboriginal people throughout the region, and which link them to the generations who have gone before them. In actual fact, conversion seems likely to be far more a syncretic process than the either/or quality of the message would seem to indicate, but the passion surrounding the Christian message tells us that people hold it to be a life and death issue.

Hobbles died in 1988, and in 1990 a few Yarralin residents invited the missionaries to come and live there. They built a tabernacle, and they began holding church services and other church-related activities as often as they liked. During the 1990s the settlement was split. As residents explained the split to me: there were those who refused to convert, and they were classed as 'culture way' people; then there were those who had converted, and they were classed as 'church way' people. The split was geographically defined, with one portion of camp being identified as church way, the other as culture way. It turned out, however, that some of the converts were actually quite sceptical of missionary dogma. The sceptics took an instrumental approach to conversion, seeing church as a way of facilitating their identity as modern Aborigines. One theme common to both types of converts was the statement 'we can't live in the past'. They spoke of their living culture as a past which they were transcending.

I last wrote about missionaries in the Victoria River District in an essay entitled 'Jesus and the Dingo' (Rose 1988). There I addressed the contestation between Indigenous cosmologies of human origins and death, and a colonising cosmology purveyed by the local missionaries. I concluded that the missionaries offered a set of ideas that could be thought to resolve a problem in Aboriginal cosmology: that of locating ongoing destruction within a worldview that is all about life. At that time (before 1988), the score was Dingo one, Jesus nil. When I went back in 1991 for six months' field work the balance had shifted: Jesus rising, Dingo going downhill rapidly. Today (2004) the situation is not as clear as it was in 1991, but the Dingo still runs a poor second.

In this chapter I look at contemporary missionaries as I encountered them in Yarralin in the 1980s and 1990s. The argument is that frontier culture and missionary teachings are embedded in a similar set of time-space co-ordinates and depend on a similar concept of redemptive violence. I will discuss time-space transformation in the abstract, and then concretise it in reference to Yarralin, the battlefield of body and soul, and the place where tracks of past and future, damned and saved, sick and healthy criss-cross each other in mazes of confrontational attraction and repulsion.

I would like to say that there is irony in the fact that Aboriginal people are being pressed to make transformations into modernity at a time when many of us are sceptical of modernity's capacity in the long run to sustain life on earth. But for me this is more than ironic. I understand this press for monological transformation to be essential to successful colonisation: that all cultures must be defined by reference to the dominant cultures; that variations must either be classed as deviations, or be transformed into icons which can be subjected to market forces. It is essential to successful colonisation that the options be determined by the powerful and that they be represented as the natural outcomes of inevitable historical or religious processes. We see this in small outback settlements and we see this all over the world; it is in the newspapers and on television every day (for more information see McDonald 2001).

What Lies Behind?

In chapter 2, I developed the idea of canonical orientation: a cultural geography that locates space-time co-ordinates independently of the location of individuals. Western directional co-ordinates are my starting point here. In our culture that which is in front, that which is forward directionally, is the future (a time concept). That which is behind us, that which is backward directionally, is the past. This orientation provides a template for a great deal of colonising thought: we are familiar with the description of people as backward; they are behind us, they are slow, they are stuck in the past. At various times in our history we have classified whole peoples, whole nations, whole regions of the world, and of course many religions as backward. There is an anthropological story here that Johannes Fabian (1983) has analysed superbly. He contends that one of anthropology's great errors has been to fail to acknowledge that the anthropologist and the people who teach her are part of exactly the same time. We are coeval, in Fabian's terms: our differences are real, but they are not temporal. My point here is that the temporal classification of others as backward can only make sense to us because our thinking is embedded in this chronotope in which ahead, or in front, equates with the future, and behind, in back, equates with the past.

I discussed Yarralin people's orientation in time in chapter 3, saying that Dreaming is at the heart of time-space co-ordinates. I explained that people say that 'we here now' are the 'behind mob'. We here now come after or are behind our ancestors who came before us. Our descendants are the 'behind mob' relative to us. We precede them, they follow along behind. And the whole of ordinary life can be understood collectively as a 'behind mob' – we all follow along behind the Dreamings. This is a temporal orientation that is based on sequence. First the earth, then Dreamings, then the ancestors; we follow along behind them, and our descendants follow along behind us.

The orientation, then, is the reverse of European co-ordinates. Westerners face the future, the past is behind; the image is of generations of people marching into the future. Aboriginal people face the source; the image is of generations of people returning into Dreaming.

To change from an Aboriginal worldview to a western worldview requires a 180-degree shift which reorients human life so that it faces the future rather than the source. This shift reconfigures the source, naming it 'the past'. 'The past' is placed behind present human life and defined as a state of being which is to be transcended. The implications are massive.

Whether it is millennial thought or modernity, the message is set within a Christian pattern: it is teleological, this present is imperfect, the future will be better. And the relative evaluation of the future as better necessarily implies that now is worse, and that the past is even worse than now. Movement in time is movement into the future; it is movement through qualitative changes of state towards that which is better and away from that which is worse. This construction of the present as the imperfect contrast to the fantasised utopia of the future is a key narrative for a certain type of triumphal history. Manning Clark, for example, in his monumental *History of Australia*, wrote:

> But as industrial civilisation provided the machine with which to subdue the mighty bush, some Australians began to dream a great dream: that they could banish the Old World errors and wrongs and lies. That Heaven and Hell were priests' inventions and that they could build a paradise in the land that belonged to them. (Clark 1973: 460)

Clark's narrative is overtly and explicitly secular, but is it otherwise so different? For Aboriginal converts to Christianity, the message is that the past was the time when Satan ruled, the present is a time of transition, and the future will be radically different from both present and past. The Aboriginal culture which is alive and well in much of the Vic River District is, for converts, a past they are now transcending. It is history, and it is history in that modern sense of the term which implies that it is old, no longer living, devoid of current value. From an archeological perspective, it is the stone age. In the missionary view, Yarralin people's past is not unlike Manning Clark's Old World errors and wrongs and lies.

What Lies Adjacent?

I described a sequence of life whose temporal orientation is to face the source and to construct continuity between source and present. I need to add that this sequence is located: it all happens in the one country. Country is the matrix for the relationships I will be discussing. A country is small enough to accommodate face-to-face groups of people, and large enough to sustain their lives; it is politically autonomous in respect of other, structurally equivalent countries, and at the same time interdependent with other countries. Each country is itself the focus and source of Indigenous Law and life practice.

Country is multidimensional: it consists of people, animals, plants, Dreamings, underground, earth, soils, minerals and waters, surface water, and air. There is sea country and land country; in some areas people talk about sky country. Country has origins and a future; it exists both in and through time. Humans were created for each country, and human groups hold the view that they are an extremely important part of the life of their country. A fundamental proposition in Vic River Law and society is that the living things of a country take care of their own. All living things are held to have an interest in the life of the country because their own life is dependent on the life of their country. This interdependence leads to another fundamental proposition: those who destroy their country destroy themselves (see Rose 1996 for more detail).

The temporal dimension of country is that generations follow each other. People of this generation take the country of their ancestors; their descendants take their place in country. Each country is its own place, the subject of its own power and life, related to its own source. David Turner describes Aboriginal Australia as being made up of a plurality of promised lands, each with its own chosen people (1988: 479). No country is in a privileged position because there are no singularly privileged positions; each place contains its own privilege, its own life, its own Law. And because Law is replicated across countries, each country is morally equivalent to every other country. The lateral dimension to time-space co-ordinates requires us to think in terms of replication and pluralities.

Western spatial co-ordinates are very different. There are two aspects to consider: singularity and horizontal extent. Christian co-ordinates are focused on the Holy Land, along with a few other sacred centres such as Rome for Roman Catholics. Structurally what matters is that there is a singularity of privilege – whether it be the Holy Land versus the pagan wastes, the metropole versus the hinterland, Home versus colony. As discussed in chapter 2, the modern view of the world (and of course many Christians would agree with this view) is centred on places and people who compete as the centre of gravity for the modern world – Western European nations, Great Britain, and the United States all style themselves as leaders according to one criterion or another. What is not in doubt in modern thought is that the west collectively is the leader; it is closest to the future, and the rest of the world follows along behind.

The spatial dimension of western chronotopes has been especially well analysed by Fabian (1983), so I will just summarise briefly. In western geography, the West is the privileged epicentre; distance in space equals distance in time. Western co-ordinates thus offer a globalising, monocentric, teleological linking of time and space. The backward peoples are incorporated into this global history on the basis of what they are and what they are to become: they are pre-literate, pre-industrial, pre-scientific, and thus their future is already known: they will become literate, industrial, scientific, whatever.

Western canonical direction – facing the future – is given a precise geographical location. In so far as the future is the privileged time, those spatially closest to the future are in a privileged position.

Aboriginal converts to Christianity, and to modernity, are impelled to consider a shift in their orientation in space – from a focus on their own country (as their centre and source of life and mystery) to a focus on some distant part of the globe (as *the only* centre and source of life and mystery). Both Christianity and modernity incorporate Aboriginal life in a global structure which situates Aborigines at the periphery in time and in space, and in the rearguard of the march towards redemption or progress.

When Aboriginal people are said to be joining the modern world, the unspoken corollary is that people are being consigned to a position which, from the western point of view, is still backward. People closest to the future are agents of transformation; people in the rearguard are objects of transformation. The adjectives beginning with the prefix 'pre-' make this clear: the transformation is known, it has happened historically, only some people and nations have yet to experience it. Their role, then, is not make history but to experience the history that others have made. The lateral spatial orientation towards the privileged centre which is closest to the future entails a turning away from local sources of power and Law. This shift involves the creation of a kind of wasteland in which Aboriginal people's 'now' is already the western world's 'yesterday'.

Missionaries, one could say, are inducting Aborigines into a social formation based on progress, modernisation, and western dominance by offering a worldview which makes sense of these propositions. Government programs aimed at improving life for Aboriginal people emerge from much the same set of time-space co-ordinates, and aim to induct people into much the same social formation. But whereas government programs enter Aboriginal society as a set of directives with very little cultural information, missionaries offer a worldview in which the requisite shifts in temporal and spatial orientation are explained.

There is also a shift along the vertical axis. Yarralin people's chronotope situates power as the source, and situates the source within the earth. The source, Dreaming, brings this world into its living reality through the interactions of living things in life and in death. Missionaries require a complete turnaround of this dimension. They situate power with God in Heaven; Heaven is not only above this world, but also radically other than this world.[11] This teaching is graphically expounded in sermons and songs:

> This world is not my home, I'm just a' travelling through,
> If Heaven's not my home, then Lord what will I do?
> The angels beckon me, from Heaven's open door,
> And I can't feel at home in this world anymore.[12]

People are exhorted to think of this earth as 'just rubbish' and to keep their heart and mind focused on their home on high. Along with the many links to apocalyptic predictions ('the end of the world is nigh'), this teaching caused a lot of consternation in both practical and philosophical modes of thought. It uncannily mirrors the practice of colonisation that is destroying so much of people's living world. In that mirroring this teaching can be seen to reflect an emerging ecological fact – this earth is becoming just rubbish.

On a more philosophical side, this teaching asks a profound question. As the noted theologian Norman Habel (2003) puts it: 'What kind of God would destroy Earth anyway?' Yarralin people have asked both questions: what kind of God, and what kind of people, would destroy the world? The answer, for those who do not convert, is the same: He's the wild, just the wild. For converts, however, the answer must be different. God has a better home on high and can thus dispense with this world. And so the teachings start to make a strange proof of themselves by treating this world as dispensable even as it is becoming uninhabitable. Back in the early 1980s Big Mick Kangkinang, the oldest and undoubtedly the wisest of Yarralin men, said to me that the missionary had said that Jesus would lift up the whole world. And so Big Mick wondered: does that mean he will take the whole world, or will he just take the outer layer? And if he only takes the outer layer, might there be something left for Aboriginal people?

Hobbles and others resisted the very idea that this world no longer matters:

> Everything come up out of ground – language, people, emu, kangaroo, grass. That's Law. Missionary just trying to bust everything up. They fuck em up right through. Gonna end up in a big war. Before, everything been good – no war, no missionary. (quoted in 2000a: 57)

God's Body

In 1991 I camped in an abandoned shed that was located at the church end of town. One of my friends, and occasional teacher, Kitty Maliwa, was a convert, and she visited me early every morning as I drank my tea. She told me she was doing this as an act of kindness, because the missionaries preach kindness, and she took the time to try to help me. Fixing me in the eye, she demanded: 'Debbie, have you given your soul to Jesus?' I gave my standard reply: 'No way!' She invited me to church, and when I declined she told me how interesting it was: 'You should come, Debbie, it's really fun, we sing and drink blood and take fits.'

On this and other occasions I was torn. It did seem that a good anthropologist would go to church. At the very least one would want to see it all with one's own eyes (there was never any doubt about hearing with one's own ears, as the service was amplified with a huge sound system that meant there was no escape short of leaving town). One would want to ask questions concerning religion and conversion, interviewing missionaries and converts. I had carried out research in a small Pentecostal church in the state of Delaware for my BA honours thesis, so I knew something of what was involved, and was aware of the ethics of participation in a situation in which one's research objectives (to learn) were at such odds with the subject group's objectives towards the researcher (to convert).

Yes, a good anthropologist would have gone, but what would a good student of Hobbles have done? That was my question, and to me the answer was clear. In doing anthropology my research took me into relationships bound by ethics. Not just the ethics of anthropology, important as they are, but the ethics of the relationships between my teachers and myself. I was no longer a stranger from far away. I had been protected and taught, brought into families and given names and skin. I had been claimed, and I was now bound by awareness of fidelity. Not only was I bound to be faithful in my analysis and reporting of what people had taught me, I was also bound, I believe, to fidelity towards those people as people. My witnessing was also my limit: having been claimed, I was no longer free to do just anything that took my interest, even when it involved something as intriguing as drinking blood and taking fits. I could not turn my back on Hobbles, even though he was dead. Equally, I could not face his children and grandchildren knowing that I had engaged in actions that could be construed as support for the very people against whom he had put his life on the line by testing God.

Kitty and I talked about church, but I never went. She explained that when they drink the blood and eat the body of Jesus, they are ingesting God. When they ingest God they become stronger and better-bodied persons. Then she started naming off other people in the settlement who were sick, and blaming the sickness on the fact that their bodies were either inadequate in themselves or sullied by the fact that they did not come to church and thus did not ingest God.

Dreaming creation is the origin of bodies. Relationships of shared flesh and shared blood are relationships of consubstantiality. Persons are consubstantial with their mother, through her milk, for example, and they are consubstantial with their mother's flesh by reason of being nurtured in the mother's womb. Mother's flesh is a category of substance that cuts across species. Some mother's flesh (*ngurlu*) is catfish, others are sugarbag, or emu, or other animals and plants. One's flesh is shared with other species. These relationships, which bring people into connectivities of care and nurturance, are part of what the missionaries defined as the work of Satan. Indeed, everything that was seen to deviate from an extremely narrow norm defined by disconnection was the work of Satan. It seemed that to accept Jesus as one's personal saviour would alienate the convert from their own body, as well as from the bodies of their families and their non-human kin.

It turns out that this was not the first time 'God's blood' had been brought into the region. Charlie Schultz of Humbert River Station where Kitty Maliwa had grown up and lived much of her adult life, reported on another purveyor in an interview with Darrell Lewis:

> Ah, then there was a setup that came from Newcastle Waters. When I say a setup, there was two chaps, religious chaps, came from Newcastle Waters, across. They'd visit VRD and the Humbert and they ... I got them off me place, or put the skids under them, call it what you like. They were selling the blacks beetroot vinegar for Christ's blood. Charging 'em two shillings a nip or something like that.[13]

Why people want to drink God's blood is no doubt a very complex issue, but in a region where average life expectancies are about twenty years below the national averages, where infant mortality rates were terribly high, and where leprosy was once common, a desire for the body of God may not seem so strange. Most of the old people I knew were missing fingers and toes from leprosy, and many had spent time in the leprosarium. Then there was the tuberculosis, the influenza, the kidney failures and diabetes, the obesity, the heart failures, and the devastating convergence of problems known as 'middle-aged death syndrome'. It was not hard to discern the need, but one wondered if the 'cure' was any better. Conversion seemed designed to cut people off from all the regional systems of care and support, throwing people into the arms of Jesus, each other, and two struggling missionaries. In addition to health, conversion seemed to empty the body of the flesh and blood of connectivity, and thus the blood and body of Jesus could be understood to be replenishing these depleted bodies, replacing totemic flesh with Christian flesh.

Downstream

Some Aboriginal people in Yarralin are proposing a cultural museum, and these things are being established all over the place. The modern discourse was that the museum would be the place that would enable people to leave the past behind without losing it. Others spoke of it in a Christian mode: selected items from their culture would be preserved as reminders of who they had been before they became Christians. For both sets of people the very concept of a museum requires that living culture be transformed into objects.

The act of transforming culture into history is potentially also an act which transforms subjects into objects. Paradoxically, as I have shown, people's efforts to place themselves within history also placed them so far downstream that they were effectively out of history in any active or subjective sense. 'Yesterday' (before conversion) they lived at the centre (one of the many centres) of the world, and were the subject of their own power and their own history. 'Today' (after conversion) they are in a remote wasteland, and are the object of other people's history and other people's power, or God's history and God's power. The transformation also altered time. Formerly people lived a 'now' that was richly invested with meaningful action. After conversion, the present became stretched between a singular moment of value – conversion – and the 'end of days'.

There is also a more personal reflexivity to these transformations. The definition of living culture as a past to be transcended is happening in a small settlement. It takes little more than ten minutes to walk from one end of Yarralin to another. Starting at the church end of camp, and travelling with that worldview, one walks from salvation to damnation. Put another way, one goes from the modern world into ancient history. By contrast, starting at the culture end of camp, you walk from a living culture into an empty space. In this empty space, the church end of camp, the culture-way person becomes the primitive, the non-self, the exotic. You the culture-way person encounter living subjects – your cousins, aunties, countrymen and women. But you are not responded to in quite that way; you are perceived as a fossilised and probably damned other.

It sounds bad, and it gets worse. You, the culture-way person, probably will not go to the church end of camp any more, but your relations will come to visit you. And you will know that as they look at you they see flesh they no longer claim kinship with. They see sick or sickening flesh, and they see dying bodies that will never be resurrected. They see your death, and they know it is a death that will never twist back into life in this or any other world.

And what would you see? My imagination falters, but what I gather from Hobbles and others is that church-way people are inverting a fundamental moral principle of country, life, and Law. The principle is that a country and its living things take care of their own. Church-way people have been required to make a different choice – to take care of themselves by detaching themselves from connections in this world and connecting themselves only with God. Paraphrasing and inverting that moral principle, one might say that those who destroy connections destroy country. These are the people who are now erasing the continuities of people in place, and erasing the life of the place, and doing this either for a future in Heaven, or for a more progressive life on earth, or both. In any case, they erase the living and the dead, the here and the now, the complexity of memory and the continuity of replication and plurality. Not unlike Kiernan's experience of Lake Pedder (chapter 2), you would perhaps see your own countrymen and women in this present moment unmaking your future as well as your past.

Graveyard Report

I thought I saw an Indigenous western history begin in Yarralin in 1991. It happened this way: one of the old founding men, a senior person for the country on which the settlement is located, died. His very large family decided to have a Christian funeral for him. This entailed establishing a Christian burial ground. From settlement up to that day, the burial place had been in a closed off area of land near the settlement within which individuals were buried in unmarked graves. The body was oriented towards the person's country, and people sang them home. Except during funerals, this area was off-limits except, perhaps, to senior men. Before that, tree 'burial' had been the norm, and the bones were sent back to the dead person's country. Whether by tree or by ground, the consequence of this kind of burial was that dead people returned to their own country and eventually mingled back into the collectivity of ancestral/Dreaming figures who nourished the country and gave life to the living generations of people, their descendants. These mortuary practices turned death back into life, thereby sustaining the power of nurturing life in country (see chapter 9).

In the new burial ground individuals would have marked graves. This reworking of the interactions between the living and the dead brought the dead closer in one sense: one could go there any time and commune with them if one chose. But while fixing them spatially, it created a temporal gap that could only increase. In Aboriginal genealogical time one is always only a few generations removed from one's founding ancestors, but the new burial ground defines an absolute time-frame. From here on, one can only become more distant in time from those who are buried there. The graveyard was a first step on the road that stretches time ever more tenuously between the now and the source. Worse yet, the dead bodies can only keep accumulating in graveyards; their spirits are said to have been sent to heaven. Formerly dead people returned into country, became part of it, were reborn into new bodies, and thus remained embedded in and contributing to the flux of the life of the world.

It may be this sense of impending distance that prompted church-way people to consider how the past might be retained, and started talking about a museum. Material representatives of the culture which had been transcended would be retained as heritage. Church-way people's action no longer sustained continuity with their past, but that past might linger in objects. Among the objects they wanted to include were large portraits of some of the older people who had founded Yarralin.

In so far as people place themselves within a western mode of historical representation, they define themselves in relation to western concepts of history. On the one hand, they place themselves within global history, and on the other hand, and at the same time, these people disconnect themselves from indigenous sources of power, Law, and continuity. Ancestors become heritage objects.

The schism between converts and their unconverted kin keeps widening. It is less and less clear that they live in the same world. As a culture-way person you may have more in common with the deceased forebears of the others. The museum displays may be your community of countrymen and country women, even more so than the living people who are your neighbours.

The disenchantment of the world happens in many places and contexts, and it surely happens here where violent ontological discontinuity sunders social and ecological relations as it thrusts its way into time-space and human bodies and spirits, piling up death in the world of the living.

PART THREE

TRACKS

Aboriginal people in many parts of Australia have taught me to consider country to be a conscious entity. Place is one kind of embodiment of being, and the encounters of living things are recorded there. Signs are memories; they may become obscured, but not, perhaps, lost. We human beings construct the passages of our lives through our cultures and our actions. Different cultures, different actions: different traces. Contrasts between the concreteness of place and the elusive quality of the signatures of our lives become provocatively vivid as we learn to understand our lives as tracks. Such understanding calls us to mark out ethics and objectives, ways of life and death, time, resilience and recuperation.

These tracks are always located. In Part One I examined moral engagements with the past in the present. In Part Two I looked at claims to the future. In Part Three I examine moral engagements with place in the present.

9

FOOTPRINTS

> What is important about a death narrative is that one's own passing away becomes a gift for those who follow, as well as an address to them. Death narratives are vocative; they call to one's survivors for some mode of response. (Hatley 2000: 212)

Aboriginal people bring the gift of an ecological perspective to the moral engagement of past in present. Rather than 'death narratives' emerging solely from inter-human engagements, my Aboriginal teachers would insist on the participation of country. In this chapter I draw on my studies with Aboriginal people of Yarralin and Lingara to consider that a flourishing ecosystem is itself a 'death narrative' in the vocative mode.

In the public arena where Nature is debated, the prominent discourse of conservation and care is a discourse of management. In Australia management is fastened down by the acronym NRM – Natural Resource Management. NRM is explicitly or implicitly goal-oriented, and these days the goal is some form of sustainability. Types of sustainability clash, so there is a meta-goal of sustainably balancing conflicting types – economic sustainability to be sustained without impacting on environmental sustainability, and both to be achieved within a society that has a stated goal of moving towards increasingly sustainable forms of social and environmental security.

My theme forms a counterpoint to the NRM focus on sustainability. Whether the arguments come from bureaucrats, scientists, or politicians, or whether they come from philosophers or deep ecologists, sustainability focuses on the rights of future generations, and on the obligations on the current generations to care for the future. My contrapuntal theme looks to the past, to the moral actions of the dead towards the living, and vice versa.

Victoria River Country – Here and Now

In a great many parts of Australia today, research confirms the insight that AP Elkin brought to the study of Aboriginal Australian totemism in 1938 when he defined it as 'a view of nature and life, of the universe and man, which ... unites them [Aborigines] with nature's activities and species in a bond of mutual life-giving ...' (Elkin 1938 [1954]: 133). Today we can improve on this definition by looking to multiplicity rather than singularity, and to an enlarged sociality that includes the dead as well as the living, bringing people and other living things into bonds of mutual life-giving. Contemporary studies that enlarge Elkin's definition emphasise consubstantiality and intersubjectivity between humans and their totemic or other kin (see for example Rose 1999; Magowan 2001). At the heart of these relationships are configurations of shared body that are patterned across species to bring living things into ethical relationships within and among inter-species groups to facilitate the flourishing of life.

the dead take care ...
The first Aboriginal claim to land that I worked on was with people whose home settlements were Yarralin and Lingara. The vacant crown land that was available for them to claim was nearby. I had a fair idea of who I needed to be talking to, but as much as possible I wanted to start from scratch. The boundaries that determine which land is available to claim and which is not make no sense in terms of indigenous country, and I knew that statements of belonging shift with context. I offered people clear explanations of the boundaries of the claim area, and then I started asking:

Debbie:	Who are the traditional owners, in your understanding?
Allan Young:	They're all dead.
Debbie:	What about you?
Allan Young:	Yes, that's my country.

Allan Young explained to me, as he later explained to the lawyers and finally to the judge, that real traditional owners are the *ngurramarla* ('ngurra' means country; 'marla' is not productive of meaning in itself but relates to concepts of dweller; in this context, to permanent dwelling and belonging). Sometimes he identified the Dreaming creators as the *ngurramarla*, sometimes an undifferentiated set of ancestral people/Dreamings, and sometimes his own direct ancestors. Another person in the area explained: 'he's the *ngurramarla* when he's dead – to take care of the country' (see Rose 2000a: 88, 107).

Allan's response was not atypical. Claimants made statements like this in many claims and the opposition loved it. Often an opposition lawyer would ask in an aggressive tone: 'who are the *real* owners for this country?' The question would often elicit the response 'they're all dead now', and it would take a certain measure of follow-up questions to ensure that the judge understood that a statement about the priority of ancestral presence was not, in fact, a statement that the land-owning group had died out.

the living call out ...

Jessie Wirrpa took me under her protection and guidance, and was a friend and teacher for sixteen years. When she took me walkabout she called out to her ancestors. She told them who we were and what we were doing, and she told them to help us. 'Give us fish', she would call out, 'the children are hungry'. When she was walking through country she was always with a group, and that group included the dead as well as the living. As her brother Allan Young said:

> At night, camping out, we talk and those [dead] people listen ... When we're walking, we're together. We got dead body there behind to help ... Even if you're far away in a different country, you still call out to mother and father, and they can help you for dangerous place. And for tucker they can help you. (Rose 2000a: 73)

Ancestors do not run around everywhere. People when they die are said to return to their country, and to live there as 'dead bodies' who take care of the country. Their beneficence is sought by their living descendants. In addition, every place is part of some story or other. Jessie Wirrpa spoke to the Dreamings too, calling out to them to let them know that the people who were there belonged there, that strangers were accompanied, that this was all lawful.

As discussed elsewhere, Dreamings established countries. I use the term 'eco-place' to speak to a locatedness that is not human-centred and that is attentive to the many living things who participate in the life of a given place. Country in which life is flourishing is sometimes called *ngurra punyu*. 'Good country' is the usual gloss, but *punyu* also means healthy, Lawful, and beautiful. Good country is a matrix of mutual life-giving. Ancestors are extremely significant personages in country, as people's words and deeds indicate. Paraphrasing William Faulkner, we might say that the dead are not gone, they're not even dead.

fidelity ...
Riley Young Winbilin is an intense and passionate man, and his views are always vigorous. In about 1982 he decided to convert to Christianity. As discussed in chapter 8, the missionaries preached a strongly dualistic worldview: you could either go for Jesus or you could go for Aboriginal culture. There was no way you could do both. Aboriginal culture was the work of the devil, and those who followed it were condemning themselves to eternal hell. They spoke of the suffering of hell, and begged Jesus to save them all. Their message went against the here and now of this world: this world is 'just rubbish', they hollered, and those who devote themselves to it will lose out on the only home that really matters.

Riley converted in a period when there was a lot of conversion fervour. Later, however, he gave it away. He said that he'd thought about it long and hard. He didn't want to go to Heaven, and if that condemned him to hell he would face the consequences. What he really wanted, though, was to stay in his country, as his forebears had done. At any rate, he said, generations of people had raised their children for country, had done the Law business and put the boys through initiation. His father had done that, and his father before him. Riley was going to do that for his son. If continuing in the way of his forebears meant going to hell, then he would have to endure it, but in so far as he had a choice, his decision was to remain faithful to the dead people who had nurtured him and his country (discussed further in Rose 1985, 1988).

some things don't change ...
Riley was often critical of Whitefellas, and he enjoyed drawing contrasts and declaring his position. He was against dams, against what

NRM experts would call management through the regulation of rivers. In Riley's view, the ground (which one might also gloss as 'Nature' or as 'Earth') is a non-negotiable force in the world:

> Why that government reckon he gonna change em everything? Change him round? How you going to change em round? You can't change ... that big hill there. You can't change em this ground. How you going to change em? How you going to change that creek? ... Put that creek this side, he'll come back to flood this side. You can't! No way! ...
>
> I know government say he can change em rule. But he'll never get out of this ground. (quoted in Rose 2000a: 57)

some things are in flux ...
The idea that the ground does not change is one part of the story. Another part is that everything is in a state of flux – of life and death, of nurturance, care, hunting, dying. Burning practices are a good example.

There is now a strong interest on the part of scientists, land managers, and pastoralists in indigenous fire regimes in North Australia. It has been shown conclusively that Aboriginal burning was responsible for sustaining the biodiversity of much of the continent. Eco-systems that were richly life-supportive were sustained by detailed fire practices that protected fire-sensitive plant species, promoted the well-being of fire-dependent plant species, sustained a large number of eco-tones with high levels of habitat diversity, and provided fresh grass ('green pick') for herbivores at crucial times of year. Whitefella interest is a response to savanna degradation, as well as to proof of indigenous efficacy (see Bowman 1995, 1998 for reviews of these issues).

Out in the savannas the pastoralists' desire for Aboriginal knowledge is paradoxically situated. For over a hundred years many of them did their best to suppress indigenous fire regimes. It was believed that fire was detrimental to Mitchell grass, which was the preferred pasture; only recently have scientific studies shown that correct burning enhances Mitchell grass (see Lewis 2002: 79). The fine-grained detail of the fire regimes implemented by the ancestors of Yarralin and Lingara people is probably lost. As Dora Jilpngarri, the oldest woman in Yarralin, explained, to work with fire was to risk death: 'No, they never used to burn. They weren't allowed to. Policeman would kill them, or manager would kill them. They weren't allowed to burn. They never used to burn.'

People talk about the knowledgeable use of fire as a system of mutual life-giving. Out here in the grasslands people only ever burnt small areas, aiming for an extremely patchy effect. The goal was to clear dead grass (lacking nutrition) and thus to promote new green grass. The further goal was to maintain a mosaic of patches so that hunters had clumps of grass to hide behind when they stalked the animals. The animals would come to feed on the 'green pick', and the hunter would sneak up. Animals not killed would benefit from the nutritious grasses, and people would benefit from the hunters' skill and the animal's good condition.

responsibility ...

Big Mick Kangkinang was close to ninety years old when I met him in 1980. He had been born and raised in the bush, and was probably one of the last of the people in the region to have had that experience. He had seen a huge amount of change in his life, and he enjoyed talking about it. His great detachment no doubt contributed to his longevity. On the subject of environmental change, however, his detachment was moderated by a sense of responsibility. Like many people in the region, he noted the loss of food plants, of animal species, and of general richness of country. It just wasn't as life-giving as it used to be, in his view and in the view of many others.

Big Mick suggested that the reason might be that people were not doing the mortuary rituals properly any more. Formerly the dead person's bones were rubbed with red ochre and returned to their country. These days, the body is buried in a coffin, as official regulations require. Big Mick explained: 'We never think about that bones, [we] not take 'em out anymore and put red ochre and fat. That [used to] make it good for anything, goanna, sugarbag, that makes fat food that country' (Rose 2000a: 70). Big Mick's words suggested that flux is motion that brings life out of the country and into the bodies of the living things; death is part of this flux, as it returns people (and some animals too) back into country, where they continue to nurture the living.

Aboriginal people in other parts of Australia have speculated in similar ways. T.G.H. Strehlow (1978: 49) reported on ecological damage and dwindling social responsibility in the Central Desert of Australia:

This geographically-based and uniquely Australian system of religion collapsed ... Its animals were shot at, often purely for 'sport', and its trees and grasses were ravaged by short-sighted overstocking ... 'Our country has been turned into a desert by the senseless whites', many of the older Aranda used to tell me ... as they pointed to a land sadly reduced from its former state of fertility by years of unprecedented drought and overstocking, and by millions of introduced rabbits. They commented bitterly on the swift and complete extinction of many of the formerly abundant species of marsupials, and said sadly – 'The old men who knew how to summon the rain clouds, how to create the animals, and how to keep the country green, are dead now; and our land is dying too.'

Bonds of mutual life-giving are indeed mutual – country and people take care of each other. If people fail to take care, country starts to falter too. If country starts to fail, it may be that people are failing or faltering too.

degradation ...
In the 1990s I thought that Yarralin and Lingara people may not have had a concept of exponential change. As I understood things, people looked at the changing world around them and expected it to right itself. Paraphrasing Tim Ingold (1994), one might say that they waited with trust. In 2001 people were struggling with explanations for changes that seemed to be accumulating rather than righting themselves. Riley Young Winbilin had an explanation, and while a lot of the people listening to it laughed at his choice of words and may (I think) have been sceptical of his effort to find an explanation for things that were looking pretty inexplicable, they did not fault the underlying logic:

> Used to be this country bin all clean, and today, round about two years or a year, you can see everything, different plants growing.
> And why? We got too different cattle la [here in] this country. Brahma, Santa Gertrude, all kinds of breeds. All kinds of horse breeds. And country was change ... You can see everything all changed. And you can see too many white man. Too different white man. Too different ... some of them good eye, some of them small eye, some of them big eye [laughter]. That kind make you wrong.

Riley contrasted the state of the country before the 1970s with its current state:

> And when I bin go long this land, land was really good. He was really good ... But now ... when we bin start again, country was little bit funny that day, I bin looking at country was little bit funny that day. I bin looking at, 'what's wrong this one? Something wrong.' And after that I bin look now, one year's time I bin see em plants bin get up. You go longa bush now looking for fruit, you can't see em fruit. You see em all these trees now ... And even if you go round la bush here, you can't see that karil, gooseberry, kilipi, tipil, purlkal, ngaringari, that kind bin too much longa this – yarkalayin, mintarayij, that bin already bin clear. But you can't see em this time now. That's from what I bin say: 'country bin change. Ground bin change.' Because no fruit now. Where him gottem good fruit longa this ground, country was look good. But fruit going away, country gone, finish.[14]

Riley spoke of a process that I would gloss as intensification. The social aspect of intensification concerns land use and social services. Tourism is increasing rapidly since the conversion of a few stations into National Parks (Gregory National Park, Keep River National Park). In addition there is a growing scientific presence, and investigations and activities by people from numerous other branches of government. As we talked about ecological change in 2001, we were surrounded by army personnel who were building houses and roads as part of a government effort to standardise living conditions in the outback.

There is also a process of intensification of vegetation, referred to in this region as 'thickening'. In other regions it is called woody weed invasion; radically disturbed land is taken over by opportunistic native and introduced scrub (mainly Acacia spp). In the Vic River District, the woody weed invasion is accompanied by an increase in the number of trees. The savanna is rapidly losing its 'clean, clear' character (Lewis 2002 provides an excellent discussion of these processes in the Vic River District; see also Goodall 2000). Current scientific studies are documenting the changes, but the causes are not yet fully understood by anyone. It is probable that numerous factors are involved: global warming, suppression of indigenous fire regimes, intensification of land use, and new breeds of cattle, among others.

Along with thickening, there is also loss – of topsoil, riverbanks, and, ultimately, of many of the species and habitats that supported indigenous life. Country is becoming wild. When Daly spoke of the eroding wild he went on to speak of quiet country – the country in which all the care of generations of people is evident to those who know how to see it. Both erosion and invasion involve loss. Riley listed a number of plant foods that are not available any more. Daly looked at the disappearance of country as it washed down into the bare gullies.

Fluidity and Fidelity

The significance of ancestral tracks in Australian Aboriginal culture is well documented (for example, Morphy 1991; Watson 2003). The emphasis for the most part has been on the forms that tracks take in ritual and in art. Here I want to consider the form that tracks take in ecological systems. I want to be clear, as well, that I am not separating humans from ecosystems. I am using the word 'ecosystem' to include living things, their sustenance, and their relationships with other living things.

Flourishing, or 'quiet', country is an ancestral track – it shows the care that has been or is sustaining it. Ancestral footprints sustain the living generations. In the Vic River District, people say that their country gives them body. The relationship is reciprocal: they take care of the country, the country takes care of them. People's ability to keep on living from day to day is embedded within the relations between past and present, and is actualised in living country in the daily life of every present moment (see Povinelli 1993 on the salience of daily life in encounters between people and origins).

The generation of life is the process by which life is unfolded by the actions of transient living things in interaction with Dreaming and ancestral presence. The process rests on subject–subject reciprocity: an intersubjectivity of bringing forth. Persons are immanent in those portions of the world which are theirs, and those portions of their world are immanent in them (see also Ingold 1986: 139). Ephemeral persons are embedded in the world, and by the work of their lives they bring forth the life of the world. This process is nurtured and sustained through cultural procreation. Flourishing life is evidence of current and ancestral labour, but it all can come undone when the organisation fails.

Dreaming creation exists in dynamic and fluid reciprocity with the ephemeral life of the created world, and today the connectivities are increasingly stressed. M Kat Anderson notes that the question of losses is not just about species but also, and perhaps more significantly in the long run, about losses of connections. Drawing on evidence from North America, Anderson notes several factors that are equally pertinent to the Vic River District: loss of cultural practices that benefit rare and endangered plants, loss of ecosystem diversity, and loss of patchy environments (Anderson 1997: 21).

Resilience

So fragile are the relationships that sustain the world: eco-place is immensely vulnerable because the ongoing life of the place happens through the actions of ephemeral living beings. This means that life doesn't just happen to happen. And it doesn't just happen to work itself into patterns, and it doesn't just keep returning like an automaton. Ephemeral beings are crucial actors in all these processes: bringing life forth and sustaining patterns in life and in death.

My Aboriginal teachers can be understood to work with life processes in a way that generally accords with the practice of facilitated resilience as discussed in chapter 2. Under their intellectual and ecological life practice the concept can be enlarged in two main ways. The first is to note that human action really does matter; there is no suggestion that country abandoned by, or sequestered from, people is better able to take care of itself than country in which people are active participants. Quite the opposite, in fact. People are deemed to be an integral part of the life of country. The question is not 'people or no people', rather the pertinent question is 'what kind of action?' The view that Aboriginal people are key participants in flourishing life processes is attested also by evidence from science; conclusions drawn in many contexts show that through their burning practices (in particular) Aboriginal people sustained high levels of biodiversity across the continent (Langton 1998; Gammage 2003).[15]

The second enlargement is that it is not only humans that work to the mutual benefit of flourishing life. This point takes me into details of ecological thought that go beyond my purpose here, but that can be summarised under the idea of mutual benefit. This idea articulates a point that is also addressed from a science perspective.

Wilson (2002: 108) notes that 'the more species that inhabit an ecosystem ... the more productive and stable is the ecosystem'. In parallel, it is fair to say that the more species that inhabit an ecosystem, the more densely entwined and stable are the benefits. The work of facilitating resilience is undertaken by interacting (human and non-human) species.

Big Mick's discussion of mortuary rituals, like discussions of other people, offers the idea that death is most properly turned towards resilience. Mortuary rituals twist death back into life; this ecology of emerging life sets up recursive looping between life and death; country holds both, needs both, and most importantly, keeps returning death into life.

Thus the time-space matrix of the living world is a set of eco-places in which life is brought into time, and in which time and life are bound into place. The ephemeral in its fidelity returns into place, and the 'dead bodies' sustain country in its life-giving propensity. Eco-place does not exist from nothing; it is an ancestral footprint – a living sign of past action.

Double Death

The current western emphasis on sustainability – that future generations should have some means of life support, has stimulated a great green literature along with all the policy discussions and negotiations. Aboriginal thought impresses upon us consideration of the thought that to fail is to be doubly at fault: to fail the future is also to fail the past. Human beings, in this orientation towards life, are the footprints of the ancestors who died and who still nurture the country and their descendants. Failure works back into time, as well as forward. To kill off chunks of species and connectivities that form the matrix known as country is to start a process that works to erode the traces of the life that preceded us.

Riley Young spoke about continuity between generations as a set of links. From the beginning right up to today people have sustained responsibilities between themselves and their country. Failure to sustain those links not only in their social but also in their ecological context starts to unravel those links. In a degrading and dying world, from this moment now it is all disappearing right back to the beginning.

The multiplication of effect that Riley Young described in the context of ecological change can be seen as doubled up death work. His analysis suggests that eco-systems could cope with one invasion, but that these multiple invasions are triggering longer-term changes. The multiplying invasions are producing loss across place – erasing species and habitat diversity and replacing them (if at all) with rampant opportunists. The multiplying invasions are equally producing erasures across time, wiping out the life-giving systems that were the signs of the ancestors, and ultimately, we must imagine, wiping out the living presence of the dead. The dead who are left with no living descendants to call out to them and whose lives they can nurture will become doubly dead: having already died, they now become lost to the present because the present itself is becoming lost.

The concept of double death implies a plurality of responsibilities in the present – both towards the past and the future. Further, this extensive responsibility in the present suggests a desired congruence between past and future. In a recent article on mining in Arnhem Land, Ian McIntosh draws on Bakhtin's theory of history, bringing it into conversation with the late David Burrumarra around the idea of 'historical inversion'. Bakhtin defines this type of inversion as a perspective in which history (the past) is something yet to be achieved. David Burrumarra tells stories about Macassans to show a potential for 'how things should be if the law is followed' (McIntosh 2001: 28).

One of Burrumarra's great gifts was to offer stories that spoke to confrontational situations in a rapidly changing world. The idea of history as future, however, need not be confined to crisis events. History as future can suggest continuity and adaptability, as Morris & Boccara (2000) indicate in the subtitle of their book on Aboriginal Australia: *L'ancien futur de l'Australie.*

Abstract questions of time detached from place and responsibility portray structure, but life in country equally concerns process. Within the matrix of country, the concept of future history indicates connections of mutual life-giving across time and within place, and demands of the living that they work towards making new tracks and prints following those of the ancestors.

Dialogue

In cross-cultural dialogue, zones of apparent convergence frequently offer up sharp divergences. Take footprints, for example. In contemporary natural resource management the concept of the 'ecological footprint' is an 'accounting tool for ecological resources'. It is a way of measuring the amount of resources that a nation or other unit is consuming (Wackernagel & Rees). In Daly's world, the footprints or tracks of the ancestors are visible as quiet country. His ancestral footprint is a signature of ecological coherence, human care, and mutual life-giving, whereas NRM's ecological footprint is a quantifiable measure of impact. Stephen Muecke notes that this pervasive binary crops up all over the place, as Aborigines are 'called upon to be the "human side" to our industrial nightmare – the *eros* to our *thanatos*' (Muecke 1997: 15).

There is a romantic temptation here, of course, along with the seductions of despair and abdication, but one need not slip into fantasies of otherness and redemption. Divergences are also provocations, and from an ecological point of view, provocations are exactly what is needed for new knowledge to come into the world. A provocation is an unanticipated perspective. It enriches thought, conversation and discovery.

In settler societies, the lives of settler and Indigenous peoples are entangled, but in some of the most significant contexts our discourses are not. The major entanglement, in my view, is around our ecological well-being in this period of impending crisis. And yet the conversations we most need to have are barely happening. In Australia the early focus on resource management (Williams & Hunn 1982) accomplished the necessary and immensely important political objective of reframing hunter-gatherers as active agents rather than the 'parasites' that Elkin (1938: 15) and others had asserted. There are today a few studies of contemporary Aboriginal caring for country on Aboriginal land, and a growing literature on co-management in parks and elsewhere (for example, Langton 1998; Baker et al. 2001; Rose 2002). But in many co-management contexts the monologue of NRM tends to dominate both practice and epistemology, framing the questions as well as the answers.

Paradoxically, it may be that talking about 'the environment' or 'resource management' is not the best place to start the kinds of dialogue I am arguing for. Short-term NRM issues are being negotiated case by case. The long-term issues constitute the big questions, and I believe that conversations that circle around, but do not necessarily become limited to, NRM themes will be most productive of new knowledge. Enlarged conversations still require some ground of contact. It is therefore necessary to be alert to zones of convergence that erupt unexpectedly and with unpredictable possibilities. One such possibility is that the current interest among western scholars in refiguring moral engagements of past in present is part of a recent turn in western thought towards the living past (for example, Gordon 1997; Neuman 2000; Taussig 2001; Tumarkin 2002).

Convergences around questions of time, history and death offer scope for greatly enlarged thought and practice. Dialogue in this domain has deep implications, as I have sought to show. At the very least, Indigenous people are likely to insist on including the Earth. The logic of the fragility of the relationships that sustain the living world impels me to turn the analysis around onto my own society. A series of appalling questions rises up in my face. If all the connectivities that sustain life are undone in our lives, if that which follows us can only falter and perhaps fail utterly, then what is our 'death narrative'? If the present living world in its ecological complexity exists as the footprints or tracks of the life that has gone before, then we are faced with this terrible question. Are we, today, the living ones who will leave no tracks? Will our deaths even have an ecological narrative? And if not, how will other narratives survive? Is this the legacy of the wounded space of colonisation and development: that having come into the world as signs of our forebears' lives, we now remake ourselves, and all who are enmeshed in our damage, as trackless ghosts?

10

JOURNEYS

> The Bible and the Cross help us to remember Christianity and to believe in God ... They are like eyeglasses. Without these glasses would we see God in our image (and vice versa) or would God look different? Would he look like the natural world?' (David Burrumarra, in Burrumarra & McIntosh 2002)

The late David Burrumarra, one of the great sages of Arnhem Land, believed that human and ecological rights are most properly embedded each within the other. One cannot speak in a holistic way about human rights without speaking also of ecological rights, and vice versa. He outlined the three main principles which he taught to young people, and he defined them as the 'real human rights':

> Do the ceremony properly for your homeland and for yourself.
> Understand the land and everything on it so you can manage it properly.
> When you are a bungawa [leader] you will stand up and do the business properly for your homeland and Australia. (quoted in McIntosh 1994:78)

I understand Burrumarra to be saying that these human/ecological rights apply, or should apply, to every Australian. His vision was inclusive, and at the same time powerfully provocative. It fills us with questions, and arouses a desirous curiosity: what does one do in response to his request for us to learn the land and to learn the practices of care, to work properly for ourselves and our country? If we were to accept his view of the 'real' human rights, how would we implement them in our own lives, communities and country?

Following Michael Ignatieff's (1999) proposal that 'human rights' are a ground for dialogue rather than a narrative of triumphal achievement, I approach Burrumarra's words as an invitation for response and action. From this perspective, Burrumarra's 'real' human rights offer an opportunity for reconciliation at deep and momentous levels. In exploring some of the social, ecological and philosophical issues that are entailed by Burrumarra's statement of the real human rights, I offer outlines of possible paths rather than signposting a one-way street. In what directions, I ask, could such life-enhancing footsteps start to take us? Burrumarra's injunctions are indeed words in dark times, and in this and the following chapter I develop more specific stories that respond to issues of reconciliation and the 'real human rights'.

Modernity's Legacy

Dialogue in an ethical mode begins where one is. It acknowledges the legacies that form one's history and ground, seeking from that grounded position to turn towards others in an attitude that welcomes change. The legacy of modernity is so vast that it cannot be fully encapsulated here (or anywhere), but three dominant ideas are especially pertinent to Burrumarra's challenge.

One dominant idea is *fragmentation*. Western knowledge today is oriented towards mastering the world through the disciplines of differentiation, separation, fragmentation. Mastery of these disciplines is internalised (Cuddihy 1974), as well as being practised outward on the world (Hornborg 1994). Many of our research techniques approach an inert world in order to dissect, rearrange, classify, typologise, and remake. This knowledge system is highly successful in producing technologies and economies that feed and fuel desire. We live today in a world that is in many ways delightful in its technological opportunities, and delightful for some in its economic rewards. But by the same process of fragmentation, modernity also produces pitiless and alienated selves – persons whose well-being is increasingly at risk, whose desires must be always unsatisfied, whose optimism requires a bruising indifference to others. We live in a world that is forever being dismantled, ostensibly in the service of our desires but more potently in the service of wealth, and this broken and fragmented world is increasingly unable to hold systems of life together. As the development expert Frédérique Apffel-Marglin (1996b: 173) puts it, this disengaged and fragmenting form of knowledge 'has proved dramatically successful at creating material abundance and technological advance, but disastrous at maintaining social and natural ecology'.

Hand in hand with fragmentation we encounter a longing for a lost wholeness. This is a hunger for wholeness, to use Peter Gay's (1968) term, a dream of unity and of a world that has not been subjected to modernity. Wholeness hunger is itself part of modernity, and it slips into longing for a world that one can only encounter in dreams. Here in Australia, as in other settler societies, one form of wholeness hunger manifests as the desire to attribute to Indigenous people a reality that conforms to the very dreams of wholeness that are themselves brought into being by fragmentation. These dreams are structured by reversals: modernity fragments, so Indigenous reality must be whole; modernity destroys, so Indigenous people must conserve; modernity impels us towards instrumental relationships with others and requires of us an extreme callousness, so Indigenous people must be kind, thoughtful and knowing. In this kind of reversal, Indigenous people are configured as a sort of 'us' without modernity; 'us' as we dream of being when our minds recoil from our own loneliness and alienation.

I want to be clear, therefore, that I am not suggesting that Aboriginal people in Australia or on any other continent can be understood as a reflex of modernity's desire for wholeness. I am not suggesting, in fact, that Australian Aboriginal people live in a world of wholeness at all, as I have made clear in earlier chapters. Nor do I suggest that all the answers to modernity's problems are to be found among Indigenous people. In Australia today every person, settler-descended and Indigenous, knows brokenness in the wake of modernising violence. And still, there are differences between settler-descendants and Indigenous people: these differences are real, and they do matter.

A second dominant idea is *isolation*. As Melbourne philosopher Freya Mathews discusses in her book *The Ecological Self* (1991), Newton's physics implied, and became, a cosmology and a worldview. It posited atoms – isolated and bounded singularities – as the irreducible elements of the cosmos. Each was separate and distinct, and logically independent (p. 8). The Newtonian theory of matter was mechanistic, and depended on some form of mind outside matter not only to observe and analyse, but also to provide the impetus to motion. This theory and its correlates were worked into a theory of society by philosophers such as Thomas Hobbes, who posited the individual as the metaphoric atom of society (pp. 25, 39). Atomism is connected with fragmentation minimally through the theory that because atoms are the basic 'building blocks', the best path towards understanding is to disassemble structures to get to the basics.

The social and cultural implications of atomism constitute pillars of Enlightenment thinking: the transcendence of reason (mind over matter, culture over nature), the disembedded (and disembodied) subject, and faith in the existence of a site of objectivity which exists beyond historical and cultural contingency (Benhabib 1992: 4). These points are connected: the disengagement of mind from matter enables the concept of a disembodied subject, and a disembodied subject is required in order to occupy an imaginary site of total externality. Rationality was held to be the main tool of the mind; it was equated with the mind of God or cosmos, and offered the promise of complete understanding. These key points underlie our contemporary social thinking: our scholars have aimed for universal theories, and our major models of economy and democracy are built on atomism. How we understand and achieve justice, and even how we imagine and allow for compassion are embedded in atomism. It is thus extremely difficult to think about major changes in our basic understandings without also imagining some sort of descent into chaos.

On the other hand, the incredibly powerful forms of technological mastery that we have developed with rational science constitute today the very causes for concern about crisis. An objectivity which requires the erasure of self and purports to calculate the incalculable (Marglin 1996: 241) can only produce fragmented knowledge, some of which is extremely useful. The effects of such knowledge, when linked to the confidence and technological seductions of high modernity, and to the political and economic power of global capitalism, are devastating, as a number of excellent new studies in 'development' show (Apffel-Marglin & Marglin 1996; J. Scott 1998). As Hans Jonas wrote in 1984: 'the danger of disaster attending the ... ideal of power over nature through scientific technology arises not so much from any shortcomings of its performance as from the magnitude of success' (quoted in Bauman 1993: 221).

A third dominant idea is *denarrativisation*. Modernity rests on a mind/matter hyperseparation that progressively empties from the non-human its own self-presence or intentionality. Matter becomes 'sheer externality, devoid of subjective interiority ... this world is [the modern person's] object, an ever-changing artefact of his passing whims' (Mathews 1999a: 247).

Martin Jay (1993: 51) uses the term 'denarrativisation' to describe a western intellectual development by which people ceased to regard the world as having its own story (exemplified, for example, in the idea of the 'book of Nature'), and started to look at the world as a story-less object. This development relied on hyperseparations, and the result is a commitment to there being a gap between the mind and the world; from this gap arises the idea that the world is devoid of mind. The extreme form of this gap would see the world as expressively inert (Merchant 1980; Apffel-Marglin 1996a: 3).[16] Carried to this extreme, denarrativisation asserts that the world is meaningless, in the sense of having no meanings of its own, but only the meanings we humans attribute to it.

This is disenchantment in the secular mode, and is not that different, perhaps, from disenchantment in the fundamentalist Christian mode (chapter 8). It asserts that 'the world is silent as the good or the beautiful. The cosmos became ... a despiritualized mechanism to be grasped by concepts and representations constructed by reason' (Apffel-Marglin 1996a: 3).

Denarrativisation is a negative legacy for us on two counts. The first is social: as settler-descended peoples we inhabit country for which other people already have stories. This is not empty or unstoried land. The second is ecological. My argument in this chapter is that the belief that the world is expressively inert does *not* destroy the world's expressivity. Modernity may damage our ability to hear, even as our violence damages the world's ability to communicate, and we become caught up in an amplifying process of reduction: the refusal to hear stifles or destroys living things, thereby reducing the multivocal expressivity of the world. Nevertheless, it is essential that we not mistake an inability to hear for an absence of communication, and not mistake loss for total death.

If atomism, wholeness hunger and denarrativisation are part of modernity, and part of the way of thinking and being that impels us into ever more violence, are there paths that lead into a different legacy? I read Burrumarra's provocation as an urgency for stories. One set of stories would turn us towards expressivity, connection, and recuperative action. Another set would sustain our awareness of loss and thus help us avoid complacency. Each of these sets would engage us with Aboriginal people whose capacity to listen to the world's expressivity is both local and fine-tuned.

Reconciliation

Many thoughtful participants in the contemporary movement towards reconciliation describe the process as a journey. I understand people to be emphasising the open-ended quality of reconciliation – that there is no tribunal, no final determinations of guilt, innocence, and clemency, and no formal declarations of closure. Rather, there is this ongoing domain of our lives in which we sustain an open commitment to social and cultural change. Reconciliation consists of efforts to acknowledge the harm of the past and its links to the present, to undo some of this painful history and to work towards new relations between and among us – relations as yet not fully imagined.

The word 'journey' is thus extremely important for us, but a journey is always more than a metaphor, and in the case of reconciliation, I think that the term is meant quite literally. If the first dimension is social, the second is temporal, with the past and the future both implicated in the present. The third dimension is spatial. Where this journey takes place matters greatly: not only because it is an Australian journey, unique to our entwined and painful history, but also because it takes place within the environments of Australia.

Taking Burrumarra's concept of real human rights into the domain of reconciliation, he shows us that we must include the environment in our journey. I offer four main reasons, each of which is complementary to Burrumarra. The first is that without an inhabitable world for the future there is no point even to thinking about change. This would seem to be self-evident, and I do not discuss it further. The second is that Aboriginal people ask us to do this: to promote land rights, land care, co-management, ecological restoration, and protection of sacred sites. To the extent that reconciliation truly engages us, we must work to respond to the issues that matter to Indigenous people. The third is that society and environment are inextricably connected. Changes in one area cause changes in another. The outcomes are open. Life-enhancing feedback between social change and environmental change is one possibility; damage is another. There are possibilities for informed choices, and the choices we make really matter. The fourth is that Aboriginal people over the millennia have developed many ways of enhancing both their own lives and the lives of other beings and life support systems. This knowledge is not 'lost': Aboriginal people keep offering to share their knowledge for the mutual good of country and people. In general it is neither possible nor desirable to try to mimic their ways of being in Australian environments – both because of the quantitative and qualitative social and environmental changes that are taking place, and because mimicry will fail to get at the deeper meanings. But it is still possible, I believe, to seek together to reshape relations between people and environments. Reconciliation, I am saying, for each of these four reasons, makes a moral ecological claim on us.

Commitment

Reconciliation draws our attention to the war against Indigenous people, and shows us the legacy of conquest: this great divide on one side of which are the survivors of this undeclared and untreatied war, and on the other side of which are the descendants of those who waged the war, and may include today people who continue to hold the powerful view that Indigenous people will have to assimilate in order to become part of the nation.

This great divide is both profoundly present, and yet strangely non-existent. It constitutes much of our history, and it continues to tell us more about ourselves than we really want to know. But at the same time, the lives of many of us are enmeshed in tangled webs of connection that undermine the idea and the experiences of a clear divide. Many settlers both dispossessed and protected Aborigines. Many settler family photo albums contain photos of Indigenous people who were once 'like part of the family'. Many Australians today are descended from both settler and Indigenous ancestors. And of course, many people today actively seek reconciliation as a positive good for themselves, their regions, and our shared future. The project of reconciliation demands of us that we acknowledge the divide and the violence, but it simultaneously demands that we explore the entanglements of memory, connection, and commitment.

The complexities of this social web of division and entanglement are similar in an environmental context. Environmental historians have long drawn our attention to the war against Nature. The great divide of 'us' and 'them' constructed and sustained through violence is equally pertinent to settlers' relations with Nature. Here, too, the destruction has been immense. We know, for example, of the many exterminations (some intentional, many incidental to the project of colonisation), and we know of the 'acclimatisation societies'. We know of the careless introductions of species that cause irremediable harm, and the difficulties of containing what has gone feral. Across this divide we also know of the entangled histories of conservation, reclamation, preservation, and restoration. Social and environmental entanglements come together in current moves towards co-management.

I have used the concept of a dual war to highlight the violence that underpins the need for reconciliation and is constitutive of so many of our social and environmental problems. But reconciliation really aims for new forms of connectivity. Provided connectivity is understood in a proactive way to mean relationships of mutual benefit and mutual flourishing, it offers an excellent alternative to war.

Land is Law

The Aboriginal philosopher Mary Graham has written a compelling article entitled 'Some thoughts about the Philosophical Underpinnings of Aboriginal Worldviews'. She identifies two basic precepts. Each one is at once deceptively simple and extraordinarily complex:

- The Land is the Law.
- You are not alone in the world. (Graham 1999: 105)

The first precept is based on a very inclusive concept of land. Within the word 'land' there is water, plants, animals, indeed the whole of what we generally call the natural world. Graham expands on this precept with this explanation:

> The two most important kinds of relationships in life are, firstly, those between land and people and, secondly, those amongst people themselves, the second being contingent upon the first.

> The land, and how we treat it, is what determines our humanness. Because land is sacred and must be looked after, the relations between people and land becomes the template for society and social relations. All meaning comes from the land. (p. 106)

This precept offers huge challenges to all of the West's great thought systems: philosophy, religion, and science. But it also puts forward a very pragmatic challenge: to give the land priority in all our practice.

The second precept is given substance in Aboriginal worldview and practice through the fact that kinship includes the natural world, including land and water, plants and animals, and other phenomena, as I have discussed in other chapters. This precept is non-dualistic; as Mathews and others show, it challenges fundamental premises of modernity. Looked at from this perspective, modernity would claim that we are alone – as a species, and as individuals also (Mathews 1991). Graham counters modernity with this explanation:

> Aboriginal people have a kinship system which extends into land ... Every clan group has its own Dreaming or explanation of existence. We believe that a person finds their individuality within the group. To behave as if you are a discrete entity or a conscious isolate is to limit yourself to being an observer in an observed world. (Graham 1999: 106)

The challenges of these two precepts raise for us profoundly unsettling questions about ourselves and Nature. What would it mean to think of ourselves as one species among many rather than as the highest species? Is it possible within western knowledge systems to become more than an observer in an observed world?

Ethics and Ecology

Mathews (1991) reminds us that Einstein's theories of relativity knocked Newtonian physics out of position, thereby destabilising the intellectual infrastructure of the Enlightenment worldview. Much of our cosmology may yet be Newtonian, and to that extent it is out of sync with emerging knowledge not only in physics but in other sciences as well. One of the greatest achievements of western science and philosophy in the last century was to overcome the subject/object binary. This achievement calls for 'abandoning the ontologies of our time', as Levinas (1996: 24) so forcefully puts it. Some of the most arresting shifts in science have taken place in biology and ecology; they take us far away from the Cartesian position of being a disembodied observer.

I will summarise a few of the basic properties of life as they are now understood from a western ecological perspective, drawing first on the work of Gregory Bateson. The new ecology starts with this fundamental assertion: that the unit of survival is not the individual or the species, but is the organism-and-its-environment in relationship. It follows from this that an organism that deteriorates its environment commits suicide (Bateson 1973: 436; Harries-Jones 1995: 66). The further implication is that being is inherently, inescapably, and necessarily relational. Relationships entail mutual causality: organism and environment shape and sustain each other. Relations between organism and environment are recursive, meaning that they are densely and mutually entangled through time.

The shifts in thinking are revolutionary: from building blocks to relationships; from concepts of equilibrium to concepts of pervasive disequilibrium; from concepts of objectivity to concepts of intersubjectivity; from visions of deterministic prediction to an awareness of fundamental uncertainties such that predictions must be probabilistic (Ciancio & Nocentini 2000). Inherent in this shift is the subversion of the concept of a universal knowledge. Frank Egler is reported to have said that 'ecosystems may not only be more complex than we think, they may be more complex than we can think' (quoted in Dietrich 1992: 110). One cannot remove one's self from the system under examination, and because one is a part of the system the whole remains outside the possibility of one's comprehension (summarised from Mellor 1997). The consequences of this understanding are enormous, and are only beginning to shape new forms of environmental science and practice.

Scholars from a range of disciplines and perspectives approach these big issues: anthropologists such as Ingold (1996), historians such as Merchant (1980), eco-feminists such as Cuomo (1997), Mellor (1997) and Warren (2000), environmental philosophers such as Mathews (2003a & b) and Plumwood (2002), activists and analysts such as Mies & Shiva (1993), and deep ecologists such as Naess (1989). This scholarship (and much more) seeks to demonstrate the history, power and consequences of the epistemological error that asserts that humanity is fundamentally separate from, and can control, Nature. The work seeks to undermine the universality of western knowledge and to seek new forms of dialogue that will enable us to find alternatives in our current epistemological-ecological crises.

Mary Graham's second precept – you are not alone – addresses the kinds of relatedness and relational thinking that underpin the new ecology. Resilience is a key issue. In this context the word is intended to convey the idea that what matters in relatedness is not just parts of a living system but rather the capacity of a living system to be self-organising and self-repairing. Processes of resilience are not static: they are extremely active and far from equilibrium. As discussed in chapter 3, they are dynamic and are always embedded in time and in the real.

The process of overcoming the subject/object binary poses three important challenges that take on special shape and pertinence in our settler societies. As Levinas argues, and as new scientific knowledge also implies, ethics become primary. Ethics involve relations between self and other, and thus actively abjure homogenisation, appropriation, objectification, and manipulation. 'Self' and 'other' matter in the here and now of their life and their difference. In our societies ethics includes relationships between Indigenous and settler-descended peoples, and relationships between our knowledge systems. It includes our moral engagements with our past and future, and with our ecosystems.

The second challenge is how to engage with the world in a mode of intersubjectivity. Donna Haraway's (1988: 593) point – that we need some account of the world as an active subject – is the focus of vigorous contemporary research. The implications for settler societies have been discussed above: our 'New World' homelands are already storied places. Indigenous people here and elsewhere already have accounts of the world as an active subject (for example, see Scott 1996). We cannot ethically pretend that the places with which we engage, whether cities or so-called wilderness, are empty places either ecologically or socially.

The third challenge is that subjects are always situated. The new ecology, like Aboriginal teachings, situates us ethically and situates us physically. The subject is emplaced, and to be emplaced is to be both vulnerable and empowered, as I discussed in relation to Lake Pedder in chapter 2.

Nativism

Freya Mathews has been exploring these themes from the perspective of western philosophy. Her context is that of 'becoming native' (Mathews 1999a). Her premise is that 'from the viewpoint of nativism, every human being has the "right" to resist or overcome the existential alienation of modernity, and to preserve or restore her relation of belonging to the world through a particular place or set of places' (p. 265). To be native to a place, she points out, can mean simply that one was born there. Mathews is exploring a deeper engagement with place: to belong to a place, to be made of its matter and steeped in its character (p. 245). In this sense, nativism entails a relationship of connectivity that is countermodern.

Nativism lives within continuity and connectivity between humans and their place in the world. One of Mathews' (2000) finest achievements is to pursue her argument in the context of the city. As discussed in chapter 2, she actively seeks to work with the real as it is given – in the bush, in towns and cities, in places that thrive and places that are not thriving. Becoming native, she contends, requires making a commitment to one's place. This countermodern work is:

> a way to beat modernity while conceding the inescapability of its effects – the cities, technologies, industries, the litter and junk it has spawned. For while modernity is the process of converting the hitherto sacred order of matter and place into commodities, cash and property, our affirmation, forgiveness, preservation and enhancement of the given converts commodities and property back into the sacred order. We shall also in this way re-enter that order ourselves. (1999a: 255)

Mathews acknowledges that becoming native in a settler society requires reconciliation between colonisers and colonised. She is not proposing unilateral action here, but rather full acknowledgment of past and present. She looks for Indigenous guidance, but at the same time acknowledges that Indigenous people will choose – to share or not, as they see fit (see chapter 11). For this reason, among others, she is also dedicated to exploring new ways in which settler-descended peoples can reinhabit the places of their lives. That is, she seeks to expand the settler repertoire of 'real human rights' while also seeking dialogue with Indigenous people.

Graham (1999: 107) advises settler-descended Australians who are concerned with forming new relationships with people and place:

'The best way of achieving these ends is to start establishing very close ties with land, not necessarily via ownership of property but via locally-based, inclusive, non-political, strategy-based frameworks, with a very long term aim of simply looking after land'.

Report from a Pilgrimage

In the essay on becoming native, Mathews (1999a: 268) differentiates between tourist travelling and journeying. The tourist experience, she suggests, involves a 'packaging or purchasing of certain prescribed geographical and cultural sights and sounds. Tourism is one of the paradigmatic pursuits of modernity...' The journey, in contrast, 'involves a voyage into vulnerability ... [and is] open to serendipitous direction by the world ...' (p. 269). Her beautiful book *Journey to the Source of the Merri* (Mathews 2003b) recounts her journey to get to know the land locally. The Merri Creek runs through Mathews' neighbourhood in Melbourne and has been part of her work towards 'becoming native' in the city (for example, Mathews 2000). In 1999 she and two friends set off to walk to the source of the creek.

Freya notes that pilgrimage is not tied in any necessary way to landscape. A philosopher, she suggests, might make a pilgrimage to Athens in honour of Socrates. In contrast, she defines her pilgrimage as a work of reinhabitation; it was a gathering of the journey into a poetic unity (2003b: 31). Rather than looking for a lost wholeness, she walked through shattered land, gathering a narrative that became a relationship and a testimony. Hers was a 'journey into our own country; the land itself was our destination' (p. 31). She also contrasts her journey with bushwalking. The bushwalker, she suggests, is seeking a particular experience of a particular kind of 'natural' world. Freya, in contrast, walked with, for, and to the creek:

> Pilgrimage ... was shaping up as an exercise in the acceptance of the given. After a single initial choice, that of one's sacred destination – one hits the road. Once on the road, however, one takes whatever comes. There is no preference for the non-human over the human here, nor is there any sense that the human is less a part than the non-human of the numinous, the sacred, the absolute other. One rejoices in nature and the open skies, but trudges through industrial darkness and urban labyrinths if that is where the way leads. (p. 29)

A pilgrimage of reinhabitation thus poses questions that I would love to have taken back to Burrumarra. Few people have spoken as mysteriously and provocatively as he did. You can read his words and ponder them, have conversations with them and dream about them, but you never really fathom the depths of his insight. In another essay he tells us about *Motj*: *Motj* is power; it is the flow of life towards growth, of stories towards the real, of a person towards awareness ... *Motj*, he says, is the source of all life. In comparing his sense of power with Christianity, Burrumarra said: 'The Bible and the Cross help us to remember Christianity and to believe in God ... They are like eyeglasses. Without these glasses ... would God look different? Would he look like the natural world?' (Burrumarra & McIntosh 2002).

I understand Burrumarra to be affirming that without these particular eyeglasses we would see the natural world as God. What would he say about industrial darkness and urban labyrinths? Can *Motj* also be discerned in these places? Can these different worlds interpenetrate each other? Metaphorically speaking, what would be the situation if the Dreamtime Magi (chapter 7) came to the surface only to find that they were in a parking lot? Would they hasten away, or would they stay and work with it? In my mind's eye I see cracked asphalt with a few weeds and the odd blade of grass. I imagine the Dreaming ancestors unpacking their sacred objects, perhaps taking out a coolamon with a grass seed design, and starting to sing. They would be lifting up the *Motj*, facilitating resilience in this impoverished area.

If the power of the living world is a power that is the source of all life, then resilience is surely one of the most significant powers in the world. I wonder if work that facilitates resilience may not be one of the most powerful and life-affirming forms of reconciliation available to us. If so, it would not seem to make sense for us to privilege the 'natural' world over and above the industrial wastelands. As Freya suggests, we could be 'singing up the city' (Mathews 2000) as well as caring for the bush. In working towards connectivity we engage in work that has the potential to facilitate in the here and the now the growth of legacies that defy modernity's fragmentation, isolation, denarrativisation, and destruction. In the process we would begin to assert our 'real' human rights.

11

LOVE AND RECONCILIATION IN THE FOREST

> A genuinely ecological approach does not work to attain a mentally envisioned future, but strives to enter, ever more deeply, into the sensorial present.
> (Abrams 1996: 272)

Different cultures, different tracks and paths. Mary Graham's philosophical analysis raises the question: how would we live, as persons and as a society, if we accept that we are in connection and that we are not primary? In an important sense this question is not answerable in the abstract. The answers, if they come at all, will come in life as people seek to make the shifts towards connection with and commitment to the non-human world. The project of recuperation that I advocate depends on the view that time is braided to the extent that there are people in Australia today who are making these shifts. In this chapter I examine one such story.

On the south coast of New South Wales social and environmental justice are coming together around an Aboriginal sacred site. Here two sets of people – settlers and Indigenous people – live side by side, sharing neighbourhoods, landscapes, commitments and concerns. Neither group is homogeneous, and this chapter examines some significant conflicts, but people of each group have found ways to collaborate for protection of the ecological and spiritual integrity of the sacred mountain Gulaga. In this chapter I follow the conflicted histories, and conclude with a series of interviews that I conducted with a local dairy farmer, a White man by the name of Mal

Dibden. Mal describes the changes he has undergone in articulating a moral presence for himself, and he discusses his efforts to inscribe his life into place and time.

It will become clear that the resilience of the mountain has been a significant part of the story, and I will suggest that the resilience of individual human beings and of groups of humans in all their complexity is equally part of the story. The story of the mountain includes the story of reconciliation among people and with Nature, and thus tells us that alternatives to the status quo not only exist among us, but exist in wounded and contested places such as forests. Such stories show us how to imagine resilience in a recuperative mode, how to imagine alternative futures, and thus how we might work step by step towards decolonisation.

Resilience of a Mountain

Captain Cook came sailing up the eastern coast of Australia in April 1770. He saw 'a pretty high mountain' that looked to him remarkably like a camel, and so he named it Mt Dromedary (Forestry Commission 1987). According to the local Aboriginal people, Captain Cook discovered neither their mountain nor them. They had been advised of his journey, and many of their compatriots from the inland had joined them at the coast to watch him sail by. The Aboriginal people responsible for this mountain are the Umbarra people (People of the black duck) of the Yuin nation. These people call their mountain Gulaga. Today the mountain is a National Park.

The mountain is an extinct volcano, linked geologically to a smaller hill named Little Dromedary and to Montague Island. From the perspective of Yuin people, the mountain – Gulaga – is a Dreaming woman, and she is linked by story to her two sons Little Dromedary and Montague Island. Gulaga is a Dreaming place, a sacred site, for local Aboriginal people. It is a place to which they are uniquely connected as a consequence of creation.

The mountain is located near Central Tilba and Tilba Tilba, and is seen from all the neighbouring communities: Narooma, Bermagui, Cobargo, and a few others. This is a rural area of farms, state forests, national parks, and, increasingly, of tourism and retirement homes. Central Tilba is a heritage town; it is an attractive and popular tourist site. Many local people in the area have successfully made the shift out of primary production – dairy farming and logging – and into the kinds of economic ventures that work with tourism: wood-turning galleries, bed and breakfast cottages, and so on.

The Aboriginal people and the mountain have both experienced the full gamut of colonisation since the 1840s when White people first settled in the grassy plains around Narooma. I will discuss the history of the mountain first. Between 1877 and 1910 it was the site of intensive mining: 335 kilograms of gold were extracted in that period. Much of the rainforest was destroyed in the area where miners worked, and the damage to ecosystems was severe. According to foresters, however, it has now regenerated (Forestry Commission 1987). Mal Dibden, the dairy farmer to whose words I will return, described this period:

> The place was totally raped, turned upside down, burnt everywhere. It was just like the action of a mob of pigs. The mountain had sat there for 80 million years minding its own business, and then came this twenty years of damage. It must have been reeling.

Timbergetters have been active on the mountain for most of the history of settlement. During the period 1880–1970 when this area was a thriving dairy community, farmers cleared up the slopes to the point where it just was not viable any more. Human disruptions opened areas on the mountain that were subsequently swept by violent fire, and there have been some savage fires. The 1952 fire is remembered vividly: people down at the coast at Bermagui said that the mountain went up like an atom bomb.

In spite of these impacts, the mountain is botanically rich. There are three major types of rainforest as well as several types of Eucalypt forest. According to the Working Plan of Management: 'Botanically, Mt Dromedary Flora Reserve is of unusual interest and of high conservation significance ... It includes a large and diverse range of plant communities, and in particular, for its latitude, of rainforest communities. A number of these communities are quite disjunct and separate from similar stands elsewhere on the South Coast.' A number of the species recorded are at their southern most known occurrence in the Reserve, while many others are uncommon or rare (Mt Dromedary 1985: 6).

In the 1960s Mal Dibden started agitating to get some protection for the mountain. In 1966 it was incorporated into Bodalla

State Forest, and as part of that transfer, the eastern side of the mountain and the summit were designated 'Mount Dromedary Flora Reserve' under the Forestry Act in recognition of the unique concentration of different plant communities. The Flora Reserve was managed by a committee whose members included a few local White people, a few local Aboriginal people, and a few foresters. The ecological significance of the Flora Reserve led to its inclusion in the Register of the National Trust and listing by the Australian Heritage Commission. In 1986 the NSW Government nominated the Flora Reserve for inclusion in the World Heritage List (Forestry Commission 1987). By 2001 it had become Gulaga National Park, as it is now constituted.

Resilience of a People

The history of the mountain reflects the history of White people in this region: mining and logging were sporadic activities while small-scale farming endured until the collapse of the rural communities in the 1960s. The White people with whom I spoke looked back on the time before mechanisation as a time when they had close and often warm relationships with local Aboriginal people. In contrast, the Yuin people with whom I spoke emphasised their sense of apartness throughout the 20th century.

The colonisation history of the local Aboriginal people is punctuated by two main periods of concentrated brutality. The first was in the mid-19th century. Devastating epidemics, dispossession and some massacres caused the loss of about 90 per cent of the population. There followed a period of adaptive coexistence in the last decades of the 19th century. During this interesting period some Aboriginal people became owners of land under Anglo-Australian title. Farming and fishing were the two main activities that articulated with a cash economy, for Whites and for Aborigines. There were Aboriginal cricket teams and musical events. Aboriginal people asked for and were allocated a school. At the same time, the ceremonial life, while diminished, was still a rich part of the Aboriginal culture of the region. This period of adaptive coexistence came to an end early in the 20th century with a new wave of dispossession and confinement on reserves under the rule of the Aborigines Protection Board. In this period language and formal ceremonies were curtailed and suppressed, and Aboriginal ownership of land under Anglo-Australian title was extinguished. By the 1950s assimilation policies and practices were actively moving people into White society, and at the same time a lot of the former reserve land was sold off (summarised from Cameron 1987 and Goodall 1996). The battles for Yuin people's bodies and souls were similar to those I have discussed in Part II. Christianity was thrust upon people as they were confined to missions. Many of today's adults were taken from their families and institutionalised for greater or lesser periods, and many families are now struggling to regain their cohesion and sense of community.

Yuin people of this region inhabit a homeland dominated by two major sacred mountains: Gulaga and Biamanga. In addition to the cultural significance of the mountains, there is an historical significance to the fact that through all of these years of conquest, policy shifts, and enforced evictions, the mountains have remained constant. They are visible from surrounding communities, so that even people who were moved into White settlements like Cobargo were still in sight of the mountains. They were there on the horizon: a visible presence signalling identity, belonging, responsibility, and people's relationships to the sacred. The perduring relationship is one of connection. Gulaga, in particular, is understood and experienced as an active presence that exerts a hold on people. Yuin people say that no matter where they go, the mountain calls them back (see Byrne 1984).

One of the men I interviewed in 1989 said that in one way it is like homesickness. When you are away your thoughts begin to wander, and they wander to Gulaga and you want to go home. In another way, according to this same man, it is like a magnet. No matter how far you go (and this man has been very far away at times), you feel a pull that draws your thoughts and your feelings back to the mountain. He explained that this calling back is part of the living power of Gulaga.

Yuin people's efforts to protect both of these mountains are well documented (for example, Byrne 1984; Kelly 1975; Egloff 1979; Rose 1990; Rose et al 2003). At this time, each mountain is a National Park, and their hand-back to Yuin people is being negotiated. Visitor access to Gulaga is defined as open to walkers; cultural tours are run by the Umbarra Aboriginal Cultural Centre in Wallaga Lake. The tours take visitors to Gulaga, or to Biamanga, or out onto Wallaga Lake.

'Respect Law'

In 1989 the Forestry Commission of New South Wales (hereafter referred to as Forestry) began a timber removal project on the west side of the mountain. Yuin women and their relatives sought to ban that logging, and they were joined in their action by White people from all of the communities within sight of the mountain.

The women took their concerns to Forestry, and to the NSW National Parks and Wildlife Service. Forestry agreed to halt logging while the matter was investigated. There was already a precedent for restraint from logging on the grounds of cultural significance in relation to nearby Biamanga (Egloff 1979). I was approached by the Umbarra women and formally asked to assist; once Forestry agreed that in their view I was a suitable person, I began the task.

The main basis of the women's action was that the mountain is a sacred place, one of a series of sacred mountains along the south coast. Gulaga is a Dreaming woman; the mountain is her body. There are portions of the mountain where men can go, and portions where only women can go. The main division is into two sides, east and west, and the west side – the side that was being logged – is exclusively for women. The mountain is ringed with tall standing stones called guardians, some of which are male, some female. The trees are gendered too. As well, the mountain is home to a number of extraordinary beings who guard it, and whose presence sustains its spiritual integrity. The mountain was an initiation and teaching place 'from time immemorial', and in recent years people have publicly organised teaching and other ritual activities there.

The late Guboo Ted Thomas, one of the senior Yuin people with responsibilities for Gulaga and other sites, explained:

> There are powerful places in the mountain, blessed by the Great Spirit. There are rocks I call my cathedral. It is more powerful than a man made church. We don't have glass windows or statues of angels, to make it sacred. These rocks were not put here by cranes they were put here by Mother nature. These rocks are where you should sit and meditate to understand the Great Spirit. (c, 1999: 15)[17]

Underlying the action to stop logging, there was a sustained belief among Yuin people that the mountain is theirs: they belong to it, and it belongs to them (discussed in Rose 1990). As Ann Thomas explained in the Umbarra Cultural Centre's video 'Journey to the Dreamtime', made in 1996:

> Our creation stories on the south coast tell of Tunku and Ngardi coming down from the star. They came from the star to this beautiful land. They became this, this Earth. They became part of the stones, the rocks, the clay. They became part of the trees and the mountains itself, and the ocean. And they developed from the Earth. All our energies and everything else that we are, are part of the rocks at Gulaga and every other teaching place.

Aboriginal people's opposition to logging action on Gulaga was powerfully felt and powerfully expressed. One woman with whom I worked closely said: 'you've got to understand. I'd give my life for that mountain.'

The convergence of opposition to Forestry was striking. Most of the settler-descended people in the area also opposed logging activity. This situation would probably have been different if a significant proportion of the local population was engaged in logging, as Peace's work on forestry disputes indicates (Peace 1999). Local people formed several action groups; the most prominent were the Gulaga Protection Group, and the Women's Forest Action Group. While there was a convergence of opposition, there was no unanimity in the reasons. Many White people, who in fact did not believe that the mountain was sacred but who still thought it was significant for one reason or another, opposed the logging. They spoke of the need to protect water supplies, to control erosion, and to sustain biodiversity.

Yuin people spoke of these issues too. Gulaga was and still is a protection area for all sorts of plants, animals, and birds. Historically, Najanuga (Little Dromedary) and Barunguba (Montague Island) off the coast functioned as bird sanctuaries (Rose 1990: 67). In the video 'Sites We Want to Keep' Guboo Ted Thomas stated that the name Najanuga means 'powerful home'. The significance of Najanuga as a resource site for birds' eggs is documented there as well as by Kelly (1975: 4). According to Guboo Ted, birds were protected in the area around Najanuga; only old people gathered eggs from Najanuga, and they always took a limited number. Najanuga is thus one of the original bird sanctuaries of the continent. Women also possess knowledge concerning Najanuga which deepens the understanding provided by Guboo Ted and which is strictly their own.

Just as there was convergence around ecological issues, so too was there a degree of convergence around the matter of the sacred. Many of the settler-descended people involved in these groups knew many of the local Yuin people, and had known for some time that the mountain was sacred to them. Some of these White people had also come to their own understanding that this was a sacred mountain. That is, some of the local White people understood the mountain to be sacred in reference to themselves as well as to Aborigines. Some of them understood themselves to have been drawn by the power of this place. Thus while they deferred to the Aboriginal people's statements of sacred significance, and regarded Aborigines as the primary spiritual custodians, many of them asserted that the mountain was sacred to them too, that it influenced their lives, that they had assumed responsibilities towards the mountain, and that their lives would be diminished if the mountain were damaged. Some of these people had participated in teaching and healing events organised by Yuin elders Ann and Guboo Ted Thomas; these events have included Indigenous and settler-descended people.

The teachings of both the women and men concern Law and respect. According to Merv Penryth, also speaking on the Umbarra Cultural Centre video:

> Darama's creation is all our relations. What we're going through is the respect Law: respect to the elders. Respect to the trees, to the rocks, to the water, to all sacred and significant sites that we have.

The convergence of concern for the sacred significance of the mountain was quite clearly the result of the generosity of local Aboriginal people. They shared stories and teachings, and they shared the place in the richness of its power. They are aware that shared knowledge can readily be appropriated, and thus become subjected to violence. Frédérique Apffel-Marglin (1996b: 142–43) shows us that there is a possibility of doubled violence in appropriation. The first violence is theft, and the second, she writes, is an 'invisible violence' that robs people 'of their power to be perceived as possible resources for alternatives to modernity' (p. 143). The violence alluded to here is the violence I have been discussing throughout as an abrogation of ethics: appropriation deprives people of their power to be present to others in their own history and knowledge.

I want to be clear that Yuin people have their own restrictions on what they will share, and that these restrictions include a number of factors in addition to the quantum consideration that they will not share everything. Other factors include context, gender, age, and trust. People negotiate a fine line between generosity and appropriation, and at this time their trust has largely been reciprocated, and their sharing has helped them and others to achieve goals towards which they have worked with enormous passion. The fact that Aboriginal and settler-descended people were asserting, separately and together, the sacred quality of the mountain bears out the thesis put forward by Alf Hornborg (1994: 250) that Indigenous people make a pivotal contribution to environmental discourse by having 'redefined its framework so that it is becoming increasingly legitimate to evoke concepts of sanctity'.

In addition, Yuin elders have given permission to local groups to use the mountain. This has meant that people whose spiritual practice was not Aboriginal, but who approached the elders and the mountain with respect, were given permission to conduct their practice there. In this context permission is an important term. Nothing in the western legal system prevents people from engaging in spiritual practice on the mountain as long as they obey the standard park rules. The permission of the elders is more in the nature of a blessing – consent confers its own power.

To return to Forestry and logging: I completed my investigations and offered two main proposals. The first was that Forestry desist from logging, and the second was that they liaise with the Yuin women to develop workable mechanisms for consultation so that they could jointly determine a boundary beyond which there would be no logging. Forestry agreed to these proposals, and the western side of the mountain is not logged.

In January 2001 the whole mountain was incorporated into a new National Park, named Gulaga, that also comprised the Wallaga Lake and Goura reserves. Wallaga Lake itself is not included in the National Park and many residents are worried about the future of this important estuarine ecosystem. Their concern is that development may overtake the lake in spite of its award-winning plan of management that excludes further lake-side development. The area within the Park is managed by the NSW National Parks and Wildlife Service and is scheduled to be handed back to Yuin people for joint management. This organisation has a superb statement of reconciliation, and it is actively seeking to implement its reconciliation commitments in daily practice and in specific policy. It is now experiencing changes to itself as a result of its reconciliation endeavours. The 'Statement of Reconciliation' from the staff of the NSW National Parks and Wildlife Services acknowledges the violence of the past, and the pain of today, as well as the need to move forward with care and respect:

> We acknowledge the suffering and injustice that resulted from colonisation and that this continues today for many Aboriginal people. We feel regret and sorrow that the loss of their traditional lands has been a source of enduring pain to Aboriginal people. As people working in a government land management agency, we acknowledge a special responsibility in finding creative and positive ways to move forward together with a shared understanding of the past.[18]

The integrity of the mountain and the generosity of the Yuin people have drawn other people with a spiritual orientation towards the area. Thus, along with tourism and other industries, the sense of sacred place also contributes to the quality of the local community. Recently, for example, the Dzogchen Community of Australia purchased a large block of land in the foothills of the mountain and established a residence and teaching centre for the Rinpoche Chogyal Namkhai Norbu.

It came as a shock to many people in the area when, in 2001, a local shooting club announced plans for a shooting range in the foothills of the mountain. The proposal would have had people circling the mountain on narrow dirt roads to get to the western side, and then shooting across a gully into another low hill. Gulaga's distinctive presence and shape would have been the immediate backdrop to the target range, and the sounds of shooting would have pervaded the mountain and the surrounding region. The gender of the gun hit me like the return of the repressed. The gun folk chose a site and vista that could not possibly have better captured the battlefields of colonisation: the guns, the sacred site, the woman's body as a target range – it was almost like, but never actually was, a parody.

Local people formed a new action group, Narooma/Tilba Residents' Action Group, to co-ordinate opposition to the shooting complex. Again, alliances of settler and Indigenous people worked together, not without difficulties but with success. This proposal was set aside.

Mal's Stories: Report on 'Earth Logic'

Mal Dibden had worked to get the Flora Reserve put in place, and was on the Advisory Committee; he was active in working against logging but tried to keep a low profile, in keeping with his status as a local farmer. In 1990 the historian Peter Read and I worked together on a pilot project investigating White Australians' attachments to place. We decided to go to the Tilba area and interview Mal Dibden in depth. Pete Read and I conducted most of the interviews I am drawing on here with Mal in 1990 (see also Read 1992).

Mal started off with a 400-acre farm called Spring Hills that had been in his mother's family. It is right up against Gulaga, and much of it is too steep to farm. His father purchased the place in 1948, and Mal worked there with him. He had spent his childhood holidays there, and the place was already dear to him. Over the years he bought more and more properties. Some are on the flatter land near Wallaga lake and are pretty good dairy country. Most, like Spring Hills, are poor dairy country, with a lot of bush. On most sides his land is bordered by national parks, state forests, wildlife preserves, and the lake, so that, as he says, the boundaries aren't really boundaries at all.

He had 1300 acres in 1990, of which only about 300 were cleared. That is to say that less than a quarter of his land was economically productive, and since then he has had to sell more land. In this area property values and property taxes are rising very rapidly, and Mal needs a cash income. Like many farmers, he operates under a large financial debt.

The philosopher Emil Fackenheim (1994: 5) says that in dark times we have to go to school with life. Mal has done exactly that. He calls the school Nature, and he has worked out for himself a philosophy of life that he shared with Pete Read and me in extended interviews. Nature, in Mal's view, is more powerful than humans, and a human life lived well is a life that has been 'knocked into shape' by Nature. He seems to be saying that society offers ideas, expertise, and directions for action that allow us to kid ourselves that we're in charge. Getting knocked into shape by Nature is a process of realising the folly of thinking you are in control.

In chapter 2, I discussed Mathews' proposal that we would better understand Nature as a process than as a thing. I linked her philosophical approach to research in conservation biology, suggesting that resilience is a key concept and process in understanding Nature's way of doing things. Mal takes a similar approach. For him, Nature is an active force which he encounters with pleasure, awe, and humility.

Much of Mal's thinking moves between the extremes of the forest and the cleared land. The farmers, and the former farming communities that he loves so much, were thoughtless in their clearing of the bush, and Mal lives that legacy. Thus, for him, farm and forest are strongly alternative modes of engaging with Nature. Mal loves them both, but valorises them differently. It is a tension he does not try to resolve, minimise, or justify.

The ratio of bush to cleared land on Mal's blocks means that most of the land does not produce a cash income:

> It's a privilege to own and burden to try and hold.
>
> It doesn't produce much, unless you want to cut the trees down, and the rates around here are enormous. So, you've just got to be crazy to kid yourself that you can hold onto it in the long term.
>
> You've got to be honest with yourself, really. For me, my beef effort, and even the dairy effort are only efforts I'm making to kid myself and kid the banks that I'm a farmer.

The original farm of 400 acres only had 160 cleared acres, but as Mal says, what was cleared was beautiful in his eyes.

> It was amazing how tidy it was, and what a good job they did do, as far as keeping it tidy was concerned.
>
> I'm still not convinced that it ever should have been cleared in any way, ever. But it was cleared, and it did look nice.
>
> I like to remember and think of sections that really looked wonderful. You get that mountain country tidied up, and the granite rocks poking out through the green grass, and it's fantastic mountain country, mountain gazing country. To look at. Not for any other purpose, but to look at.

Mal treasured the aesthetics of it, and also the self-supporting community that was associated with it.

> They were only small dairies. And they didn't make much money, and they didn't have much money. It wasn't economically all that wonderful ... It was a particularly close knit community, particularly in a cheese-making district because you

> delivered milk to a factory every morning. So you met every farmer, practically every morning, seven days a week ... You had community effort on each individual farm, and you had community involvement because people met almost every day.
>
> But thinking since, when you think of all those farms around the mountain, that steep country that should never have been cleared in the first place. When you think of the numbers of people that it supported, just for a short period, you know, only thirty or forty or fifty years. And the work that was involved in doing it, and the soil that must have eroded away as a result of all their efforts ploughing hillsides. It was just crazy.

The rural way of life that Mal treasured has collapsed, and he speaks of a double shame: the shame of clearing in the first place, and the shame of losing those self-supporting communities to mechanisation and development.

> If you look at it one way, you'd have to say it was a waste and a shame. You can look at it in so many different ways. You can say well it's a shame now the way it's gone, neglected, only rabbits and regeneration; but you can look at it and be honest and say, its a shame it was ever cleared in the first place.
>
> So, maybe it's all a shame.

Mal started life as a keen farmer:

> You get knocked into shape by droughts and financial situations, and, yeah, I did some things that looked pretty good, and I was pretty cocky about it for a time. Like, I raised cattle for beef, extra beef efforts that went along with what agricultural scientists said I should be doing. I had things that I thought were looking pretty good at one stage. And then Whang, four years of drought, and these lovely cattle that I'd raised, and the nice pasture that looked good, it turned to dust, and the cattle ended up most of them dead. Most of them dead over four years. That comes as a pretty fair message. When it's all over, that is. When you're going through it you keep kidding yourself that it can't go on much longer, it's going to rain soon, you're going to get out of it, and you're going to be a good farmer, when really you're a dreadful farmer. Because droughts come every so often no matter what.
>
> When you're young you don't know. [You only learn] because you've been knocked into shape by the lessons of Nature.

To get a closer look at Nature, we have to go to the mountain. Gulaga/Mt Dromedary has been part of Mal's life since childhood as a presence that towered above him. He did not actually go up onto the forested areas of the mountain till after the 1952 fire. It was easy to travel up the mountain then, and he and his father rode up on horses. They came to one part that had not been burnt, and it had a great impact on him.

Mal compared the impact of his first time in the mountain forest with what he thought it might have been like for Aboriginal people to have been taken up there for religious purposes. This event was for him a transformative experience which would be with him for the rest of his life. Here as elsewhere, when Mal spoke of his deepest experiences and beliefs, he expressed himself in conjunction with Aboriginal people, as if talking about Aboriginal people enabled him to articulate a spirituality that he was hesitant to claim for himself.

> The impact on young people would be such that they never would forget; a very deep feeling straight away; they could feel the sacredness. Not to live there, but to keep it in reverence in their hearts and in their minds for the rest of their lives. That's the sort of impact it had on me.

Mal started returning to the mountain in the 1960s and he kept coming back. In his words:

> I didn't come back again for quite a long while. It was in the sixties or so before I started becoming interested in it again. Rough times on the farm, disappointments, pasture improvements that did badly, the drought, the cattle dying, that changed my life. Thinking back on it now, it doesn't mean a thing. You're mad to get worked up about those things, but when you're younger, you put a fair bit of work into it, and think you've done a good job over it, and if it's all wiped out by Nature with a few years of drought, it has an impact on you. I don't know why I started coming up here again, really.
>
> As the Aboriginals say, it seemed to draw me back.

Mal took Pete and me up the mountain, and we spent a day straggling along behind him with camera and tape recorder, while he took off his thongs and leaped around as nimble as a goat, picking leeches off his feet, and pointing out to us particular places and trees that he had been visiting and observing for decades.

> I feel that it's so beautiful, and it looks after itself. It's completely natural, a natural perfect garden. Nothing looks out of place except intruders, and I class myself as being an intruder.
>
> I feel it is a very spiritual place, really. It has more spiritual – if that's the right word – more spiritual meaning to me than walking into a church anywhere. I think this particular type of forest, being such a lovely tranquil cool temperate rainforest ... I feel more tranquil and peaceful and responsible in appreciating the values of it, so I'm even careful about where I put my feet. There's a responsibility to the beauty, and to the values it must have meant to Aboriginals, and does now.

Mal was not sure if 'spirituality' was the right word. I am not sure either. We simply do not have a vocabulary that works well for us in talking about these relationships to place. However, looking at the term in context, Mal's 'spirituality' requires that Nature be understood as an active force, something living, something to be encountered. I find three interconnected dimensions of Mal's word 'Nature'. The first is that Nature is self-organising. For example, he contrasts the mountain forest with the rainforest in the National Botanic Gardens in Canberra, saying that they try, but they just don't succeed in making something that is anything like the real rainforest. The more important point concerning self-organisation is that the forest is perfect, as it is.

> It never needs human attention. It is beauty which just works itself out without anyone picking up the sticks or putting things in order. It's all in order anyway, even a stick that's fallen on the ground out of a tree. A new object on the ground still doesn't look like a foreign thing.

A second dimension is that the forest is active on its own behalf. This is part of resilience: it is self-repairing. Nature takes its own back and re-forms and replenishes itself. An example is all the old farm equipment around Mal's place. The pig pens are caving in and covered with vines, the old World War II trucks are up to the axles in soil, and have weeds growing out the windows. Mal's concept of taking care of place is non-interventionist: he is not looking to restore the land to an imaginary perfection; he lets Nature 'take its own back'.

The third dimension is that as Nature is a living and active presence, it reaches out to people. It is not only present in its self-organising life, but seeks to organise those within its ambit as well.

> You've got to get the impact, be hit by the beauty. It's almost got to startle you, I reckon, to stop you in your tracks and just make you change yourself to a degree while you're enjoying the beauty of it.

Nature, then, organises relationships. The fact that the mountain does not need you to organise it is counterbalanced by the fact that if you put your body into the place with an attitude of attention, the place will organise you by requiring you to make changes in yourself.

> The hard knocks have sorted me out. I can see my mistakes, and the good values have come into my head. I can take [the lessons of the mountain] with me. I'll never lose it. And it was in the minds of the Aboriginals too. The mountain drew them back.

The lessons that Mal has learned by getting knocked into shape by Nature and by going to the mountain inspire him to keep on working to protect the land and waters of his region.

The tension between forest and cleared land is a tension between reverence and labour. His reverence for the perfection of Nature is in contradictory tension with the labour of clearing/transforming the land. Mal's great respect for Aboriginal culture is founded in his view that they had developed a form of reverential labour. That is, there was no contradiction for them, as there is for him, between reverence and labour. He stated the contrast vividly:

> I'm sitting on the edge of the lake where Aboriginals have lived for probably thirty or forty thousand years without cutting one single tree down – not thousands, but one single tree. And they were healthy and happy people, healthier, probably than I am now and healthier than most Europeans are who've tipped the place upside down to make a dollar out of it.

Most of the current evidence of human labour in the area is degradation: the lakes are silting up, the water systems are becoming fouled, and so on. In contrast, Mal is still searching for a form of reverential labour. His compromise is to work part of his land and keep the much greater portion of it out of production. So his life problems circle back around to economics, and the terrible pressure to be commercially viable:

> I don't own this land at all. In no time at all somebody else will be scratching their head and worrying about how to hang on to it. So I don't own it, I'm just the galoot who's trying to hold it

together. If you think of it that way – that you do own the land – you start thinking of monetary values and it really becomes upsetting in the end. I try to disregard it because you do realise that it is worth a heap of money. And you just love it so much you don't want to sell any of it, so what's the point of it being worth a heap of money? It only makes it harder to hang on to it.

As Nature reached out and changed Mal, he had to query everything about himself, his society, and the public values that surrounded him. His conclusions are related to his lifelong problem of holding land in a commodity economy:

> We've all been conned. I'm pretty sure we've all been conned into a system where we've got to have heaps of money just to maintain the basics.
>
> I think it's going to be extremely difficult to coast along with it and survive. The pressures are too great.

Pete and I asked Mal if he would do it all again – all the farming, all the clearing – and he said 'No'. Pete told Mal about some other people we interviewed who in the 1950s had dropped out of city life and gone to make a farm in the country, and who now express an awareness of the damage they did as well as feeling pride in the work of their lives. Their view was that in the 1950s government policy and general social knowledge had it that it was a good thing to be in primary production and to feed the world. These folks said, 'sure we cut a lot of trees down. Maybe it was wrong, but we enjoyed it, and we had a good life.'

We put this proposition to Mal, and he would not agree. Rather, he insisted on a deeper and more problematic engagement:

> I'm not sure of the logic. I'm not sure of the Earth logic. The relationship of humans to the Earth. That's the serious question, I think, really. And, it scares me. I think things are running riot, really, and out of hand. It's showing up all over the world, where economics is governing people's relationships with the Earth. It shouldn't be economics at all. It should be sensibilities and responsibilities.

School of Life

Stories of Gulaga and Mal Dibden are not paths that take us to known places. Rather, they help us put one foot in front of the other in dark and risky times. Mal's life exemplifies in an extremely positive way what I take to be the great problem for settlers: that of regrounding our accountability in time and place. I have wanted to show that his way in the world is not without anxiety, conflict, and bouts of despair. And yet I see that Mal shows us what it means to be a settler with a conscience and with enormous love for a particular place in this world. In light of Mal's testimony, I would want to use the word 'decolonisation' in an extremely strong sense to mean the unmaking of the regimes of violence that enforce the disconnection of moral accountability from time and place. These stories unfold in real time and are not over. They tell themselves differently to different people, and cannot be encapsulated once and for all. I see four significant stories unfolding at Gulaga.

One story concerns *reconciliation*. It involves Indigenous people whose connections to place and to the knowledge of sacred places is alive and well. At the same time, it involves settlers who, in their own lives or the lives of their forebears, actively or passively promoted the practices that sought most specifically to eradicate these Indigenous people, to wipe out their knowledge, and to destroy their connections to place. How these people manage to come together across this abyss is itself a phenomenon of settler societies that cannot fully be accounted for by conventional analysis.

Reconciliation started long before Forestry threatened the mountain. The work that Mal and others undertook to protect the place in the plurality of its ecological, historical, and sacred dimensions was a form of decolonising reconciliation that began before either of the words had a public profile. Forestry itself promoted reconciliation, first by generating the need for people to come together, and then by their responsiveness to the local communities. The action taken to protect the mountain keeps rolling along: there were nature protection zones, and now there is a National Park. Increasingly, there is the understanding that these precious landscapes are connected, and that the zones of protection must connect and incorporate broader ecological and sacred landscapes.

A second story concerns *resilience*. The mountain had been dug up, turned over, and filled with tracks and flying fox conveyances during the brief period of mining. It had been filled with coupes and skids in the course of forestry. Whole sections of forest had been taken out and replaced with uniform and crowded little nurseries. It had been burnt deliberately and accidentally, and had gone up 'like an atom bomb'. The biological legacy of diversity remained and has reasserted itself. The rainforests are taking over mine sites, forests return into the coupes, and the dynamic interaction between wet and dry forests continues its delicate dance. The power of the mountain is perhaps more evident today than ever before: not only has it endured, it has recuperated the life-giving dedication known as resilience.

A third story concerns *the sacred*. People who experienced the mountain as a sacred place worked together without demanding a dogma of belief. This is a story that is full of respect (and contestation) for place, and respect (and contestation) for people. It is full of reverential labour to sustain the integrity of place. The story of the sacred runs counter to the regimes of violence that are labelled development, and thus seems to fit what Mal calls the Earth logic. The sacred bends the world towards a balance that sustains relationships between humans and the earth in life-giving propensity.

A fourth story is about *love*. It looks like a love story on first glance because that is what people say it is. Mal says that he loves the place so much. That is what Yuin people say, and that is what many other settler-descended people in the area are saying.

We can think back to the great migrations in which settlers detached themselves from their home places, or were forcibly expelled, and in which they conquered other people's homes. The wounded space of our lives is doubled up: one dimension consists in the rupture of an indigenous cultural system of geography; of sacred geographies as well as the social and ecological geographies. The other dimension of wounding is the effects on European geography of transporting it to the antipodes, and imposing it on a colony. Here at Gulaga, improbably, the wounding has not yet been mortal for Indigenous people, for settlers, or for country.

We are in the midst of immense harm, after more than a century of damage, and in a time when regimes of violence are becoming ever more powerful. We are listening to a man who cleared the land, cut down rainforest, and loves the farming community which used to be the context of his life. This damage, and the various moments of shame that Mal identifies, provide a context in which his love springs forth with improbably greater power.

Mal talks eloquently about Nature, and in light of the ecological and social history and the contemporary life of the place, we need to amplify and contextualise what Nature actually is and does here. Gulaga is Nature in our conflicted settler societies. Nature is the mountain, in exemplar. She is a Dreaming woman and a sacred site. She has been wounded, torn up, and threatened with being transformed into a commodity. She has been proposed as the large target for the big guns of the advanced shooters, and she has been burnt, loved, cherished, protected, defiled, ridiculed, and yet is there today in all her resilience. Not all places have endured so well, and not all places will be able to recover in this way, or at this pace. But let us be aware always of this fact: Nature for us is history, conquest, and damage; by our own ethical presence Nature may become for us resilience, reconciliation, and love.

How we relate to Nature must always therefore be painfully complex. We may gain courage from the fact that the process of relationship is not one-way. I thought at first that Mal was inscribing himself into the mountain, and only belatedly did I come to understand how deeply the mountain was inscribing itself into Mal. This is a story of Mal's love of the mountain, as he says. But it is also a story of how Nature not only knocks you, and forces you to change yourself, but of how Nature pulls you into love.

AFTERWORD

Why do we listen to the stories of others, if not to hear? And having heard, would we not desire to respond? Simply to listen is to be drawn into a world of ethical encounter: to hear is to witness; to witness is to become entangled. I have written this book in a time when catastrophe surrounds us but has not yet hit us fully. In arguing for recuperation I have suggested that the means for change, the inspiration for change, and the desire for change are all around us. I have sought to witness for alternatives, to bring more fully into our ken some of the possibilities of our present moment.

Decolonisation, I have argued, rests on a broad interpretation of Hobbles Danaiyarri's view that these days now we can turn away from cruelty and become mates. I draw out this statement to include the non-human world, and link it to David Burrumarra's perception that if we looked properly we would see 'God' in the natural world. In seeking to sustain the connections between social and ecological decolonisation, I explore numerous paths toward decolonisation and the affirmation of life processes, as well as exploring some of the paths of cruelty and the multiplication of death work. These stories, I claim, show us how to recognise resilience, how to imagine alternatives, and how to sustain moral action in dark and risky times.

In attending to the here and now of our lives, and in working with some decolonising journeys, I argue against 'the wild' and for forms of countermodernity. The ethical challenge of decolonisation illuminates a ground for powerful presence. Against domination it asserts relationality, against control it asserts mutuality, against hyperseparation it asserts connectivity, and against claims that rely on an imagined future it asserts engaged responsiveness in the present.

Throughout the book I have argued for a particular kind of presence-to-the-world. I mean this presence to be situated in history and in place, and I mean it to be available to social and ecological 'others'. Attentive and alert to the here and now of life, the kind of presence I argue for, in addition to being situated and available, is relational, connective, mutual, and committed. I do not claim that engaging in passionately connected forms of presence can protect us or our world from the risks and violence we now confront. Ethics for decolonisation actually call us into greater vulnerability as well as greater connectivity.

In chapter 10 I proposed that work that facilitates resilience may be one of the most powerful and life-affirming forms of reconciliation available to us. Presence in the engaged mode I have been arguing for is closely akin to the connectivities of flourishing and resilient life processes. In accepting the challenge to be present in ethical relation and mutuality, we take a human stance that aligns us with the world. We acknowledge our place in and of the world and we accept that we live and die with the world. Within this place of connectivity it becomes possible for us to inscribe our moral presence, and each inscription promotes the beauty and resilience of life's struggle against the ramifying death work of contemporary local and globalising violence. In considering the possibilities for ethical action, I come to use the term 'decolonisation' in an extremely strong sense to mean the unmaking of the regimes of violence that promote the disconnection of moral accountability from time and place.

Stephen Muecke writes that writing itself is a trace of paths to be followed (1997: 231). I intend that the traces I have presented here, the results of conversation, thought, and commitment, will indicate possibilities. The paths toward decolonisation are many; and yet the ethics hold fast.

NOTES

1 Robyn Davidson used the term 'mantra' to describe this wonderful vernacular phrase; see also Mathews (1999b: 95).
2 The term 'ecocide' was brought to my attention by Grinde & Johansen's (1995) study of Native Peoples of North America.
3 This term was given prominence in Maurice Blanchot's study *Writing the Disaster*. It was rendered more accessible by Langer (1991). I use the term in a more expansive way than either of these scholars; while in no way seeking to denigrate the power of the term to denote the death world of the Holocaust, it seems to me to be appropriate to consider that wounded space is space which contains visible as well as invisible wounds, and that there is a justification for considering the visible wounds not only because they matter in their own right, but also because knowledge of their existence can lead to a more profound appreciation of invisible wounds.
4 <http://www.gg.gov.au/speeches/pdfs/2001/sp010607.pdf>
5 The sketches included here were traced directly from the tanks by Darrell Lewis. He then photographed the tracings. This technique reduces the amount of background 'noise', enabling the particular piece to be read relatively easily.
6 I am not yet aware of Aboriginal women's involvement in cattle events, although North American First Nations women compete in a number of events. Andrea Lemon (1996), however, makes a strong connection between rodeo and country music; she spotlights a number of Indigenous women musicians who are key figures in the country music scene, notably Ruby Hunter and the Mills Sisters.
7 The vernacular term 'O.P.' means overproof rum, i.e., rum over 100 proof.
8 Translated into English from the original Latin by P. Dalton, and held in the Archives of the Jesuit headquarters in Melbourne, Victoria.
9 Stanner's analysis lays the ground for his discussion of the introduction of the 'All-Mother' religious movement from the Victoria River valley. Swain (1993) takes up these issues in greater detail. Povinelli (2002) has recently brought a wonderfully critical analysis to the issues.
10 Chips Mackinolty told me about this event. I was not there at the time, and regret deeply that I was not able to witness it myself.
11 This is not the first time that Christian missionaries have encountered this shift. There have been major transformations in our thinking about the earth. Christianity reversed the Celtic orientations; whereas Celts went down to achieve wisdom and power and to be in touch with the superhuman Underworld, Christians demonised the Underworld and identified the

sky as the source of wisdom and power. Gender is implicated here as well. A poignant Irish story tells of how St Patrick sacrificed the female custodians of a sacred spring, transferring the meaning of the place from the Goddess below to the Father above (W. Brenneman 1991: 150–1). Similarly, missionaries in Yarralin are teaching people the power of God the father, and Jesus the son, and are demanding that people refuse further to acknowledge the power of the earth and of the Dreamings.

12   From memory.
13   Tape recording made by Darrell Lewis in 1990 (see also Schultz & Lewis 1995). The *Newcastle Waters Police Journal*, F493, 5-6-51, contains a report on a 'missionary' giving a mixture similar to raspberry cordial to Aboriginals and taking collections from them. There the concern was that the missionaries might have been supplying alcohol, then an illegal act.
14   The plants Riley discusses are: Karil: *Cucumis* spp, probably trigonus; Gooseberry: *Physalis minima*; Kilipi: *Leichardtia australis*; Tipil: unidentified (unable to locate a specimen); Purlkal: *Vitex acuminata*; Ngaringarin: *Pterocaulon serrulatum*; Yarkalayin: unidentified water plant (unable to locate a specimen); Mintariyij: *Nymphaea violacea*.
15   I do not address here the exact question of intent. It seems manifest that Indigenous people did *not* work towards an abstraction like biodiversity; there is ample evidence that they *do* consciously engage in practices that they found to be good for everybody (see Bright 1995, for example).
16   The authors cited refer to the death of nature, or to nature as expressively dead. I prefer the more neutral term 'inert'. As discussed in chapter 3, we rush into declarations of death (of tribe, language, culture, species, etc.) as ways of punctuating time and process, and such declarations become part of the problem (not part of the solution).
17   These and some of the other quotes in this section also appear in a recent study that Chris Watson and I undertook for the National Parks and Wildlife Service (Rose et al. 2003: 38–56).
18   <www.nationalparks.nsw.gov.au/npws.nsf/Content/Statement+of+reconciliation>

REFERENCES

Aboriginal Land Commissioner 1996, *The Malngin and Nyinin claim to Mistake Creek: Land Claim no. 133; Report and Recommendation of the Aboriginal Land Commissioner*, Australian Government Publishing Service, Canberra.
Abrams, D 1996, *The Spell of the Sensuous: Perception and Language in a More-Than-Human World*, Vintage Books, New York.
Adam, B 1994, 'Running Out of Time. Global Crisis and Human Engagement'. In M Redclift and T Benton (eds), *Social Theory and the Global Environment*, Routledge, London.
Alford, R 1989, 'The Douglas/Daly Region: A Historical Overview to 1900'. Report prepared for the National Trust of Australia (NT).
Alroe, M 1988, 'A Pygmalion Complex Among Missionaries: The Catholic Case in the Kimberley'. In Swain & Rose, *Aboriginal Australian and Christian Missions*, Australian Association for the Study of Religions, Adelaide.
Anderson, M 1997, 'California's Endangered peoples and Endangered Ecosystems', *American Indian Culture and Research Journal*, 21(3): 7–31.
Anthony, D 1986, 'The "Kurgan Culture," Indo-European Origins, and the Domestication of the Horse; A Reconsideration', *Current Anthropology*, 27(4): 291–313.
Apffel-Marglin, F 1996a, 'Introduction: Rationality and the World'. In Apffel-Marglin & Marglin, *Decolonizing Knowledge*, pp. 1–39.
—— 1996b, 'Rationality, the Body, and the World: From Production to Regeneration'. In Apffel-Marglin & Marglin, *Decolonizing Knowledge*, pp. 142–181.
Apffel-Marglin, F, & S Marglin 1996, *Decolonizing Knowledge: From Development to Dialogue*, Clarendon Press, Oxford.
Arendt, H 1958, *The Human Condition*, University of Chicago Press.
—— 1969, 'Reflections on violence'. In R Silvers & B Epstein (eds), *Anthology: Selected Essays from Thirty Years of the New York Review of Books*, NYREV, New York.
—— 1970 [1955], *Men in Dark Times*, Jonathan Cape, London.
Arthur, J 1997, 'An unobtrusive goanna'. In D Rose & A Clarke (eds), *Tracking Knowledge in North Australian Landscapes: Studies in Indigenous and Settler Knowledge Systems*, North Australia Research Unit, Darwin, pp. 37–49.
—— 2003, *The Default Country: A Lexical Cartography of Twentieth-Century Australia*, UNSW Press, Sydney.
Attwood, B, & SG Foster (eds) 2003, *Frontier Conflict: The Australian Experience*, National Museum of Australia, Canberra.

Baker, R, J Davies & E Young 2001, *Working on Country: Contemporary Indigenous Management of Australia's Lands and Coastal Regions*, Oxford University Press, Melbourne.

Bakhtin, M 1981, *The Dialogic Imagination*, University of Texas Press, Austin, TX.

Bar On, B 1993, 'Marginality and Epistemic Privilege'. In L Alcoff & E Potter (eds), *Feminist Epistemologies*, Routledge, New York, pp. 83–100.

Bateson, G 1973 [1972], *Steps to an Ecology of Mind*, Paladin, Granada Publishing, London.

Baudrillard, J 1994, *The Illusion of the End*, Stanford University Press.

Bauman, Z 1993, *Postmodern Ethics*, Blackwell, Oxford.

Benhabib, S 1992, *Situating the Self: Gender, Community and Postmodernism in Contemporary Ethics*, Polity Press, Cambridge.

Benjamin, W 1969, *Illuminations*, ed. and with an Introduction by H Arendt, transl. H Zohn, Schocken Books, New York.

Bercovitch, S 1978, *The American Jeremiad*, University of Wisconsin Press, Madison, WI.

Bernasconi, R, & D Wood (eds) 1988, *The Provocation of Levinas: Rethinking the Other*, Routledge, London.

Berndt, R 1952, 'Surviving influence of Mission contact on the Day River, Northern Territory of Australia', *Neue Zeitschrift fur Missionswissenschaft/Nouvelle Revue de science missionaire*, 8: 1–20.

—— & C Berndt 1948, A Northern Territory Problem: Aboriginal Labour in a Pastoral Area. Unpublished manuscript.

—— & —— 1987, *End of an Era; Aboriginal Labour in the Northern Territory*, Australian Institute of Aboriginal Studies, Canberra.

Bishop, P 1989, *The Myth of Shangri-La: Tibet, Travel Writing and the Western Creation of Sacred Landscape*, Athlone Press, London.

Blanchot, M 1986, *Writing the Disaster*, University of Nebraska Press, Lincoln, NE.

Boer, R, & E Conrad n.d., 'Beholden to Whom: A Manifesto for Biblical Studies'. Manuscript in preparation for publication.

Bolton, G 1981, *Spoils and Spoilers: Australians Make their Environment 1788–1980*, George Allen & Unwin, Sydney.

Bowman, D 1995, 'Why the skillful use of fire is critical for the management of biodiversity in Northern Australia'. In D Rose (ed.), *Country in Flames: Proceedings of the 1994 Symposium on Biodiversity and Fire in North Australia*, Biodiversity Unit, Department of the Environment, Sport and Territories, and the North Australia Research Unit, Canberra and Darwin, pp. 105–12.

—— 1998, 'The impact of Aboriginal landscape burning on the Australian biota', *New Phytologist* 140(3), Tansley Review #101, pp. 385–410.

Brenneman, W 1991, 'Holy Wells of Ireland'. In J Swan (ed.), *The Power of Place; Sacred Ground in Natural and Human Environments*, Quest Books, Wheaton, IL, pp. 107–119.

Bright, A 1995, 'Burn Grass'. In D Rose (ed.), *Country in Flames: Proceedings of the 1994 Symposium on Biodiversity and Fire in North Australia*, Biodiversity Unit, Department of the Environment, Sport and Territories, and the North Australia Research Unit, Canberra & Darwin, pp. 59–62.

Broome, R 1982, *Aboriginal Australians: Black Response to White Dominance*, Allen & Unwin, Sydney.
—— 2003, 'The statistics of frontier conflict'. In Attwood & Foster, *Frontier Conflict*, pp. 88–98.
Brown, P 2004, 'Global warming threatens to kill off a million species', *Guardian Weekly*, 15–24 January, p. 3.
Burridge, K 1960, *Mambu: A Study of Melanesian Cargo Movements and their Ideological Background*, Harper & Row, New York.
Burrumarra, D, with I McIntosh 2002, '*Motj* and the Nature of the Sacred', *Cultural Survival Quarterly*, 26(2): 10.
Byrne, D 1984, *The Mountains Call Me Back: A History of the Aborigines and the Forests of the Far South Coast of N.S.W.*, NSW Ministry of Aboriginal Affairs, Sydney.
Cameron, S 1987, An Investigation of the History of the Aborigines of the Far South Coast of New South Wales in the Nineteenth Century. BLitt thesis, Department of History, Australian National University.
Carter, J 1968, *In the Tracks of the Cattle*, Angus & Robertson, Sydney.
Carter, P 1988, *The Road to Botany Bay: An Exploration of Landscape and History*, Alfred A. Knopf, New York.
—— 1996, *The Lie of the Land*, Faber & Faber, London.
Casper, B 1988, 'Responsibility Rescued'. In Paul Mendes-Flohr (ed.), *The Philosophy of Franz Rosenzweig*, University Press of New England, Hanover, pp. 89–106.
Chakrabarty, D 1997, 'Minority Histories, Subaltern Pasts', *Humanities Research*, Winter: 17–32.
Chinnery, E, to J Turner, Memorandum dated 30.8.40, Australian Archive Services Series F1, Item 52/508.
Churchill, W 1992, 'The Earth is Our Mother: Struggle for American Indian Land and Liberation in the Contemporary United States'. In A Jaimes (ed.), *The State of Native America*, South End Press, Boston MD, pp. 139–88.
Ciancio, O, & S Nocentini 2000, 'Forest Management from Positivism to the Culture of Complexity'. In M Agnoletti & S Anderson (eds), *Methods and Approaches in Forest History*, CABI Publishing, Wallingford, UK, pp. 47–58.
Clark, M 1973, *A History of Australia, vol. 3, The Beginning of An Australian Civilization, 1824–1851*, Melbourne University Press, Melbourne.
Clement, C 2003, 'Mistake Creek'. In R Manne (ed.), *Whitewash: On Keith Windschuttle's Fabrication of Aboriginal History*, Black Inc Agenda, Melbourne, pp. 199–214.
Clifford, R 1972, *The Cosmic Mountain in Canaan and the Old Testament*, Harvard University Press, Cambridge, MA.
Cohn, N 1993, *Cosmos, Chaos and the World to Come; The Ancient Roots of Apocalyptic Faith*, Yale University Press, New Haven, CT.
Cole, T 1990 [1988], *Hell West and Crooked*, Angus & Robertson, Sydney.
Conrad, J 1959, *The Horn and the Sword: The History of the Bull as Symbol of Power and Fertility*, Macgibbon & Kee, London.
Conway, J 1989, *The Road from Coorain*, Alfred A. Knopf, New York.

Cowlishaw, G 1997, 'Race at Work: Reflecting on Field-Work in the Northern Territory', in *Journal of the Royal Anthropological Institute* (née *Man*), 3(1): 95–113.

Cuddihy, J 1974, *The Ordeal of Civility: Freud, Marx, Levi-Strauss, and the Jewish Struggle with Modernity*, Basic Books, New York.

Cuomo, C 1997, *Feminism and Ecological Communities: An Ethic of Flourishing*, Routledge, London.

Curthoys, A 1999, 'Expulsion, exodus, and exile in white Australian historical mythology'. In R Nile & M Williams (eds), *Imaginary Homelands: The Dubious Cartographies of Australian Identity*, University of Queensland Press, Brisbane.

—— 2003, 'Constructing national histories'. In Attwood & Foster, *Frontier Conflict*, pp. 185–200.

—— & J Docker 1999, 'Time, Eternity, Truth and Death: History as Allegory', *Humanities Research*, 1: 5–26.

—— & —— 2001, 'Introduction: Genocide: definitions, questions, settler colonies', *Aboriginal History*, 25: 1–15. (Special section: 'Genocide'?: Australian Aboriginal history in international perspective.)

DeCoste, F, & B Schwartz (eds) 2000, *The Holocaust's Ghost: Writings on Art, Politics, Law and Education*, University of Alberta Press, Edmonton.

Dahl, K 1926, *In Savage Australia*, Philip Allan & Co. Ltd, London.

Davis, R in press, 'Eight seconds: style, performance and crisis in Aboriginal rodeo'. In R Davis & D Rose (eds), *Dislocating the Frontier*, Aboriginal Studies Press, Canberra.

DeCoste, F 2000, 'Introduction'. In DeCoste & Schwartz, *The Holocaust's Ghost*, pp. xv–xix.

Denoon, D 1983, *Settler Capitalism: The Dynamics of Dependent Development in the Southern Hemisphere*, Clarendon Press, Oxford.

Dietrich, W 1992, *The Final Forest: The Battle for the Last Great Trees of the Pacific Northwest*, Penguin Books, New York.

Drews, R 1988, *The Coming of the Greeks: Indo-European Conquests in the Aegean an the Near East*, Princeton University Press, NJ.

Durack, M 1986 [1959], *Kings in Grass Castles*, Corgi Books, Transworld Publishers, Sydney.

Egan, T 1979, *A Drop of Rough Ted*, Dai Nipon, Hong Kong.

Egloff, B 1979, *Mumbulla Mountain: An Anthropological and Archaeological Investigation*, National Parks and Wildlife Service, Sydney.

Elkin, AP 1938 [1954], *The Australian Aborigines: How to Understand Them*, Angus & Robertson, Sydney.

—— 1950, 'Ngirawat, or the Sharing of Names in the Wagaitj Tribe, Northern Australia', *Sonderdruck Aus Beitrage Zue Gesellungs und Volkerwissenschaft*, Verlag Bebr. Mann, Berlin, pp. 67–81.

—— 1970, 'Before it is too late'. In R Berndt (ed.), *Australian Aboriginal Anthropology*, University of Western Australia Press, Perth.

Fabian, J 1979, 'The Anthropology of Religious Movements: From Explanation to Interpretation', *Social Research*, 46: 4–35.

—— 1983, *Time and the Other: How anthropology makes its object*, Columbia University Press, New York.

Fackenheim, E 1978, *The Jewish Return into History*, Schocken Books, New York.
—— 1994 [1982], *To Mend the World, Foundations of Post-Holocaust Jewish Thought*, Indiana University Press, Bloomington, IN.
Fernandez, J 1979, 'On the Notion of Religious Movements', *Social Research*, 46: 36–62.
Fiedler, L 1968, *The Return of the Vanishing American*, Paladin, Granada Publishing Ltd, London.
Fiske, J, B Hodge & G Turner 1987, *Myths of Oz: Reading Australian Popular Culture*, Allen & Unwin, Sydney.
Forestry Commission of New South Wales 1987, *Mount Dromedary. A Pretty High Mountain*, NSW Forestry Commission, Sydney.
Franklin, J, D Lindenmeyer, J MacMahon, A McKee, J Magnuson, D Perry, R Waide & D Foster 2000, 'Threads of Continuity', *Conservation Biology in Practice*, 1(1): 8–16.
Friedlander, S 1993, *Memory, History, and the Extermination of the Jews of Europe*, Indiana University Press, Bloomington, IN.
Frye, N 1982 [1981], *The Great Code: The Bible and Literature*, Harcourt, Brace, Jovanovich, San Diego, CA.
Fullerton, T 2001, *Watershed: Deciding Our Water Future: Juggling the Interests of Farmers, Politicians, Big Business, Ordinary People – and Nature*, ABC Books, Sydney.
Furniss, E 1999, *The Burden of History: Colonialism and the Frontier Myth in a Rural Canadian Community*, University of British Columbia Press, Vancouver.
Gamkrelidze, T, & V Ivanov 1995, *Indo-European and the Indo-Europeans: A Reconstruction and Historical Analysis of a Proto-Language and a Proto-Culture*, Part I, Mouton de Gruyter, Berlin.
Gammage, B 2003, *Australia Under Aboriginal Management*, Australian Defence Force Academy, University College, UNSW, School of Humanities and Social Sciences, Canberra and Sydney.
Ganguly, D 2001, *Hierarchy and its Discontents: Caste, Postcoloniality and the New Humanities*. PhD thesis, Australian National University
Gay, P 1968, *Weimar Culture: The Outsider as Insider*, Secker & Warburg, London.
Geertz, C 1973, 'Thick Description: Toward an Interpretive Theory of Culture'. In C Geertz (ed.), *The Interpretation of Cultures*, Basic Books, New York, pp. 3–30
Gibson, R 1992, *South of the West: Postcolonialism and the Narrative Construction of Australia*, Indiana University Press, Bloomington, IN.
—— 2002, *Seven Versions of an Australian Badland*, Brisbane: University of Queensland Press.
Gill, N 1997, 'Pastoralism, A Contested Domain'. In D Rose & A Clarke (eds), *Tracking Knowledge in North Australian Landscapes: Studies in Indigenous and Settler Knowledge Systems*, North Australia Research Unit, Darwin, pp. 50–67.
Glowacka, D 2000, 'The Shattered Word: Writing of the Fragment and Holocaust Testimony'. In DeCoste & Schwartz, *The Holocaust's Ghost*, pp. 37–54

Goodall, H 1996, *Invasion to Embassy: Land in Aboriginal Politics in New South Wales: 1770-1972*, Allen & Unwin, Sydney.
—— 2000, '"Fixing" the Past: Modernity, Tradition and Memory in Rural Australia', *UTS Review*, 6(1): 20–40.
Gordon, A 1997, *Ghostly Matters: Haunting and the Sociological Imagination*, University of Minnesota Press, Minneapolis, MN.
Graham, M 1999, 'Some Thoughts about the Philosophical Underpinnings of Aboriginal Worldviews', *Worldviews: Environment, Culture, Religion*, 3: 105–118.
Gray, G 2001, 'Abrogating responsibility? Applied anthropology, Vesteys, Aboriginal labour, 1944–1946', *Australian Aboriginal Studies*, 2: 18–26.
Gray, J 2003, *Al Qaeda and What it Means to be Modern*, New Press, New York.
Griffiths, T 2001, 'Cooper Clay'. In M Martin, J Carruthers, G Fizhardinge, T Griffiths and P Haynes, *Inflows: The Channel Country*, Mandy Martin, Publisher, Mandurama, NSW.
—— 2003, 'The Language of Conflict'. In Attwood & Foster, *Frontier Conflict*, pp. 133–49.
Grinde, D, & B Johansen 1995, *Ecocide of Native America; Environmental Destruction of Indian Lands and Peoples*, Clear Light Publishers, Santa Fe, NM.
Grosz, E 1994, *Volatile Bodies: Toward a Corporeal Feminism*, Allen & Unwin, Sydney.
Gunn, J 1954, *We of the Never Never*, Robertson & Muller, Melbourne.
Gurevich, A 1985, *Categories of Medieval Culture*, Routledge & Kegan Paul, London.
Habel, N 2003, 'What kind of God would destroy Earth anyway? An ecojustice reading of the flood narative'. Paper presented to the Bible and Critical Theory Symposium, Adelaide, June 2003.
Haraway, D 1988, 'Situated Knowledges: The science question in feminism and the privilege of partial perspective', *Feminist Studies*, 14(3): 575–99.
Harney, W 1945, 'Report on Patrol Western Stations', Australian Archives, NT Region, CA 1070 Administrator, NT (11) General Registry, CRS F1 Item 44/275.
—— 1946, *North of 23°*, Australasian Publishing Company, Sydney.
Harries-Jones, P 1995, *A Recursive Vision: Ecological Understanding and Gregory Bateson*, University of Toronto Press.
Hatley, J 2000, *Suffering Witness: The Quandary of Responsibility after the Irreparable*, State University of New York Press, Albany, NY.
Hedrick, K n.d., 'The American West: Contested Landscapes and the Power of Identity'. Paper prepared for the American Anthropological Association Annual Meeting, Chicago, 2003.
Healy, C 1997, *From the Ruins of Colonialism: History as Social Memory*, Cambridge University Press, Melbourne.
Hill, E 1955 [1951], *The Territory*, Angus & Robertson, Sydney.
Hokari, M 2002, 'Images of Colonialism: Interpretation of Colonial Landscape by an Aboriginal Historian'. In H Stewart, A Barnard and K Omura (eds), *Self- and Other-Images of Hunter-Gatherers*, National Museum of Ethnology, Osaka, pp. 153–69.

Hornborg, A 1994, 'Environmentalism, ethnicity and sacred places: reflections on modernity, discourse and power', *Canadian Review of Sociology and Anthropology*, 31(3): 245–67.
Horowitz, T 1987, *One for the Road: A Hitchhiker's Outback*, Harper & Row, Sydney.
ICTR (International Criminal Tribunal for Rwanda) 1996, The Prosecutor Versus Jean-Paul Akayesu, Case No. ICTR-96-4-T.
Ignatieff, M 1997, *The Warrior's Honor: Ethnic War and the Modern Conscience*, Henry Holt & Co., New York.
—— 1999, 'Human Rights: The Midlife Crisis', *New York Review of Books*, 20 May: 58–62.
Inglis, K 1998, *Sacred Places: War Memorials in the Australian Landscape*, Melbourne University Press, Melbourne.
Ingold, T 1986, 'Territoriality and tenure: the appropriation of space in hunting and gathering societies'. In T Ingold (ed.), *The Appropriation of Nature: Essays on Human Ecology and Social Relations*, Manchester University Press, Manchester.
—— 1994, 'From Trust to Domination: An alternative history of human–animal relations'. In A Manning and J Serpell (eds), *Animals and Human Society: Changing Perspectives*, Routledge, London, pp. 1-22.
—— 1996, 'Hunting and Gathering as Ways of Perceiving the Environment'. In R Ellen and K Fukui (eds), *Redefining Nature: Ecology, Culture and Domestication*, Berg, Oxford, pp. 117–55.
Irigaray, L 1985, *This Sex Which Is Not One*, Cornell University Press, Ithaca, NY.
Iverson, P 1999, *Riders of the West: Portraits from Indian Rodeo*, photographs by L MacCannell, foreword by C Buffalo, Graystone Books and University of Washington Press, Vancouver and Seattle, WA.
James, B 1989, *No Man's Land: Women of the Northern Territory*. Collins Publishers Australia, Sydney.
Jay, M 1993, *Downcast Eyes: The Denigration of Vision in Twentieth-Century French Thought*, University of California Press, Berkeley, CA.
Kaplan, H 2000, 'The Metapolitics of Power and Conflict', in DeCoste & Schwartz, *The Holocaust's Ghost*, pp. 65–74.
Keen, I 1980, *The Alligator Rivers Stage II Land Claim*, Northern Land Council, Darwin.
Kelly, R 1975, 'Investigations of Aboriginal Sites in the Wallaga Lakes Area of New South Wales', NSW National Parks and Wildlife Service.
Kepnes, S (ed.) 1996, *Interpreting Judaism in a Postmodern Age*, New York University Press, New York.
Kiernan, K 1990, 'I saw my temple ransacked'. In C Pybus & R Flanagan (eds), *The Rest of the World is Watching*, Pan Macmillan, Sydney, pp. 20–33.
Kimber, R 1990, Entry in D Carment, R Maynard, A Powell (eds), *Northern Territory Dictionary of Biography*, vol. 1, Northern Territory University Press, Darwin.
Kinsella, T (translator) 1969, *The Tain*, Dolmen, Dublin.
Kittredge, W 1996, *Who Owns the West?* Mercury House, San Francisco, CA.
Koepping, K 1988, 'Nativistic Movements in Aboriginal Australia: Creative

Adjustment, Protest or Regeneration of Tradition?'. In Swain & Rose, *Aboriginal Australians and Christian Missions*, pp. 397–412.
Kristen, A 1899, Aboriginal Language. Manuscript (copy held at the Australian Institute of Aboriginal and Torres Strait Islander Studies).
Kristeva, J 1982, *Powers of Horror: An Essay on Abjection*, Columbia University Press, New York.
La Capra, D 1998, *History and Memory After Auschwitz*, Cornell University Press, Ithaca, NY.
LaFarge, P 1991, 'Rodeo Hand' on the CD 'Cowboy Songs on Folkways', Compiled and Annotated by G. Logsdon, Smithsonian Folkways, Washington, DC.
Langer, L 1991, *Holocaust Testimonies: The ruins of memory*, Yale University Press, New Haven, CT.
Langton, M 1998, *Burning Questions: Emerging Environmental Issues for Indigenous Peoples in Northern Australia*, Centre for Indigenous Natural and Cultural Resource Management, Northern Territory University, Darwin.
Lattas, A 1990, 'Aborigines and Contemporary Australian Nationalism: Primordiality and the Cultural Politics of Otherness', *Social Analysis*, 27: 50–69.
Lavender, T n.d., Young Bill's Happy Days: Reminiscences of Rural Australia, 1910–1915. Unpublished manuscript, introduced, edited and annotated by Peter Woodley.
Lawrence, E 1982, *Rodeo: An Anthropologist Looks at the Wild and the Tame*, University of Chicago Press, Chicago.
Lemon, A 1996, *Rodeo Girls go Round the Outside*, McPhee Gribble, Penguin Books, Melbourne.
Levinas, E 1988, 'Useless Suffering'. In R Bernasconi & D Wood (eds), *The Provocation of Levinas: Rethinking the Other*, Routledge, London, pp. 156–67.
—— 1996, *Proper Names*, transl. M. Smith, Athlone Press, London.
Lewis, D 1992, 'The Ghost Road of the Drovers: Report on the History and Historic Sites of the Murranji Stock Route'. Report prepared for the National Trust of Australia (NT).
—— 1997, *A Shared History: Aborigines and White Australians in the Victoria River District, Northern Territory*, Timber Creek Community Government Council, Timber Creek, NT.
—— 2002, *Slower Than the Eye Can See: Environmental Change in North Australia's Cattle Lands. A Case Study from the Victoria River District of the Northern Territory*, Co-operative Research Centre for the Sustainable Development of Tropical Savannas, Darwin.
Lincoln, B 1981, *Priests, Warriors and Cattle: A Study in the Ecology of Religions*, University of California Press, Berkeley, CA.
—— 1986, *Myth Cosmos and Society*, Harvard University Press, Cambridge, MA.
Lines, W 1991, *Taming the Great South Land: A History of the Conquest of Nature in Australia*, Allan & Unwin, Sydney.
Linklatter, W, & L Tapp 1997 [1968], *Gather No Moss*, Hesperian Press, Perth.

Littleton, C 1982, *The New Comparative Mythology; an Anthropological Assessment of the Theories of Georges Dumezil*, University of California Press, Berkeley, CA.
Lomax, A, & E McCurdy n.d., *Cowboy Songs of the Old West* (collected and sung by Lomax & McCurdy), Legacy CD.
Loomis, R 1956, *Wales and the Arthurian Legend*, University of Wales Press, Cardiff.
Low, T 1999, *Feral Future: The Untold Story of Australia's Exotic Invaders*, Penguin, Melbourne.
—— 2002, *The New Nature: Winners and Losers in Wild Australia*, Penguin, Melbourne.
Luban, D 1983, 'Explaining Dark Times: Hannah Arendt's Theory of Theory', *Social Research*, 50(1): 215–48.
Lyle, E 1990, *Archaic Cosmos: Polarity, Space and Time*, Polygon, Edinburgh.
MacCulloch, J 1991 [1911], *The Religion of the Ancient Celts*, Constable, London.
McDonald, H 2001, *Blood, bones and spirit: Aboriginal Christianity in an East Kimberley Town*, Melbourne University Press, Melbourne.
McGrath, A 1987, *'Born in the Cattle'*, Allen & Unwin, Sydney.
McGregor, W 1990, 'Another view of Mr Taylor's colonial image', *Australian Aboriginal Studies*, 1: 72–6.
McIntosh, I 1994, *The Whale and the Cross: Conversations with David Burrumarra M.B.E.*, Northern Territory Historical Society, Darwin.
—— 2001, 'The Iron Furnace of Birrinydji'. In A Rumsey & J Wiener (eds), *Mining and Indigenous Lifeworlds in Australia and Papua New Guinea*, Crawford House Publishing, Adelaide, pp. 12–30.
Mckillop, D 1892–93, 'Anthropological notes on the Aboriginal tribes of the Daly River', *Transactions of the Royal Society of South Australia*, 17: 254–64.
Magowan, F 2001, 'Waves of Knowing: Polymorphism and co-substantive essences in Yolngu Sea Cosmology', *Australian Journal of Indigenous Education*. 29(1): 22–35.
Margalit, A 2002, *The Ethics of Memory*, Harvard University Press, Cambridge, MA.
Marshall, A 1966, *The Great Extermination: A Guide to Anglo-Australian Cupidity, Wickedness and Waste*, Heinemann, London.
Mathews, F 1991, *The Ecological Self*, Routledge, London.
—— 1999a, 'Becoming Native: An Ethos of Countermodernity II', *Worldviews: Environment, Culture, Religion* 3: 243–71.
—— 1999b, 'Editorial Introduction', *Worldviews: Environment, Culture, Religion*, 3(2): 95–6.
—— 1999c, 'Letting the World Grow Old: An Ethos of Countermodernity', *Worldviews: Environment, Culture, Religion*, 3(2): 119–38.
—— 2000, 'CERES: Singing up the city', *Philosophy, Activism, Nature*, 1: 5–15.
—— 2003a, *For Love of Matter: A Contemporary Panpsychism*, State University of New York Press, Albany, NY.
—— 2003b, *Journey to the Source of the Merri*, Ginninderra Press, Canberra.
Meggitt, M 1955, 'Notes on the Malngin and Gurindji Aborigine of Limbunya, N.W., Northern Territory' *Mankind* 5(2): 45–50.

Mellor, M 1997, *Feminism and Ecology*, Polity Press, Cambridge.
Merchant, C 1980, *The Death of Nature: Women, Ecology, and the Scientific Revolution*, Wildwood House, London.
Merlan, F 1998, *Caging the Rainbow: Places, Politics, and Aborigines in a North Australian Town*, University of Hawai'i Press, Honolulu, HI.
Michener, J 1956, 'Today's Wild West: The Great Australian North', *Reader's Digest*, April.
Mies, M, & V Shiva 1993, *Ecofeminism*, Spinifex, Melbourne.
Milton, S 1997, 'The Transvaal beef frontier: environments, markets and the ideology of development, 1902–1942'. In T Griffiths & L Robin (eds), *Ecology and Empire: Environmental History of Settler Societies*, Keele University Press, Edinburgh, pp. 199–212.
Molony, J 1980, *I Am Ned Kelly*, Allan Lane, Penguin Books, Melbourne.
Morphy, H 1991, *Ancestral Connections: Art and an Aboriginal System of Knowledge*, University of Chicago Press, Chicago.
Morris, D, & M Boccara (eds), 2000, *Reve et politique des premiers Australiens; L'ancien futur de l'Australie*, L'Harmattan, Paris.
Morris, M 1988, 'Panorama: The Live, the Dead and the Living'. In P Foss (ed.), *Island in the Stream: Myths of Place in Australian Culture*, Pluto Press, Sydney, pp. 160–87.
Mount Dromedary Flora Reserve N. 79948; Bodalla State Forest No. 606; Working Plan. 1985.
Muecke, S 1997, *No Road (Bitumen all the way)*, Fremantle Arts Centre Press, Fremantle.
—— 1999, 'The Sacred in History', *Humanities Research*, 1: 27–37.
Mulvaney, J 1991, 'Visions of Environment: An Afterword'. In DJ Mulvaney (ed.), *The Humanities and the Australian Environment*. Papers from the Australian Academy of the Humanities Symposium, Occasional Paper No. 11, Australian Academy of the Humanities, Canberra, pp. 111–22.
Naess, A 1989, *Ecology, Community and Lifestyle*, Cambridge University Press, Cambridge.
National Inquiry in the Separation of Aboriginal and Torres Strait Islander Children from their Families 1997, *Bringing Them Home*, Commonwealth of Australia.
Neumann, K 2000, 'Haunted Lands', *UTS Review*, 6(1): 65–79.
Newcastle Waters Police Journal, Northern Territory Archives Service, F493, 5-6-51.
Newton, A 1995, *Narrative Ethics*, Harvard University Press, Cambridge, MA.
Nicholson, S 2001, *The Love of Nature and the End of the World: The Unspoken Dimensions of Environmental Concern*, MIT Press, Cambridge, MA.
Niemann, Mrs J 1920, 'An Australian Lotus-Land: Reminiscences of life in the Northern Territory of Australia', compiled and edited by M. Varr, *The Leader*, 16 May: 29.
O'Kelly, G 1967, The Jesuit Mission Stations in the Northern Territory 1882–1899. BA Honours Thesis, Monash University, Melbourne.
Oxenstierna, E 1967, *The World of the Norsemen*, transl. J. Sondheimer, Weidenfeld & Nicolson, London.

Paris, E 2000 [2001], *Long Shadows: Truth, Lies and History*, Bloomsbury, London.
Parkes, H 1890 *The Federal Government of Australasia: Speeches Delivered on Various Occasions (November 1889–May 1890)*, Turner & Henderson, Sydney.
Patrick, P 2003, 'Statement of Peggy Patrick'. In R Manne (ed.), *Whitewash: On Keith Windschuttle's Fabrication of Aboriginal History*, Black Inc. Agenda, Melbourne, pp. 215–17.
Peace, A 1999, 'Anatomy of a Blockade: Towards an Ethnography of Environmental Dispute (Part 2): Rural New South Wales', *Australian Journal of Anthropology*, 10(2): 144–62
Petri, H, & G Petri-Odermann 1970, 'Stability and Change: Present-day Historic Aspects Among Australian Aborigines'. In R Berndt (ed.), *Australian Aboriginal Anthropology: Modern Studies in the Social Anthropology of the Australian Aborigines*, University of WA Press, Perth.
—— & —— 1988, 'A Nativistic and Millenarian Movement in North West Australia'. In Swain & Rose, *Aboriginal Australians and Christian Missions*, pp. 391–96.
Plumwood, V 1993, *Feminism and the Mastery of Nature*, Routledge, London.
—— 1994, 'The Ecopolitics Debate and the Politics of Nature'. In K Warren (ed.), *Ecological Feminism*, London: Routledge, pp. 64–88.
—— 1997, 'Prospects for a Liberatory Political conception of Nature'. Paper presented at the Environmental Justice Conference, Melbourne, 1–3 October 1997.
—— 2002, *Environmental Culture: The Ecological Crisis of Reason*, Routledge, London.
Povinelli, E 1993, *Labor's Lot: The Power, History and Culture of Aboriginal Action*, University of Chicago Press, Chicago.
—— 2002, *The Cunning of Recognition: Indigenous Alterities and the Making of Australian Multiculturalism*, Duke University Press, Durham, NC.
Puhvel, J 1988 [1987], *Comparative Mythology*, Johns Hopkins University Press, Baltimore, MY.
Read, P, & J Read 1991, *Long Time, Olden Time: Aboriginal accounts of Northern Territory history*, Institute for Aboriginal Development Publications, Alice Springs.
—— 1992, 'The look of the rocks and the grass and the hills; A rural life site on the south coast of New South Wales', *Voices*, 37–48.
—— 1996, *Returning to Nothing: The Meaning of Lost Places*, Cambridge University Press, Melbourne.
—— 2000, *Belonging: Australians, Place and Aboriginal Ownership*, Cambridge University Press, Melbourne.
—— 2003, *Haunted Earth*, UNSW Press, Sydney.
Rees, A, & B Rees 1989 [1961], *Celtic Heritage; Ancient tradition in Ireland and Wales*, Thames & Hudson, London.
Report of the Inspector of Police for the year ending 30 June 1922. In *Report of the Administrator of the Northern Territory year ended 30th June 1922*, Parliamentary Papers 1923, pp. 1877–1935.
Reynolds, H 1981, *The Other Side of the Frontier*, Penguin Books, Melbourne.

Ricoeur, P 1985, 'The history of religions and the phenomenology of time consciousness'. In J Kitagawa (ed.), *The History of Religions: Retrospect and Prospect*, Macmillan, New York, pp. 13–52.
—— 1995, *Figuring the Sacred: Religion, Narrative, and Imagination*, transl. D. Pellauer, ed. M. Wallace, Fortress Press, Minneapolis, MI.
Rifkin, J 1992, *Beyond Beef, The Rise and Fall of the Cattle Culture*, Viking, Melbourne.
Rolls, E 1984 [1981], *A Million Wild Acres*, Penguin Books, Melbourne.
Rose, D 1984, 'The Saga of Captain Cook: Morality in Aboriginal and European Law', *Australian Aboriginal Studies*, 2: 24–39.
—— 1985, 'Aboriginal Identity vs Christian Identity', *Australian Aboriginal Studies*, 2: 58–61.
—— 1988, 'Jesus and the Dingo'. In Swain & Rose, *Aboriginal Australians and Christian Missions: Ethnographic and Historical Studies*, pp. 361–75.
—— 1990, 'Gulaga: Report on the significance of Mt Dromedary to Aboriginal people'. Unpublished report prepared for the Forestry Commission of New South Wales.
—— 1991, *Hidden Histories. Black Stories from Victoria River Downs, Humbert River, and Wave Hill Stations, North Australia*, Aboriginal Studies Press, Canberra.
—— 1994, 'Ned Kelly Died for Our Sins', *Oceania*, 65(2): 175–86.
—— 1996a, *Nourishing Terrains: Australian Aboriginal views of Landscape and Wilderness*, Australian Heritage Commission, Canberra.
—— 1996b, 'Rupture and the Ethics of Care in Colonised Space'. In T Bonyhady & T Griffiths (eds), *Prehistory to Politics: John Mulvaney, the Humanities and the Public Intellectual*, Melbourne University Press, Melbourne, pp. 190–215.
—— 1999, 'Indigenous Ecologies and an Ethic of Connection'. In N Low (ed.), *Global Ethics for the 21st Century*, Routledge, London, pp. 175–86.
—— 2000a [1992], *Dingo Makes Us Human: Life and Land in an Australian Aboriginal Culture*, Cambridge University Press, Melbourne.
—— 2000b, 'Signs of life on a barbarous frontier: intercultural encounters in North Australia'. In R Torrence and A Clarke (eds), *The Archaeology of Difference: Negotiation of Cross-Cultural Engagements in Oceania*, Routledge, London, pp. 251–37.
—— 2001a, 'Aboriginal Life and Death in Australian Nationhood', *Aboriginal History*, 25: 148–62.
—— 2001b, 'The saga of Captain Cook: remembrance and morality'. In B Attwood and F Magowan (eds), *Telling Stories: Indigenous History and Memory in Australia and New Zealand*, Allen & Unwin, Sydney, pp. 61–79.
—— 2002, *Country of the Heart: An Indigenous Australian Homeland*, Aboriginal Studies Press, Canberra.
—— 2003, 'Oral histories and knowledge'. In Attwood & Foster, *Frontier Conflict*, pp. 120–132.
—— in press (a), 'New World Poetics of Place along the Oregon Trail and in the National Museum of Australia', In A Coombes (ed.), *Making History Memorable: Past and Present in Settler Colonialism*, Manchester University Press, Manchester.

—— in press (b), 'The Redemptive Frontier: A long road to nowhere'. In R Davis and D Rose (eds), *Dislocating the Frontier*, Aboriginal Studies Press, Canberra.

—— & L Ford 1995, 'The Way We Are (Working in Flux)', in *Work in Flux*, E Greenwood, K Neumann, & A Sartori (eds), University of Melbourne History Department, Melbourne, pp. 10–19.

——, D James & C Watson 2003, *Indigenous Kinship with the Natural World*, National Parks and Wildlife Service, NSW, Sydney.

Rosenberg, J 1986, *King and Kin: Political Allegory in the Hebrew Bible*, Indiana University Press, Bloomington, IN.

Rosengarten, M 1996, *Blood and the Fragility of Identity*. PhD thesis, University of Technology, Sydney.

Roth, J 1999 (ed.), *Ethics after the Holocaust: Perspectives, Critiques and Responses*, Paragon House, St Paul, MN.

Rowley, C 1974 [1970], *The Destruction of Aboriginal Society*, Penguin Books, Harmondsworth.

Ryan, S 1996, *The Cartographic Eye: How Explorers Saw Australia*, Cambridge University Press.

Salleh, A 1992, 'The ecofeminism/deep ecology debate: a reply to patriarchal reason', *Environmental Ethics*, 14: 195–216.

—— 1997, *Ecofeminism as Politics: Nature, Marx and the Postmodern*, Zed Books Ltd, London.

Scarry, E 1985, *The Body in Pain: The Making and Unmaking of the World*, Oxford University Press, New York.

Schultz, C, & D Lewis 1995, *Beyond the Big Run*, University of Queensland Press, Brisbane.

Schwartz, R 1997, *The Curse of Cain: The Violent Legacy of Monotheism*, University of Chicago Press, Chicago.

Scott, C 1996, 'Science for the West, Myth for the Rest? The Case of James Bay Cree Knowledge Construction'. In L Nader (ed.), *Naked Science: Anthropological Inquiry into Boundaries, Power and Knowledge*, Routledge, New York, pp. 69–86.

Scott, J 1998, *Seeing like a State: How Certain Schema to Improve the Human Condition Have Failed*, Yale University Press, New Haven, CT.

Shiva, V 1993, 'Impoverishment of the Environment: Women and Children Last'. In Mies & Shiva, *Ecofeminism* Zed Books Ltd., London, pp. 70-90.

'Sites We Want to Keep'. Video produced by the Australian Heritage Commission, 1988.

Slotkin, R 1992, *Gunfighter Nation: The Myth of the Frontier in Twentieth Century America*, Harper Perennial, New York.

Stanner, W 1979a, 'Continuity and Change among the Aborigines' [1958]. In W Stanner (ed.), *White Man Got No Dreaming: Essays 1938–73*. Australian National University Press, Canberra, pp. 41–66.

—— 1979b, 'Durmugam: A Nangiomeri' [1959], in *White Man Got No Dreaming: Essays 1938–73*, Australian National University Press, Canberra, pp. 67-105.

Stokes, J 1846, *Discoveries in Australia: With an Account of the Coasts and River Explored and Surveyed during the Voyage of H.M.S. Beagle, in the Years*

1837-38-39-40-41-42-43, vol. 2, TW Boone, London.
Strehlow, TGH 1978, *Central Australian Religion: Personal Monototemism in a Polytotemic Community*, vol. 2, Australian Association for the Study of Religions, Special Studies in Religions, Adelaide.
Swain, T 1993, *A Place for Strangers*. Cambridge University Press, Melbourne.
——, & D Rose (eds), *Aboriginal Australians and Christian Missions: Ethnographic and Historical Studies*, Australian Association for the Study of Religions, Adelaide.
Tacitus, 1970 [1948, H Mattingly], *The Agricola and the Germania*, Penguin Classics, London.
Taussig, M 2001, 'Dying Is an Art, Like Everything Else', *Critical Inquiry*, 1(28): 305–16.
Thomas, G c. 1999, *Come to the Centre and Open your Heart: The Best is Yet to Come*. Photocopied booklet illustrated by Lynne Thomas, Wallaga Lake.
Thomas, M 2003, *The Artificial Horizon: Imagining the Blue Mountains*, Melbourne University Publishing, Melbourne.
Thomas, N 1997, 'Home Décor and Dance: The Abstraction of Aboriginality'. In R Coates & H Morphy (eds), *In Place (Out of Time): Contemporary Art in Australia*, Museum of Modern Art, Oxford, pp. 24–28.
TCPJ (*Timber Creek Police Journal*), Northern Territory Archives Service, F302.
Tumarkin, M 2002, Secret Life of Wounded Spaces: Traumascapes in the Contemporary Australia. PhD thesis, University of Melbourne.
Turner, D 1988, 'The Incarnation of Nambirrirrma'. In Swain & Rose, *Aboriginal Australians and Christian Missions*, pp. 470–84.
Turner, F 1994, 'The Significance of the Frontier in American History' [1893]. In J Faragher (ed.), *Rereading Frederick Jackson Turner*, Henry Holt & Co., New York.
Turner, J, to E Chinnery, Memorandum dated 12 December 1940, Australian Archive Services Series F1, Item 52/508.
Umbarra Cultural Centre 1996, *Umbarra Cultural Tours: Journey to the Dreamtime*, (video 14 minutes.) Bermagui, NSW.
Wackernagel, M, & W Rees, n.d.,<www.ire.ubc.ca/ecoresearch/ecoftpr.html>
Wagner, R 1979, 'The Talk of Koriki: A Daribi Contact Cult', *Social Research*, 46: 140–65.
Walcot, P 1979, 'Cattle Raiding, heroic tradition, and ritual: the Greek evidence', *History of Religion*, 18(4): 326–51.
Walker, K, J Puckridge, & S Blanch 1997, 'Irrigation development on Cooper Creek, central Australia: prospects for a regulated economy in a boom-and-bust cycle', *Aquatic Conservation: Marine and Freshwater Ecosystems*, 7: 63–73.
Ward, R 1970 [1958], *The Australian Legend*, Oxford University Press, Melbourne.
Warren, K 1990, 'The Power and the Promise of Ecological Feminism', *Environmental Ethics*, 12: 125–46.
—— 2000, *Ecofeminist Philosophy: A Western Perspective on What it is and Why it Matters*, Rowman & Littlefield, Lanham, MD.
Watson, C 2003, *Piercing the Ground: Balgo Women's Image Making and*

Relationships with Country, Fremantle Arts Centre Press, Fremantle.
Watson, P 1998, *Frontier Lands & Pioneer Legends: How Pastoralists gained Karuwali Land*, Allen & Unwin, Sydney.
Williams, N, & E Hunn 1982, *Resource Managers: North American and Australian Hunter-Gatherers*, AAAS, Washington, DC; Aboriginal Studies Press, Canberra.
Willshire, WH 1896, *The Land of the Dawning: Being Facts Gleaned from Cannibals in the Australian Stone Age*, WK Thomas & Co., Printers, Adelaide.
Wilson, E 2002, *The Future of Life*, Alfred A. Knopf, New York.
Worster, D 1991, 'Beyond the Agrarian Myth'. In P Limerick, C Milner & C Rankin (eds), *Trails: Toward a New Western History*, University Press of Kansas, Lawrence, KS.
Wyschogrod, E 1985, *Spirit in Ashes: Hegel, Heidegger, and Man-Made Mass Death*, Yale University Press, New Haven, CT.
—— 1998, *An Ethics of Remembering: History, Heterology, and the Nameless Others*, University of Chicago Press, Chicago.

INDEX

America(s) 4–6, 39, 41, 44, 59, 62, 75–76, 81, 88–89, 133, 174, 214
Anderson, MK 174
Anthony, D. 75
Apffel-Marglin, F. 181–83, 200
Arendt, H. 1, 19, 23–24, 37
Arthur, J. 37, 64, 128
Attwood, B. 11–12, 19

Bakhtin, M. 37, 176
Bateson, G. 188
belonging 45, 47, 51, 90, 117, 121–22, 127, 129–30, 166–67, 190, 197
Benjamin,W. 4, 16, 25, 27
Berndt, R, & C. 67–69, 109, 144–45
Bible 59–61, 149, 179, 192
Bididu, Johnson 56–57
Big Sunday 131–32, 143–47
binaries, *see* dualisms
Brigalow Bill 112–13
Bringing Them Home 110
Buchanan, N. 121–22, 214
Burrumarra, D. 176, 179–80, 184, 192, 213
bushman 102, 105–7, 119–24

camp draft 74, 80, 88–90, 94
Canaan 84, 139
Canada 6, 90
Captain Cook 3–4, 6, 11, 53, 57, 61, 149, 194
Captain Starlight 74, 82–3
Carter, J. 82–3
cattle 75–80, 89–90, 111
'Cattle Raid of Cooley' 82
Celts 38, 40, 74, 76, 215
Christianity 15–16, 38–41, 58–63,
66, 105, 132–44, 149–55, 159, 161, 179, 183, 192, 197
chronotope, *see* time/space
Cole, T. 108–110
Conway, J. 38
Cooper Creek 87
countermodernity 6–8, 46, 49–50, 74, 88, 93–94, 190, 213
country, defined 153–54
 quiet country 4, 173, 177
cowboys 59, 74–75, 89–90, 92
 Indigenous cowboys 74, 89–90, 92
crimes against humanity 110–11
Curthoys, A. 12, 26, 35, 44

Daguragu 69
Dahl, K. 133, 136–37
Daly River 95–98, 106, 131–35, 138–48
Danaiyarri, Hobbles 3–4, 6, 11, 17, 31, 53, 57, 61, 74, 107, 149–50, 156–57, 160, 213
dark times 1, 23–24, 180, 203, 209, 213
Davis, R. – 89
death 2, 4–9, 12, 22, 26–30, 32, 36, 49, 55, 57–71, 94, 107, 135, 142, 144, 146, 149–50, 155, 159–70, 174–78, 183, 213–15
 death narrative 165, 178
 double death 144, 175–76
denarrativisation 183, 192
dialogue 20–22, 24, 30–31, 119, 176–78, 180, 189–90
Dibden, M. 193–95, 203–12
disenchantment 162, 183
doubling 6–7, 18, 22, 144, 175–76, 200, 205, 211

Dreaming 2, 54–57, 65, 67, 70, 145, 148, 152–53, 155, 158, 161, 167–68, 173–74, 187, 192–94, 198–99, 212, 215
Drews, R. 76, 80
dualisms 19–20, 43, 89, 93, 121, 177, 187, 189
Dumezil, G. 41
Durack family 58, 63, 66, 84, 86, 103

ecocide 34–6
ecological footprint 177
Eden (Garden) 39, 44
Egan, T. 97–8
Elkin, AP 66–7, 146, 166, 177
England (Home) 43–46, 57, 104, 154
ethics 3, 5–8, 11–14, 17–18, 21–22, 28–34, 130–32, 142, 157, 163, 166, 180, 187–89, 200, 212–14
'Eumerella Shore' 81–82, 85
Exodus 44
extinctions 22, 35–6, 48, 105, 110, 171

Fabian, J. 25, 138, 151–52, 154
Fackenheim, E. 21, 30, 32, 203
farming communities 62, 195–96, 204–5, 211
Fiedler, L. 39–40, 117, 129
Forestry Commission of New South Wales 198–99, 201, 210
fragmentation 47, 65, 180–82, 192
frontier 4, 53, 58–59, 61–65, 68–69, 73, 82–83, 85–89, 94, 98, 101–3, 106, 115, 117, 119, 121, 130, 136, 142, 144–45, 147–48, 151
Frye, N. 59–60
Furniss, E. 89
future orientation 18

Gay, P. 181
genocide 12, 27, 35
Gibson, R. 37–8, 42, 45, 101
Gill, N. 87
Graham, M. 186–87, 189–90, 193
Griffiths, T. 29, 88
Grosz, E. 93
guilt 12–13, 84, 184

Gulaga 193–99, 201–3, 206, 209, 210–12

Harney, B. 97, 109, 146
Hatley, J. 12–14, 17, 23, 26–28, 30–32, 51, 61, 111, 165
Healy, C. 3
Hill, E. 104–7, 119–20, 123, 125
Hobbes, T. 182
home, *see* England
hope 5, 18, 22, 25, 31–33, 63, 70, 73
Hornborg, A. 180, 201
Horowitz, T. 115
Humbert River (station) 4, 112–14, 158

Ignatieff, M. 29, 180
Indra 74, 80
Ingold, T. 171, 173, 188
irrigation
    Daly River 133–34, 141
    irrigation proposal, Cooper Creek 87–88
isolation 20, 181, 187, 192

Jay, M. 93, 183
Jesus 60, 81, 131, 138, 140, 144–45, 147–48, 149–50, 156–59, 168, 215
Jinimin, *see* Jin-man
Jin-man (Tjiniman, Jinimin) 140, 143–44, 147–48
Judy 112–14

Kangkinang, Mick 156, 170, 175
Kaplan, H. 14, 73
Kiernan, K. 51–52, 160
Kimber, R. 98–99
Kimberly Region 64, 66, 71, 80, 89, 103
King Arthur 37–38, 40
Kristen, A. 136, 138–40, 143, 147

LaFarge, P. 92
Lake Argyle 64
Lake Pedder 50–52, 160, 189
Land Rights (NT) 1, 65–66, 68–71, 87, 130, 166–67, 184

Lattas, A. 45
Lavender, 'Young Bill' 64–65
Lawrence, E. 89
Levinas, E. 7, 12–14, 17, 20, 32, 61, 187, 189
Lewis, D. 77–78, 130, 158, 169, 172, 214–15
Limbunya (Station) 67–69, 71
Lincoln, B. 41, 76–77, 82–83
Lingara 1, 56, 114, 165–66, 169, 171
Linklatter, W. 80–81

Manngaiyarri, Jimmy 69–70, 72
Mathews, F. 47, 40, 181, 183, 187–88, 190–92, 203, 214
McGregor, W. 100
McIntosh, I. 176, 179, 192
Messianic concepts 19, 53, 66
Michener, J. 86
miscegenation 103, 106, 123, 125
modernity 7, 16, 25, 35, 47, 50, 58, 62, 65, 93, 151–52, 155, 180–83, 187, 190–92, 200
monologue 14, 19–25, 28–30, 44, 51, 53, 61, 151, 177
Morgan (Fraser) 53–54, 56
Morris, M. 104
Mt Dromedary, *see* Gulaga
Muecke, S. 26, 29, 31, 177, 214
Murranji 77–80, 91, 112

National Parks 48, 172
National Parks and Wildlife Service, NSW 194, 196–98, 201–3, 210, 215
Native Americans 32, 35, 62, 89, 214
Nature 2, 19–20, 25, 34, 38, 46–51, 53, 88–92, 94, 98–99, 101–3, 105–7, 116, 165–66, 169, 182–83, 186–87, 189, 191, 194, 198, 203–12 , 215
Ned Kelly 83
NRM (Natural Resource Management) 165, 169, 177

O'Kelly, G. 133, 136, 139–40
Otherworld/Underworld 37–38, 46, 215

outback 64, 74, 76, 80–83, 88, 98, 103–9, 115–20, 122–24, 127, 151, 172

palindromic structure 59–62
Penryth, M. 200
Pigeon Hole 1, 9
place 1–9, 18, 21–22, 26, 36–40, 43, 46–52, 56–57, 62, 64–65, 85–86, 98, 120, 130, 148, 151–52, 154, 160, 163, 167–68, 170, 174–46, 184, 189–92, 194–95, 198–203, 206–14, 215
Plumwood, V. 20, 35, 43, 47, 92, 188
Povinelli, E. 21, 28, 70, 95, 99, 109, 131–32, 138, 145–46, 173, 215
Prendergasts 78
progress 4–5, 16–17, 19, 29–30, 42, 46, 53, 57–58, 63, 65–68, 85, 92, 125, 155, 160, 183
Proto-Indo-European 75–76
Pulkara, Daly 4, 112, 114, 173, 177

quiet country, *see* country

Rainbow Snake 53–54
Ramayana 77
Read, P. 47, 50–51, 113, 203
Reconciliation 8, 71, 130, 180, 184–86, 190, 192, 194, 202, 210, 212, 214
recuperative work 11–12, 23–25, 27–28, 31, 33, 50, 70, 129–30, 163, 184, 193–94, 211, 213
removal of children 110–12, 197
replacement 2, 28, 60, 62, 66, 68, 84, 87, 89, 104, 107, 117, 121, 123, 130, 159, 176, 210
resilience 2–3, 6–7, 46, 48–51, 131, 163, 174–75, 189, 192, 194, 196, 204, 207, 210–14
Reverence 27, 206, 208, 211
Ricoeur, P. 32, 53, 59
Rig Veda 74
rodeo 74, 80, 88–94, 214
Rolls, E. 85
Roma Jury 82–83

Rosenberg, J. 59–60

Scarry, E. 23
Schwartz, R. 84
settler societies 2, 4–6, 21, 24, 30, 34, 47, 58, 76, 85, 146, 177, 181, 189–90, 210, 212
sexuality 102–3, 106–9, 111, 145–46
sexual violence 102, 109–11, 128, 130
shame 13, 27, 72, 205, 211
Slotkin, R. 4, 73
South Africa 85
space/time, *see* time/space
space
empty 39, 63, 111, 160
liminal or ritual 117–18, 120, 127
wounded space 34, 36, 148, 178, 211, 214
Stanner, WEH 98, 131, 142–45, 147, 215
Stokes, J. 62–63, 66, 99, 105

tabula rasa 62, 131, 134
Tacitus 4
Thomas, A. 198, 200
Thomas, GT 198–200
Timber Creek 116, 118–20, 124, 127, 130
time 1–2, 5–6, 8–9, 14–19, 22–28, 30–31, 33, 37, 39–40, 48–49, 52–70, 73, 84–86, 111–12, 115–16, 118, 130, 151–55, 159, 161–63, 175–76, 178, 188–89, 193–94, 198, 210–11, 213–14, 215
time/space 2, 24, 37, 39, 55, 59, 64–65, 115–6, 118, 151–55, 162, 175
Tjiniman, *see* Jin-man
Turner, D. 154
Turner, FJ 62, 85

Underworld, *see* Otherworld

Victoria River and district 2, 9, 11, 53–5, 57, 61–64, 66–67, 69, 95, 98–99, 103, 105, 108–9, 119–20, 149, 150, 153, 166, 172–74, 215
Victoria River Downs (station) 64, 86, 99, 105
violence 4–5, 7–8, 12–17, 19, 22–24, 29–34, 36, 49, 57–8, 61, 64–66, 68–71, 73–74, 88, 95, 98, 101, 104, 112, 114, 128–30, 132, 136, 142, 151, 181, 183, 185–86, 200, 202, 210–11, 214
see also sexual violence
VRD, *see* Victoria River Downs (station)

Wagga, D. 127–29
Wave Hill (station) 68–69, 109, 121
Ward, R. 44
Ward, W (*see* Brigalow Bill) 112–13
whiteness 43, 125
wholeness–hunger 24, 181, 183, 191
the wild, people and places 3–4, 6, 17, 36, 89, 92, 99, 101, 104, 112, 131–32, 138–39, 145, 156, 173, 213
wilderness 4, 58, 63, 65, 85, 92, 120, 148, 189
wildlife 98, 116, 118, 203
see also National Parks and Wildlife Service
Willshire, W. 98–109, 129, 139
Wirrpa, Jessie – 167
witness 25, 30–34, 50–52, 68, 100, 112, 157, 213
Wyschogrod, E. 4, 26, 28

Yarralin 1, 149–62, 165–66, 169, 171, 215
Year Zero 57–59, 61–64, 68, 71, 73–74, 85, 89, 92
Young Bill Lavender, *see* Lavender, 'Young Bill'
Young, Allan 166–67
Young, Riley 168–69, 171–73, 175–76, 215
Yuin people 194–202, 211

Zero Point 39, 41–43, 46

Also published by UNSW Press

LOOKING FOR BLACKFELLAS' POINT
Mark McKenna

Winner of:

Book of the Year NSW Premier's Literary Awards 2003
Douglas Stewart Non-Fiction Prize NSW Premier's Awards 2003
Australian Cultural Studies Award 2002

Blackfellas' Point, once an Aboriginal camping ground and meeting place on the Towamba river in south-eastern New South Wales, is the starting point for this poignant exploration of Australian cultural identity and history. From the familiar vantage point of Blackfellas' Point McKenna unravels his history of Australian identity: a history that resonates with a sense of place.

Through intimate, descriptive prose McKenna unveils the politics of injustice and oppression intrinsic to our cultural history and identity. In doing so he expresses the desire of both Indigenous and non-Indigenous Australians to reconcile this history through political and social change in the 20th century and beyond.

'A powerful meditation, in local and national terms, on the continuing meaning of dispossession . . . McKenna's book burns with a fierce and loving commitment to the place, its history and all its people.'
– Peter Read, *The Age*

'McKenna's ambition is . . . amply fulfilled. To hear the silences, to see the absences, to be hopeful in awful circumstances takes a special sort of sensitivity. McKenna tells his true stories with gentle grace.'
– Greg Denning, *The London Review of Books*

ISBN 0 86840 644 9

Also published by UNSW Press

ANCIENT AND MODERN
Time, Culture and Indigenous Philosophy

Stephen Muecke

How might we think and talk about indigenous philosophy? Why has Aboriginal knowledge not been given the status of philosophical knowledge, but treated by whites rather as culture or history?

This is the starting point for the essays contained in Stephen Muecke's original and challenging book. Blending anecdote, theory and personal reflection, Muecke moves from film to travel to politics to religion, gathering knowledge, revisiting theory and recasting key assumptions.

With passion and conviction, and a sense of experiment and discovery, *Ancient & Modern* calls for a new kind of modernity.

Stephen Muecke holds a Personal Chair in Cultural Studies at the University of Technology, Sydney, and is a Fellow of the Australian Academy of the Humanities. His books include (with Paddy Roe and Krim Benterrak): *Reading the Country: Introduction to Nomadology* (1984, 1996); *Textual Spaces: Aboriginality and Cultural Studies* (1992); the fictocritical *No Road (bitumen all the way)*; a translation of José Gil's *Metamorphoses of the Body* (1998); and the children's story *About this little devil and this little fella*, edited for Albert Barunga (1999). He recently edited (with Adam Shoemaker) *David Unaipon's Legendary Tales of the Australian Aborigines* (2001). He is co-editor of *The Cultural Studies Review*.

ISBN 0 86840 786 0

Also published by UNSW Press

THIS COUNTRY
A Reconciled Republic

Mark McKenna

Australia needs a new vision of a republic. A republic worth fighting for and a republic worth voting for. A republic that will make a difference.

This Country argues for a republic that encompasses reconciliation, acknowledges our history as a nation and embraces who we are as a people – a republic that expresses the values and principles of a distinctly Australian democracy; that includes a constitutional commitment to the land in which we live; and that links this country with the people who live here.

Passionately written by one of Australia's leading commentators on the republican debate, *This Country* expands the discussion of an Australian republic beyond the limitations of previous models that assume the need for an Australian Head of State.

McKenna argues for and clearly maps out an achievable path of reform for Australian politics. *This Country* is a book that will ignite debate over Australia's future.

Mark McKenna is the award-winning author of *Looking For Blackfellas' Point*.

ISBN 0 86840 551 5

www.ingramcontent.com/pod-product-compliance
Lightning Source LLC
Chambersburg PA
CBHW031738230426
43669CB00007B/392